CW00348418

FERGIE
UNDER THE HAIRDRYER

OUR UNTOLD TALES OF A FOOTBALL GENIUS

FERGIE

UNDER THE HAIRDRYER

John Richardson

Reach Sport

Reach **Sport**

www.reachsport.com

First published in Great Britain and Ireland in 2021 by Reach Sport, 5 St Paul's Square, Liverpool, L3 9SJ. Paperback edition published 2021.

www.reachsport.com
@Reach_Sport

Reach Sport is a part of Reach PLC. One Canada Square, Canary Wharf, London, E15 5AP.

ISBN: 978-1-914197-07-9
eBook ISBN: 978-1-914197-08-6

Photographic acknowledgements: Reach PLC (Mirrorpix), PA Images.

Edited by Simon Monk, Chris McLoughlin

Printed and bound by CPI Group (UK) Ltd, Croydon, CR0 4YY.

Contents

Introduction

'You can **** off! You're finished here. Now get out of my sight!'

As first impressions go – and the prospect of a future compatible working relationship – I would say judging on marks out of ten, myself and the then plain Alex Ferguson would be rated a solid zero.

It was July 1986 and I'd been summoned by my *Daily Mail* sports editor to 'doorstep' (as they call it in the trade) the Aberdeen manager, a certain Alex Ferguson. I knew from afar of Alex's incredible success north of the border and his dismantling of the Old Firm's monopoly of Scottish football.

Anyway, this assignment had seemed straightforward enough. Alex had ventured south to Manchester for a tribunal to decide the transfer fee of one of his players, Neale Cooper, who had signed for Aston Villa under freedom of contract. The only problem was that Alex had quickly left the tribunal without saying a word, probably fuming at the £350,000 fee for his key midfielder when Aberdeen had been asking for £400,000.

I was in luck. I was tipped off that Alex wasn't heading straight back to Aberdeen because he was planning to stay the night after booking himself into the Four Seasons Hotel, which I knew well, near Manchester Airport. A little friendly chat with the receptionist informed me that Alex was in his room so off I went in pursuit of a man I'd never met before.

I knocked on the door, silence from within. I tried again, this time louder to be met by a Scottish snarl, "Who is it?" The next thing the door opened and I was confronted with a semi-naked Alex Ferguson who was clearly angry that he had been disturbed. "What is it?" he enquired. I was barely able to spit out my question about what he felt about the tribunal verdict when he slammed the door shut in my face, "Go to hell, I'm trying to get some sleep," he yelled, red-faced and clearly not up for any further interrogation.

Sadly, and a little shaken, I had to deliver the bad news to my sports desk that there would be no comment from the Aberdeen manager. The only saving grace for me was, thank goodness, I didn't have to deal with him every day and it was unlikely our paths would cross again. My only relief was then watching the film of Alex's rage at his Aberdeen players after they had beaten – yes beaten – Rangers in the 1983 Scottish Cup final shortly after securing one of the greatest results in their history, the European Cup Winners' Cup triumph over Real Madrid. Rage appeared to be the default setting of the man causing upsets in the Granite city.

So imagine my fear just four months later when Ron Atkinson was sacked and Alex Ferguson – he who was full of hell on that summer afternoon – was to take over the reins at Manchester United. Although I wasn't the regular Manchester man, having now moved to *The Sun* – that was the preserve of a brilliant colleague Peter Fitton – I was expected to cover the United press conferences, which were staged on Fridays. Luckily a switch of newspapers must have fooled him and in any case I could have only been in his eyeline during that fateful hotel rendezvous for a few seconds.

Already the conferences, which in those embryonic Ferguson days were only covered by a few hardened national newspaper reporters and the odd radio man, were turning prickly – a far cry from the easy going, enjoyable affairs with Big Ron. It was clear that the man from Govan wasn't a big fan of the press who he hoped to control in the same way that he was trying to implant his methods on the club.

We also quickly discovered that the 'hairdryer treatment' wasn't reserved for his players. John Bean, a diligent reporter for the *Daily Express*, often copped it because, unluckily for him, his paper was the one that arrived through the Ferguson household's letterbox every morning. I would later discover that wasn't ideal when I moved to the *Sunday Express*, his paper of choice on the Sabbath.

Alex's idea of trying to control the media was to hand out bans like confetti. One Friday lunchtime, Beano was on his bike – but not before a showpiece exit. A clearly grumpy Fergie had been upset by something Beano, who could have come straight out of a Dickensian novel with his looks and manners, had written. "Bean, you're a fucking has been," Fergie growled before poor Beano had chance to take his seat in one of the small rooms inside Old Trafford we occupied every Friday lunchtime.

The seats were carefully positioned around a low wooden coffee table. Without blinking, John quietly said to Fergie in his dulcet tones, "Alex, matey, before I go can I be allowed to present you with my very own soft shoe shuffle?" Fergie looked bemused and perplexed, not having the foggiest idea about what was coming next.

He was in good company as neither did the assembled hacks! Within a few seconds John had stepped onto the coffee table and treated us all to his one-man shoe shine shuffle. We were trying to stop ourselves laughing, but thankfully Fergie couldn't suppress his own feelings and broke into a huge smile. It still didn't save Beano. When his act had come to a close Fergie ranted, "You can still fuck off. You're banned!"

My first blast of the hairdryer arrived on a Friday after covering Wales in midweek, my international beat. After breaking onto the scene at both club and international level, Ryan Giggs was a prized Manchester United asset – the new George Best in many people's eyes. With that in mind, and knowing the dangers that encircled Bestie, Alex was determined that Ryan shouldn't go down the same road. It was why he had forbidden any interviews with his young Welsh winger. Not that it stopped anyone trying to get one, especially amongst those of us who covered Wales. We would always try and cajole the Wales manager Terry Yorath into allowing us to have a few words with Ryan.

Terry had tragically lost his 15-year-old son Daniel to an undiagnosed heart problem in May 1992 while they had been playing football in the garden together. Terry was understandably vulnerable and after one game he felt that a group of us conducting an interview with Ryan wasn't the biggest thing in the world after what had happened to his family.

So it was set up and there was nothing spectacular said, but we had the interview and there it was in *The Sun* on the Friday morning – a two-page spread of a Ryan Giggs exclusive by John Richardson. None of the other reporters on the Wales beat were based in Manchester so it would be just me in the firing line later that day.

I had already been warned that Fergie had gone ballistic at the training ground after seeing the Giggs interviews and when I got to Old Trafford I didn't even make it into our normal interview room. I was headed off into what was aptly called for this occasion 'The Grill Room'. He was angrily pointing his finger at me as we were about to move towards our Friday room.

"You can fuck off and never come back. You're fucking finished here," he exploded. "You've gone behind my back. Now get out of my sight." I just about managed, "Alex, have you read it? It's fine, there's nothing controversial." Back came, "I've seen the headline, that's enough, now get out of here."

In those early years you quickly learned that you never debated anything. If he didn't like something you had written you were out, but we did have our very own Eric Cantona figure – someone who was spared the verbal blast – in former Blackpool and England player Jimmy Armfield.

'Gentleman Jim' had moved into journalism having done it the proper way, going through the training system. We all loved Jimmy, so much that I would work out an intro for him if he was ever stuck following our Friday conferences. He more than paid that back because if Jimmy was present then Alex was calmer. He had respect for Jimmy and wouldn't dream of yelling at him and was loath to rant when he was around.

Despite an often spikey atmosphere, the majority of the Manchester crew wanted Alex to succeed because we all knew how hard he worked. We also knew what made him tick. He loved confrontation, but also had respect for those in the media who he felt did the job well. I was privileged to cover, in different forms, his whole career as Manchester United manager and enjoyed the banter, especially in my time as the *Sunday Express* chief football correspondent where he appeared more relaxed with the Sunday fraternity.

It was probably because a number of us had covered him from the start of his Old Trafford career and were then older than many of our daily colleagues. The hairdryer treatment wasn't as scattergun as it once was. Peace generally reigned amongst the Sundays. He was great company and loved a chat once his other duties had been completed.

We always went in to bat last. Before the official business started we would have some general banter. It would often end up going left field. Not that it always worked. Jonathan Northcroft had just joined *The Sunday Times*, where he was to become an erudite journalist well respected by his peers. But in the early days naturally he wanted to try to forge a relationship with the United manager. One day he mentioned to the group of us that we generally appeared to get on well with Alex because he appeared relaxed in discussions before we got to the on the record business.

We told Jon that he had a head start because he was from Aberdeen, where Fergie had reigned supreme. Anyway, one Friday Jon seized his opportunity. Fergie had been up at Aberdeen during the week. "Alex, I see you were in Aberdeen. Did you enjoy yourself? What were you doing there?" he said in an innocent tone.

"Mind your fucking business. What the fuck has it got to do with you, you nosey bastard?" was the reply which left poor

Jonathan and the rest of us dumbfounded. Things could only get better for the man from *The Sunday Times* and thankfully they did.

After Alex had given an amazing eulogy at Sir Bobby Robson's memorial at Durham Cathedral, seemingly without notes, I congratulated him on it. Before his speech, Katherine Jenkins, the brilliant mezzo-soprano, had sung and captivated the audience. Modestly not wanting to dwell on his own achievement, he replied, "Did you see Katherine Jenkins' dress? It was stunning." There was a twinkle in his eye. He loved conversations away from football. He was a big music fan and regaled one of our number sitting next to him at a dinner with his love of Tom Petty and the Heartbreakers.

Just don't get him on politics. Being mates with the likes of Tony Blair, Gordon Brown and Alastair Campbell nailed his Labour roots from his days amongst the Govan shipbuilders. He is interested in history – former prime minister Gordon Brown even sent him CDs about the assassination of US president John F. Kennedy – and he once suggested Tony Blair should take a masseur on his polling battle bus to try to relax him.

His head was awash with ideas. No wonder the world renowned Harvard University invited him over many times to impart his wisdom on various subjects including the art of leadership.

Alex's sense of humour was never far away if the occasion suited. I was the victim at a press conference to announce the signing of Jordi Cruyff, son of the Dutch icon Johan, in 1996. At Barcelona Jordi Cruyff had the name Jordi on the back of his shirt, not Cruyff. It was an innocent question, but the answer would produce guffaws of laughter from Fergie and the chairman Martin Edwards.

"Why do you have Jordi on the back of your shirt?" I quizzed United's new arrival. "Because it's my name," he replied with a straight face. For weeks Fergie never let me forget it.

Despite this apparent hard veneer, deep down he loved a bit of fun, especially if it was at a journalist's expense. At times like this you could see how popular he was with many figures in the game because they had witnessed his caring side. We saw glimpses of it, especially if there had been any family upsets amongst the regular Manchester press troupe. Bouquets of flowers would often find their way to your home if there had been a serious problem.

The early days, when he fought to recapture United's glory years, were more intimate. There was just a small collection of reporters armed with notebooks in the era of shorthand, before the over reliance on tape recorders, dictaphones and smartphone voice recorders in the modern age. When a camera crew first appeared he warned us all that this was just the start of the escalation in football coverage with the advent of the Premier League just around the corner.

United's historic former training ground, The Cliff, where he would sometimes stage his pre-match briefings, was easy to access unlike the Fort Knox type security surrounding Carrington – United's current training venue. At times, if you were brave enough, you would try to sneak in past Harold the genial doorman and hide amongst the cars, hoping to grab a word with one of the players. Sometimes fans would also be around in their search for autographs – thankfully the world of selfies was years away.

One late morning myself and a colleague ventured into The Cliff, weaving and ducking between the cars in an attempt to grab an interview with a player. Helping our cover were a small group of schoolgirls. Suddenly, at the window from the modest training centre, a livid Scotsman glared down at the car park. It was obvious we had been rumbled. Sure enough, breathing fire and brimstone, Fergie came marching into the car park.

"What the fuck are you two doing? Get the fuck out of here you nosey bastards." Midway through the verbal blast he noticed the innocent girls who could hardly believe what they were hearing. "Oh sorry girls. I apologise for the bad language." Fair enough, we thought as he turned back towards the changing rooms, but then he addressed the girls again. "But it's the only fucking language these fuckers understand!"

Sadly his prediction that the world and his wife would soon be turning up to report on all matters Manchester United came to pass and it was clear that Fergie became increasingly agitated with the cameras and the fact that there could be no off the record chats. When some of the young bucks decided to report a Fergie hairdryer blast that involved tape recorders being sent flying from the table, the game was up.

Previously, although some of the hairdryer tales had become legendary amongst the media, they had never been made public. Now with over-demanding sports desks to satisfy and very little being able to escape the public gaze, the whole reporting environment with the United manager changed. It was as if you were now walking on eggshells trying to wield out a story before you were sent packing.

By now, United were on a crest of a wave – the country's outstanding team – and so he was in a strong position to batten down the hatches and create the siege mentality that he and his players thrived on. Still though, there were many amusing incidents. I can still recall the look of horror on his face as he held court in the foyer of an Amsterdam hotel with the Sunday papers to preview a pre-season tournament.

Little did Fergie know, but United's visit coincided with the city's famous Amsterdam Pride – the biggest gay event in Europe. As he was talking about his ambitions for the new season he suddenly stopped in full flow. "Jesus Christ!" he muttered. Just a few yards away, going past us in a convoy, were a group of gay men and women holding hands and cuddling up to one another. I don't think he was able to collect his thoughts again – he had been knocked out of his stride completely, but it wasn't wasted. Some of us told him the hotel was famous for John Lennon and Yoko Ono's 'bed-in for peace' protest back in 1969. "Aye, but he could sing!" he said, obviously not enamoured by the goings-on around him.

There were highs and lows in the pressers, but you didn't want to miss one and after all he was such a big name that whatever he said made headlines. He made our jobs easy in that respect and even though I've never been a Manchester United fan I wallowed in the club's success with one of the greatest managers in the game and top players from around the world, including the Class of '92.

I knew I was in the presence of greatness and that's why it has been an absolute pleasure to compile this collection of stories about someone who, over the years, I grew closer to as a human being. Who doesn't have a Fergie anecdote if they have spent any time in his company?

When he announced his retirement – the second one, not the first, what was he thinking back in May 2001? – it was like someone had switched off a light. Not just at Old Trafford, but throughout the football world. There was also an obvious sense of relief in some quarters because everyone knew that no one would be able to repeat his era of domination. For David Moyes, his successor, the Manchester United job was a poisoned chalice.

Fergie's love for the game has continued in his retirement, as seen by his regular appearances at Old Trafford where he is often sat close to his all-important partner in United's successful years, former chief executive David Gill. Even his close-to-death experience, when he suffered a brain haemorrhage in 2018, hasn't dampened his enthusiasm for the game or diluted the special common touch he possesses.

I bumped into him a few years ago and it was like nothing had changed. "You still writing that shite?" he smiled. "Yes, and you are obviously still reading it as well!" I replied.

No doubt the hairdryer is poised if he ever gets to read this book – 'bloody rubbish, why are people wasting their time talking about me?'

Because you're worth it, Sir Alex.

John Richardson, 2021

1

"Alex was desperately trying to whisper the answer, but I couldn't make it out. I was completely flustered and I just blurted out, 'Lester Piggott.' You should have seen the look he gave me – he was incredulous"

Andy Roxburgh, former team-mate on the pitch and in a televised quiz show

Robert Donnelly

ROBERT DONNELLY was a player at Falkirk when Alex Ferguson arrived fresh from Rangers to add goals to the side in 1969 before eventually becoming player-coach. Robert's brother Tom, who also features in this book, played under Ferguson when he became manager of East Stirlingshire.

Alex was a player at Falkirk when I first met him. Later he became the club's player-coach. I only played for the Bairns for less than two seasons, but my pride and joy is a team photograph with Alex and myself in it. It's always a great talking point with my family and friends. If they don't believe me that our paths once crossed I quickly produce the evidence.

It was often the case that Falkirk would sign ex-Rangers and ex-Celtic players that were past their best. I was only a young boy at the time and you still looked up to these guys because they had done the business. There were no problems that they had been brought together from two deadly rivals. They all mixed fine and it was great for the club.

The good thing was that they were always on hand to help the young players develop. For me, Alex Ferguson was the one who helped even more than the others. He was always aware of you and would encourage you. If you had a problem he was the man you went to because he was also the players' union representative for the club. He was always very approachable and would help you fight your corner.

Willie Cunningham was the manager and in 1972 the first team lost 6-1 against St Johnstone. As a punishment, Cunningham came in the next day and stopped the players' bonuses and travelling expenses plus our lunch vouchers. Alex wasn't having that and he instigated a mass walk out in protest.

I've got another photo in my collection of Alex in conversation with the captain, John Markie, discussing whether the team should play in the next game. The dispute continued right until the Saturday – the day of the next scheduled fixture at home to Montrose – because Cunningham wasn't prepared to back down. Neither was Alex.

Two hours before kick off there had still been no decision. I was a reserve team player at the time and we were all ordered to meet at a hotel with the first team. Alex sensed that the manager might try to go behind the first team's backs and get us to play instead. We were told by Alex and the skipper that none of us would be playing that day. The next thing we know is that the directors had overruled the manager and that all the bonuses would be reinstated, providing the game went ahead. Alex had led the fight and was in no mood to give in. That's what he was like. You would rather have him on your side than against you as Willie Cunningham quickly discovered.

It's great now to look back on these days considering what Alex went on to achieve in his career. I'm glad I kept the cuttings of these events which can trigger the memory.

As a player he still had a lot to offer even though he had left Rangers for a club that had been relegated the previous season and was supposedly on the way down. He was someone you looked up to straight away. There was something special about him. He seemed a natural leader. There was a presence about him, an aura. Of course, we knew he had played for Rangers and carved out a reputation for himself but, there was more to him than that. At the end of the 1972/73 season I was handed a free transfer by the club. I was summoned to the ground and thought there would be a few of us there to be told what was happening over our futures. When I arrived I was surprised to see that the only person who was there was Alex. He was in the dressing room and for some strange reason it had been left to him, as the player-coach, to inform me of the club's decision to release me.

I was a little stunned, but then asked him about my two pairs of football boots which were kept at the club. He admitted that I wasn't supposed to be able to take them away with me because they really belonged to Falkirk, but then he smiled and said, "On you go with them and good luck."

It wasn't a nice thing for him to have had to tell me that I was no longer a Falkirk player, although I suspected I was on my way. And in any case there were far better players than me released at the same time. Maybe it was left to Alex because of that earlier falling out with the manager. I don't really know to this day.

I understand that Alex always said that one of the hardest jobs in football – and it stayed with him all the way to Manchester United – was having to tell players that they were being let go. I must have been one of the first players he had to tell. It wasn't a great time, but when I think back now at least I can say it was Alex Ferguson who was the one that broke the news. With everything that has happened to him since it has been easier to take. I ended up playing junior football for my local team, something I really enjoyed.

Alex went on to manage his first club, East Stirlingshire, who my brother Tom played for, so the two of us got to know him at roughly the same time – something we are proud of. And then he did us proud over arranging some tickets for a testimonial when he was later manager of Manchester United.

My brother Tom couldn't go, but he wrote to Alex explaining that our father would love to attend Mark Hughes' testimonial, which was against Celtic at Old Trafford in 1994. In the end four tickets arrived for my father, myself, my son and Tom's daughter. Unbeknown to us he had arranged for us to be shown around the whole ground.

It was a great game and Celtic took 8,000 fans down from Scotland. It was an unbelievable day, made even better by my nephew, Tom's son Simon Donnelly, scoring twice for Celtic in what was a 3-1 win for the Bhoys. It was a great gesture from Alex.

Since our connection at Falkirk I've followed his career all the way.

What he achieved at Aberdeen, taking on Rangers and Celtic, was absolutely amazing. Also, of course, he spent some time working under Jock Stein with Scotland. By coincidence, Andy Roxburgh, who also went on to manage Scotland, was a player at Falkirk at the same time as Alex and myself. So there's another wee feather in our cap. I have to say Alex was the better player, but you could see Andy was going somewhere as well in the game in the future.

For 12 months I shared a train ride with Andy to and from training. He was always well spoken and well turned out. I never knew he was going to be Scotland manager one day, but like Alex he definitely had something special.

They were enjoyable days and hopefully Alex still remembers the Donnelly brothers.

I really hope so.

Andy Roxburgh

ANDY ROXBURGH was at Queen's Park at the same time as Fergie and later went on to partner him in the Falkirk attack. He also managed the Scottish national team and for 18 years was UEFA's Technical Director.

Queen's Park was almost home for me. I lived three streets away and grew up in the shadow of Hampden Park. The club was a breeding ground for top players. Alex Ferguson was in the first team while I was in the youth squad. He was my idol. All I wanted to do was to follow in his footsteps if I was good enough. When he left in 1960 I replaced him in the first team.

Eventually we were to meet up again and play alongside each other up front for Falkirk when we both moved to Brockville in 1969. He was a great finisher. In the penalty area he was deadly and one season he ended up scoring 45 goals for Dunfermline. He had that killer instinct – even in quizzes. I don't think he has ever forgiven me for getting a question wrong in the TV series *Quiz Ball*, which was the forerunner to today's popular *A Question Of Sport*.

At Falkirk we decided to enter a team in 1970 and it comprised Alex, Bobby Ford, myself and Chic Murray, a Scottish comedian, because each side had to encompass a celebrity fan. It went out nationwide and was watched by millions. We managed to reach the semi-finals with Alex, who used to organise quizzes of his own, our star player. We faced Everton, whose team featured their manager Harry Catterick, Joe Royle, Brian Labone and famous fan Ed 'Stewpot' Stewart, a DJ.

It came down to the last question, which was mine. If I answered it correctly we would go through to the final. You can imagine the tension, especially with Alex and his will to win. My question was, "Which jockey rode the winner in last year's Grand National?"

Alex was desperately trying to whisper the answer, but I couldn't make it out. I was completely flustered and I just blurted out, "Lester Piggott." You should have seen the look Alec gave me – he was incredulous. After all, Piggott was the world's greatest flat jockey and wouldn't be anywhere near the world's greatest steeplechase. How the hell didn't I know that?

Fergie was fuming and I don't think he has forgiven me to this day. It often gets mentioned that I was the reason we didn't reach the *Quiz Ball* final. The Falkirk fans didn't forget either and at the next home game I was met with chants of 'Lester Piggott'. I wouldn't have been surprised if Alex had played a part in that.

Quiz Ball was filmed in Birmingham where Chic Murray just happened to own a nightclub, so he invited us to have a few drinks. Obviously we were expecting to get in for free and receive some VIP treatment. He charged us entry – I think something like £6 which was a hell of a lot in those days. You could say a typical Scotsman!

Alex and I both took a coaching course early in our careers to try to extend our football careers when our playing days were over. He was a leader, right from his days as a player in the dressing room and he was never afraid of pushing himself or his players.

I've still got a tape of him going in front of the TV cameras when he was at Aberdeen declaring that they would be success-ful in Europe. That was their target even though they hadn't won anything yet. That summed him up. It all depends on team selection, decision making, the ability to handle players and, of course, a bit of luck. He has been able to utilise all of these.

A little while back I walked across the Old Trafford pitch with him. The stadium was empty and I asked him what he looked for in young players? He replied that, assuming they had technical ability, he was always looking for someone who could play in front of 70,000 people every week and enjoy it.

I think that sums up his demands of a player – quality and mentality in front of a big crowd.

Iain Munro

IAIN MUNRO watched from close quarters as Alex helped to set up the Scottish Players Union. He later played under him at St Mirren, but rejected the chance to follow him to Aberdeen. Iain won seven Scotland caps and played in England for Stoke City and Sunderland. He later moved to the USA to YSC Sports, which became the official youth development partner of MLS side Philadelphia Union.

I knew Fergie from his time playing for Drumchapel Amateurs. I also turned up there a few years after him. I got to really know him from the functions involving Douglas Smith, the man who ran 'The Drum'.

When I was an 18-year-old at St Mirren in 1969/70, our fullback Tony Connell would go around collecting money for what was an embryonic Scottish PFA. It wasn't officially recognised at the time but Fergie, who was with Falkirk in those days, was on the players' committee. Tony was stepping away from doing this so he enlisted me to try to carry on his good work in collecting funds for the union. He said that because I was a budding school teacher and supposedly someone to be trusted, I was the obvious one to organise the collection of money to keep things going. So at 18 I found myself on the players' committee. In addition to myself and Fergie, Benny Rooney of St Johnstone and a load of senior pros would meet once a month.

I learned more in an hour-and-a-half in these meetings than I could ever have imagined. I would sit there and not really utter a single word. I would just look on in admiration as Fergie demonstrated his knowledge as a union leader. Without his input and the push to collect money from players the Scottish PFA would never have got off the ground. It wasn't an official organisation at the time and was struggling to give Scottish players a voice. We didn't have any proper representation but nothing was going to stop Fergie, especially as someone who had been brought up with unions through his father's connection with shipbuilding in Govan. Immediately you could see that at every opportunity he was prepared to stand up against authority. Nothing fazed him. He loved a fight for what he believed were our rights.

Until he came on the scene, players were sort of aligned to other unions, which wasn't ideal. It meant that we were often treated badly by clubs because they knew we lacked authority. The power was with the clubs and often you could only sign one-year contracts with a one-year option. But that option was weighted towards the club.

For instance, if you were being treated badly and wanted to walk out at the end of your first 12 months you couldn't. If they wanted to keep you there was nothing you could do about it. And if they wanted to get rid of you and not exercise the extra year's option, you were on your way. You didn't have a leg to stand on. The likes of Fergie and Benny Rooney slowly but surely improved the rights of players. I was so impressed with Alex, who I looked upon in those early days as a big brother to me – someone who I admired for his presence and brilliant negotiating skills.

After that I began to follow his career closely. I noticed that, after his playing career finished and he went into management with East Stirlingshire and St Mirren, he took a lad called Ricky McFarlane with him. The two of them dovetailed well. Fergie would try to cause aggravation within the dressing room – always looking to stir it up whenever he could – while Ricky would try to calm things down. Fergie was abrasive and never liked a quiet dressing room. If he thought it was too quiet he would start a fight. In any war he would have been the guerrilla fighter – ready to use any methods to win the fight.

He was so passionate and would just get players going. He didn't care if they didn't like him. It was his way of motivating them. He was never afraid to be abrasive when he felt the need to stimulate the dressing room.

After leaving St Mirren in 1973 I went to Hibernian and then on to Rangers in 1976. I thought that was me done as far as any ambitions of playing for Scotland were concerned. But in 1977 I rejoined St Mirren, who now had Fergie as their manager, and everything changed. He gave people, myself included, a belief in themselves.

He came calling for me when he noticed I had lost my place in the Rangers first team. I was only playing the odd game. His sales pitch when he contacted me was simple, but effective. "I'm going to the top and I think you should want to go there too," he said. He added that he would put me straight into his first team and together we would go places, but if I showed that I didn't share his ambitions then, "I'll drop you like a stone because nothing is going to stop me."

To be honest, I thought that was absolutely brilliant. I was leaving a huge club like Rangers and really it was a step back going to St Mirren, but this guy had convinced me that really I was going in the opposite direction.

I got to know him and his character – that drive and dedication to be the best. It might shock some people, but despite his links with Rangers from an early age then, believe me, he would have joined Celtic if it meant him making his way in the game. Nothing was going to stop him – not even the religious divide which separates the two clubs and Fergie being a Protestant. He is a football person before anything else and he wanted to be successful. I don't think it would have mattered to him how he did it or which club he played for or managed.

As a manager it didn't take long for people to recognise his potential within a few months of being in charge of East Stirlingshire. St Mirren were the first to come in for him and he completely transformed the club. He had his own way and often you would be fighting with him, but he galvanised the place. As I've already said, he loved it when he thought everyone was against him. He was a brilliant motivator in his own unique style. The players knew that if they were going out the night after a game not to bring anything decent that they would be wearing later on into the dressing room. We knew that there was every chance that cups of tea, or other objects capable of making a big mess of our suits or best clobber, would be thrown at us. So we would place our going-out gear well out of sight to keep it well protected.

He always wanted a big group of young players in his squad. That was the case at St Mirren and later at Aberdeen. At Manchester United it was his youth policy which was so important in turning the tide there. The Class of '92 was the bedrock of his future success at Old Trafford.

He also wanted a sprinkling of experience and that was one of the reasons he took me to St Mirren. There was also Jimmy Bone and Jackie Copeland and at 26 I was the third most experienced player on the books.

I was really annoyed when Fergie went to Aberdeen in 1978 because the only reason I returned to St Mirren was because of him. My game was on the up and the national team were watching me. He had told me he was going to the top and wanted me to join him. I thought that was happening at St Mirren, but obviously he decided it was going to be now with Aberdeen. He actually tried to take me to Aberdeen shortly after he had left, but I hadn't liked the way he had decided to leave after I had committed myself to his ambitions.

I know he likes to make out he was sacked by St Mirren, but some of us had known for a little while that he wanted to leave and become Aberdeen manager. He was worried about his reputation with the St Mirren fans, who held him in high esteem, so I think he manufactured a scenario where he knew he would push the St Mirren board too far, like wanting his wages tripled or something like that. In the end he was fired by the chairman.

It didn't do him any harm because, in my view, he went on to become Britain's greatest ever club manager. Some people north of the border go on about Jock Stein and others might have an honourable mention, but nobody has had the success that he has at four different clubs. You have to include what he did at East Stirlingshire and St Mirren in those formative years in addition to the numerous trophies he won with Aberdeen and Manchester United.

At St Mirren we came close to winning the Scottish title in 1979/80, with the team that he put together before leaving, which would have been unbelievable. He won the league with Aberdeen. His predecessor at Pittodrie, Billy McNeill, had done a great job, but Fergie took it on and had all the Aberdeen players believing in themselves. Although he would often fall out with them at times, he would never hold any grudges. The only thing which was unforgivable in his eyes was if you took a story to the media which was against the club. Then that was it. He would write you off for life.

You could have arguments, even fights with him, but as long as it was never revealed outside the club then you were alright. I think he invented the siege mentality tactic – circle the wagons, everyone is against us, we're all in it together.

For instance, he would tell his Aberdeen players that the Scottish newspaper football pages were dominated by reporters in the west of Scotland, that it was all about Rangers and Celtic and nobody cared for Aberdeen. Before you knew it, not only were all the players galvanised but so too were all the Aberdeen supporters. It was like he was trying to encourage the Aberdeen population to break away from the rest of Scotland – hence the rivalry which still exists today between Aberdeen and the Old Firm clubs.

On a personal level, even though I was annoyed at the manner of his departure from St Mirren and I rejected the opportunity to join him at Aberdeen, he sent me a telegram of congratulations when I was picked by Scotland in 1979. When I got transferred to Stoke City and then Sunderland he again sent his good wishes. He was terrific in that respect.

Tom Donnelly

TOM DONNELLY was at Rangers when Alex Ferguson arrived as a player and encountered him again as an East Stirlingshire player under Ferguson's management. By then he had qualified as a school teacher and was playing part-time for the club. His son Simon played for Celtic and went on to make 10 appearances for Scotland. Tom's parting shot to Fergie when he announced his departure from East Stirlingshire still brings him out in a cold sweat.

I wasn't ready to retire when Alex came to East Stirlingshire as the manager in 1974, but I was on the way down. I already knew him from the days we had been players together at Rangers. I was there for four years, but never played in the first team unlike him. I was one of the extras in the second or third team, but I'm still proud of my time at Ibrox.

I was a right-half and in those days we had John Greig, who was a right-half as well, so how the hell was I going to get in there? There was also Bobby Watson, a fine player. Then a young boy came in from Edinburgh a year later – Sandy Jardine. They were all superstars of the day so no wonder I couldn't get into the first team. On the other flank you had Jim Baxter, so it wasn't a bad side was it? Fergie arrived at the club from Dunfermline in 1967. The first thing you noticed was you didn't want to be a centre-half playing up against him. He was all arms and elbows and didn't mind where they ended up. You had to steer clear of him in training if you wanted to go home with all your teeth still intact, although in fairness he was a goalscoring centre-forward who was utilising his physical attributes to real effect.

He was 32 when came to East Stirlingshire, where we were all part-time, in 1974. My full-time job was that of a teacher. He immediately changed the training. He made it very competitive, which wasn't surprising for someone who even hated losing at dominoes. There were numerous set plays and tactics, which we had never been used to before his arrival. Before you just trained to be fit, but he introduced a professional aspect to it all. He would have us taking numerous corners and free-kicks. You'd be saying to yourself, "For God's sake what's this all about?" But he knew what he was doing.

There always used to be the odd free Saturday in the calendar because there was an odd number of clubs in the old Scottish Second Division which East Stirlingshire played in. On the first one, when he had become manager, he called us in for training. It was unknown for a part-time club, which we were, to be hauled in on a Saturday morning even though there was no game to prepare for.

Then the stories would start in order to try to get his messages across in training. I remember one of his first stories was telling us how, when he was playing against Celtic, he would always go for big Billy McNeill, who would be up against him at centre-half. He would use his elbows so it meant that Billy hated playing against him. It was a way of trying to inspire our forwards to, in effect, get their retaliation in first, try to unsettle the opposition with a few Fergie-esque arms and elbows.

Although he was only at East Stirlingshire for a short time he changed things very quickly and was constantly aware of the perilous financial state of the club. He treated their money – or lack of it – like his own, always looking at ways of saving cash or raising funds to try to bring in new players. I know it was the same when he moved on to St Mirren. Everything he did was for the good of the clubs he managed, especially in the early days, although some of my team-mates weren't happy when he stopped their expenses.

I had a car and there would often be four of the boys in it with me going to and from training. East Stirlingshire gave me £6 a week in expenses to run the car, but the other four, including Bobby McCulley, were claiming that as well, because until Fergie arrived no one knew they were getting lifts in my car. It didn't bother me picking them up because I was going through from Glasgow in any case for training.

One day Fergie discovered what had been going on and called us all into his office. He said to the other four, "You lot are getting £6 expenses, but you're travelling in with Donnelly." They had to admit it and were told in no uncertain terms that was the end of it. "You guys are getting nothing," he insisted. He said what he was saving on them would be put towards new players.

Even so, we had a great atmosphere. He had his moments, but it was generally a very close-knit group who wanted to do well. We gave Fergie everything and that continued after he left. I spent seven very happy years there and they even later paid for three trips to Wembley to watch Scotland. In his short time in charge I think Fergie changed the mindset of the club.

When he announced one day in the dressing room that he was leaving to join St Mirren I couldn't help myself. It wasn't exactly the language a teacher should use, but I just blurted out, "You bastard!" It's something he has obviously never forgotten because he mentioned it in one of his books. On page 147! It's ingrained in my brain.

He had built us up from nothing in such a short time that I didn't want to see him leave so quickly. Real professionalism had been introduced and we wanted it to continue. If you were late for training, for instance, you got fined and rightly so. We honestly thought that with him in charge we had a chance of winning the league we were in. It was such a let down to see him go, especially when you consider the success which came his way with all the clubs he went on to manage.

He never held my sudden outburst against me. Later, when he was at Manchester United, I asked him for some tickets for Mark Hughes' testimonial game because my father wanted to go. I tried to contact Fergie by phone and managed to get hold of his secretary. She listened to my request and the message came back that some tickets would be left, but Alex was sorry that he wouldn't be able to hand them over in person because he would be busy with the game.

My dad and his party were told to introduce themselves when they arrived at Old Trafford. When he arrived, as well as the match tickets there was an invitation to be shown around the Manchester United museum. That was unbelievable. I sent Alex a letter of thanks.

You could see from those first few days in charge at East Stir-lingshire that he had something special and he quickly trans-formed his next club St Mirren. We heard that he was driving around the area on a Friday night trying to get more supporters to watch St Mirren the next day. With all his teams it wasn't just about getting results. He wanted them to perform as well.

Somehow he managed to run a pub at the same time. It was near my team-mate, wee Bobby McCulley's house. We trained Tuesday and Thursday nights and played on Saturdays, so it didn't interfere with my teaching although it made it a full week. There were stories of his temper, but luckily I never saw it myself – even when I called him a bastard for leaving East Stirlingshire. He was also a very strict union man and would fight for players' rights. That came from his upbringing in the Govan shipyards, which was a hard life.

What he has done over the years has been phenomenal. I don't think his success will ever be repeated.

Bob McCulley

BOBBY McCULLEY was a midfielder for East Stirlingshire – the first club Alex Ferguson managed. In two spells at the club he made 268 league appearances. He also went on to manage The Shire in 1992/93.

I'd never been afraid of anybody before in my life until Alex Ferguson became my manager at East Stirlingshire in 1974. At times he was a right frightening bastard.

As a Rangers supporter through and through I already knew him as a no nonsense centre-forward who took no prisoners as a player. He was a battler and would fight for everything. Centre-halves knew they had been in a real scrap, players like

Celtic's Billy McNeill quickly realised they were in for a physical battering from Alex. There would be arms and elbows going everywhere. He could hold his own with anybody.

He wasn't shy in any way as a manager either. He came in and we knew straight away what he wanted from us. He didn't half give us a pounding right from the off.

The training was vicious compared to what we had been used to. Alex took us to the local park and we had to get stuck in. Our fitness levels improved straight away. We had some decent players who had been around the block a few times, but it didn't matter to the new manager – he didn't care who they were, he could handle them.

It was a team full of characters. Tom Gourlay, our goalkeeper who had been released by Partick Thistle, was a hell of a size and was in fear of nothing until he met Fergie. The full-backs were Jim Stirling, known as Stuckie, and Jim McGregor. Sadly Jim McGregor died a few years later from a brain haemorrhage.

Gordon Simpson was the captain and the guy no one answered back to. He was as hard as nails. I remember a game away to Stranraer when the cartilage in his knee popped out. He popped it back in and carried on playing. He had worked down the pits and was scared of no one. But even he used to cower in the corner when Fergie slammed the dressing room door behind him.

We had Bobby Stein, who was Rangers striker Colin's brother. He wasn't a shrinking violet either, but he would visibly shrivel in size when the manager let loose. It was fearsome and he had a habit of trapping you where you were sitting. He'd come over to within a few inches of your face and give you the treatment. If it was your turn he wouldn't shout at you across the room because that would have given you the chance to adopt a defensive position.

I have spoken to Steve Archibald, who was at Aberdeen under Fergie, and he said that was the same ploy he used at Pittodrie. Steve admitted that it induced terror the moment you saw him walking towards you. Peter Dunne, our centre-half, had a bit of money and turned up at training in a yellow sports car, which Fergie promptly told him to get rid of. I think he saw it as a bit self-indulgent. Others in the side included Dave Robertson, a fast and skilful left-sided player, and striker Billy Hulston, who cost Fergie £1,000 – half his transfer budget – from Clyde. Signing him was the first sign that he had an eye for a player.

Jim Mullen was a very fast attacking player who Fergie brought in on a free transfer, although it came back to haunt him when he scored in our 5-0 win against St Mirren in the last game of the 1974/5 season after Alex had taken over as manager there. Another member of the team was a teacher, Ian Browning. It was a good squad which enjoyed a special bond. It's still very special to this day to have been in Fergie's first team.

Alex quickly got to know what made each player tick. I am only 5ft 2in and he kept telling me I would get bigger out on the pitch. Just little things like that – it would make you feel as if you could take on the world. It was a special gift he seemed to possess. In games you knew you were now playing for him as well as yourself. You didn't want to let him down. He lifted everyone. You noticed the difference. But at times he could be one real frightening so and so.

If he asked you to do something on the field and you didn't do it he would be waiting for you in the dressing room. His face would be set and he would be looking straight at you. Honestly, he could be a frightening bugger. He wasn't a bully though – he just demanded that you lived up to his expectations.

He asked me once why I had taken an extra touch on the ball, "Why didn't you just play it inside?" he snarled. I'd lost possession and it had resulted in losing a goal. "Yes, but 16 guys touched the ball after that," I pleaded, "How can I be held responsible?"

"Aye, but you started the ball rolling to them," he answered back. I would say to myself, 'What's he going on about?' But later I realised that maybe I should have passed instead of trying to be George Best. So one thing was for certain, I didn't hang onto the ball too long the next time. There was nothing that he didn't see – he was a very clever man.

He also ran a pub at the time. I was living just around the corner from it and he would be in it regularly, taking charge. He was a leader there. It was a real rough pub that had its moments and you had to have your wits about you. It didn't bother him as he knew how to talk to people and how to win them over.

He could handle the hardest people in the pub. Before he took it over most of them were running the pub – they weren't after he became the landlord. There was only one person running it and that was Fergie. Whatever he took on he would be in charge very quickly. He was a great leader. He often played dominoes and always wanted to win – he was so competitive at everything.

His first game in charge was away to Forfar Athletic in August 1974 in the Scottish League Cup. I think his first wage was £40 a week. We were 3-0 down at half time and it looked like there was no way back – but the boss had other ideas. We traipsed in at half-time and were expecting both barrels. We knew what he was like and we were ready for the worst. He had been there long enough for us to know half-time could be interesting to say the least. I know there was no one in a hurry to be first back into the changing room. It must have been the slowest walk to a dressing room you have ever seen. Once we got there everyone was looking down at the floor not wanting to catch his eye. I think I must have tied my bootlaces at least six times. But instead of ripping into us he told us we were playing great. He filled us with confidence and a belief that we weren't beaten yet.

There was no ranting and raving – just encouragement saying that if we got an early goal then we were back in the match. Everyone was expecting, 'you cunt this and that'. It didn't happen. It was just football chat and it was such a relief that we had been given a second chance that we managed to make it 3-3. We scored three goals in six minutes and could even have won it but Billy Hulston hit the post late on. Fergie had worked his magic in his first game as manager.

As our new boss he didn't miss a trick. I used to claim expenses for getting the train to and from training. But one day he pulled me aside and wondered why I hadn't got soaked walking from the station to the training ground because it had been pissing it down. Somehow he had discovered I'd been getting a lift by car with Tom Donnelly and Davie Robertson. He gave me the eyes and there were no expenses paid the next week.

He has always been a shrewd man, but he commanded instant respect and was tireless. You couldn't get him off the training pitch. I never saw him look at his watch the entire time he was in charge of us. It was all about doing it his way and there would be no compromise. It could go dark, but we would carry on even if he couldn't afford to put the floodlights on because they were a luxury the club couldn't pay for. He had a look about him that meant you never argued because it was always his way.

We were playing one match and I had been left out, even though he had told me I had been the outstanding player in the previous game. We stopped off on the way home for a break and I decided to drown my sorrows by ordering a pint, which wasn't really allowed. Before I had even had time to touch it there was a furious Ferguson standing over me. He didn't have to say a word – the eyes said it all, 'What the fuck are you doing? I tried to pretend the pint belonged to the guy next to me – a complete waste of time.

His organisation and his attention to detail were incredible. Back at the training ground he would join in the five-a-sides and we would play on in the dark if his side were losing. If we wanted to go home it was often better to let his team win. He was ferocious in the games, elbowing and kicking.

We may have only had him as our manager at East Stirling-shire for 17 games, but it was no surprise to me that he went on to do great things. The man is nothing short of a genius. He was a leader and he could have run the country. He would have brushed any opponents aside – nothing would have stopped him in delivering his beliefs.

I also worked under his brother Martin. He came to the club in 1981. He was hard working and not a bad judge of a player, but there's only one Sir Alex Ferguson and I'll go to my grave believing that. He is a unique person. Martin was a lot quieter than his older brother, but he went on to have a good career and became Manchester United's chief European scout. It's probably unfair to compare them. Alex's mandate was to make everyone understand that the impossible was possible. That's the difference – he was great in company. He would fire off, but that was it. Once he'd had his say it was forgotten. There was no atmosphere on the bus coming back after a game. When he hit you with something that was it – it was then gone.

Another thing about Fergie is that he treated everyone the same, which included all the backroom staff. For him it was about the guy who picks the boots up. For him the guy who puts the kit in the washing machine is as important as the centre-forward. You can't pretend all that – you either have that humility or you don't. It's about letting people know they are important in the running of a football club.

He's the best manager I've ever known and also a great story teller. Very close to being perfect.

Sir Kenny Dalglish

SIR KENNY DALGLISH and Sir Alex Ferguson have known each other since the 1960s. Kenny made his name with Celtic before moving to Liverpool where he became a legendary player and manager. His Liverpool and Blackburn Rovers sides went head-to-head with Alex's Manchester United.

Our families go way back to before either of us became known as rivals in football circles. It was an era when footballers would often buy a pub to help supplement their income or help provide some security for the future. Fergie bought a pub in Glasgow. My father-in-law was already in the business and he taught Fergie the pub licence trade.

I was brought up on the north side of the city in Mingulay

Street and Fergie was brought up on the south side. It was a life of playing football whenever you could. The only time I stopped playing was when the ice cream van came around on a Friday.

When I was about 14 we moved to the south side of the city and our home was close to Ibrox. Because of that, as a youngster I used to hang around with some of the Rangers kids. Often Alex Miller, who went on to manage Hibernian, and I would head into town. Fergie, who was older than us and had joined Rangers in 1967, would give us a lift. We knew he must have cost a big fee [£65,000 from Dunfermline] as he had a big car.

I joined Celtic in 1968 and our manager, Jock Stein, took a great interest in the kids and used to move us about so we all played in different positions to add to our experience. You were sometimes playing in a position you didn't really want to play in and that's why at Celtic Park, in a reserve team game against Rangers, I found myself at centre-half up against Fergie, who had been selected for the Rangers reserve team.

I don't think I ever got off the floor to win any headers, which is no surprise when you look at the difference in our physiques. The biggest thing I can remember was Fergie using his elbows at every opportunity. They were a real nuisance. But we still ended up winning the game even though I can recall him not being too complimentary about me, telling someone, "That wee fat boy won't make a player." Despite that, he has always been someone I can approach and talk to about many subjects.

Alex was a fantastically successful manager with Aberdeen and Manchester United. I have only respect and admiration for what he achieved in more than 40 years at the sharp end. He gained great fame for the success he had, year after year. He was one of the very best in the business. The success he had with Aberdeen was incredible. I don't think it is properly appreciated. It may have been dismissed too easily by some people. He has always been someone to try to defy the odds. When he was manager of Manchester United he was a fighter and he displayed similar qualities in fighting back to health from his brain haemorrhage a few years back.

What I liked about him most as a manager is that he stood his ground for his club and his players. He defended them all to the hilt and rightly so. He was always in their corners.

Of course, we had our disagreements over the years and that happens in management. We both wanted to win – that's the way it should be. But there was always respect and friendship. Before every game we'd warmly shake hands and wish each other all the best. But deep down – under our breath – we'd be saying we hoped to win the game by a big margin! Then at full-time, win, lose or draw, we'd have a drink and a blether together. We'd tend to try to avoid talking about the game that had just taken place. I always found that to be the best way with all managers.

When I first went into management with Liverpool and achieved any success he would write a letter to me offering his congratulations. I'd do the same to him when Manchester United were successful. We were in competition – but it was never a war. When I returned to manage Liverpool for my second spell in 2011 we played United at Old Trafford in my first game in the FA Cup. Fergie shouted down the tunnel towards me before the game, "Are you coming in for a drink afterwards?" I replied, "Of course, I'm surprised you had to ask!" We laughed at that, but he went on to explain that not many managers shared a drink anymore. Maybe that's how it is now, but we're both Glaswegians and like a wee tipple at the appropriate time.

I also played under Alex for a short while for Scotland when he was assistant to Jock Stein. I enjoyed his training because he clearly knew the game. He then took over as national manager after Jock died suddenly and was in charge of Scotland at the 1986 World Cup finals in Mexico.

As everyone knows, I withdrew from the squad after damaging a knee ligament with the surgeon telling me that if I went to the finals I would jeopardise my chances of being fit for the new domestic season with Liverpool. It was said at the time that I withdrew because of a dislike of Alex, or wasn't happy with the squad he selected. It was all a load of nonsense.

So too were any suggestions that we were often at each other's throats. Like I said, we've had our disagreements, some of them played out in public, but they were always a storm in a teacup. We played Manchester United at Anfield in April 1988 on our way to winning the title, but on that day we were leading 3-1 only for United to come back to draw 3-3 despite having Colin Gibson sent off. That didn't leave me in the best of moods, but evidently Fergie wasn't happy either.

He was moaning in the tunnel that teams never get a decision at Anfield, coming out with stuff like that to the media. He was in full throttle, giving his opinions to a radio man, and I heard him when I had my six-week-old daughter Lauren in my arms. As I passed by I said to the radio interviewer, "You're better off talking to my baby. She's only six weeks old but you'll get more sense from her than him."

Fergie wasn't happy and let out a mouthful in my direction. "Careful Alex, the baby's a bit too young for that," I answered back. But there was no feud, nothing was ever carried on. Shortly after the Anfield incident Alan Hansen had a testimonial dinner and Fergie was a guest on the top table – there was no problem. My wife Marina and I also attended a tribute dinner to Alex in London. Following the Hillsborough disaster in April 1989, he was one of the first people on the phone to me. He also sent a group of supporters over to Merseyside to pay their respects, which was a wonderful gesture. Since he retired in 2013 I've seen a lot of him in the directors' box at Anfield or in the room he has at Old Trafford. He was also my guest of honour when Liverpool renamed the Centenary Stand at Anfield in my name.

Both during my time as manager of Liverpool and Blackburn Rovers, the media often portrayed us as 'bitter rivals'. Because of these constantly whipped-up stories, the public must have been fooled into thinking we were at war. Nothing could have been further from the truth. In fact when Fergie was under pressure in his early years at Old Trafford, I spoke up for him at a football writers event. I told them that, in my view, he would eventually turn things around at Old Trafford – although I never thought he would have won as much as he did! I remember the United physio Jim McGregor coming up to me shortly after my defence of his manager that night telling me that he felt Fergie had needed that support.

The way he restructured the Manchester United youth set-up was magnificent. He also led the club to their first league title in 26 years and followed that up with success after success. Although you could never for one minute call him a silky player during his career on the pitch – he was honest and industrious – the teams he managed always played with flair as well as good organisation. At St Mirren and Aberdeen he also sent out exciting teams.

Alex would always try to use psychology to unsettle his rivals.

He tried it on when I was at Blackburn and we looked a good bet to beat United to the 1995 Premier League title. I just ignored it, or tried to turn it back onto him. At one stage, in an effort to heap the pressure on us, he said Blackburn, "needed to do a Devon Loch" to miss out. I was asked about it and replied, "Is that an expanse of water in Scotland?" Of course I knew really it was the horse who inexplicably fell while leading the 1956 Grand National with the finishing post in sight, but I wasn't letting on so his piece of supposed psychology fell flat.

I had a group of positive players at Ewood Park who also joined me in laughing at Fergie's attempted mind games. But to be fair, at the end of the season – after we pipped his side to the title on the final day – he pushed aside his disappointment to send a letter of congratulations. At the end of it there was a P.S.

'Devon Loch is a horse! I'm sure your dad must have backed it – mine did!'

Frank McGarvey

FRANK McGARVEY enjoyed a love-hate relationship with Alex Ferguson during their time together at St Mirren. He moved to Liverpool then Celtic, where his goals helped them win two Scottish League titles, two Scottish FA Cups and a League Cup before he returned to St Mirren.

Alex Ferguson's famous hairdryer treatment was, I believe, tested on myself and the rest of the St Mirren players long before he turned it into an art form at Aberdeen and Manchester United. Even for an Easterhouse boy [part of Glasgow], some of the language he used seemed a bit industrial. I hated half-time talks when we weren't playing well and the bollockings at the end of games when he wasn't happy.

He would throw cups, glasses and tumblers at us. But he would aim at the wall above you so that the glass and broken porcelain would fall on our heads. He once smashed a bottle of Coca-Cola above our heads after a game at Love Street with all the Coke rolling down the wall. He had gone off on one over his pet hate, which was players drinking too much – even though he ran a pub in Glasgow called 'Fergie's' while managing us! Too much alcohol, he believed, was the scourge of any team and everyone knows that he put an end to the drinking culture at Manchester United soon after he arrived there.

After a slow start to his St Mirren management career in 1974/75 his methods began to pay dividends and we managed to scrape into the new-look First Division – the second tier – following the Scottish League's restructuring. At the end of the 1975/76 season we knew we would be going on a three-week tour to Barbados, Guyana and Suriname. But I almost missed out after giving Fergie a mouthful because I had been substituted in a game. He just stared at me as I came off because he hated anyone giving him stick, especially when all the fans were watching. Yet there I was, playing in only my first full season for St Mirren, giving it to him between the eyes in a fit of rage. I went straight to the dressing room and his assistant Davie Provan came in behind me and said to calm down, Fergie only wanted to give me a rest. Fergie continued to play me, but didn't speak to me for three weeks.

I was expecting a huge bollocking, but it never came, which made it worse because I knew he hadn't let go of what had happened. At least you knew that a bollocking – however bad – would be the end of it. I soon discovered what he had been planning.

The list of those who were going on the Barbados trip was posted and my name wasn't on it. At first I thought it was just a mistake. I looked up and down the paper, but there was no sign of my name. I then realised why I hadn't been included. I was told that I had to apologise sincerely to the gaffer or I wouldn't be going on the tour. But I wasn't going to apologise, I was too stubborn. The impasse went on until the end of the season when I still hadn't apologised. The other players were loving it, winding me up as the days went by, talking about how much sun they would enjoy and how much fun they would have while I was left behind. I pretended I wasn't bothered, but I knew that Fergie had to win or I wasn't going anywhere.

At the club's Player of the Year awards night I decided that I would swallow my pride and apologise. The other players were saying, "Right, Frank. There he is alone, up you go now." I made dummy run after dummy run. Eventually when I confronted him and apologised, he ignored me. I went back to my seat and told our physio Ricky McFarlane, Eddie McDonald, who was one of our coaches, and Tony Fitzpatrick that I had been blanked by Fergie and they fell about laughing. However, later on that night Ricky whispered in my ear, "You're going to Barbados. Don't worry." It was all a game to Fergie. He eventually telephoned my home and my mum answered and whispered to me, "It's Alex Ferguson." I thought at first for her to tell him I had gone to Spain. In all honesty, I wouldn't have had enough money to have gone to Carlisle!

It was on that tour that I played alongside Fergie up front.

He had finished playing by that time, but he was 35, still reasonably fit and he always joined in the games in training. Unfortunately the Ferguson-McGarvey partnership lasted all of 10 minutes before he was sent off against Guyana!

Fergie claims that he wasn't happy about one of our players, Robert Torrance, getting a hard time from their centre-half and he came on after half-time to sort him out with his infamous elbows. But my recollection is different. He slipped a great ball to me and the referee, a big blond-haired guy, blew for offside. Fergie shouted, "For fuck's sake, he was onside." The referee said, "What's your name sonny?"

Fergie replied, "You're not fucking booking me are you?" The referee responded, "Did you swear again? Off you go." We ended up losing the game 2-1 after going down to 10 men.

We had to agree that the press couldn't find out about the sending off. That was his only message after the game, "Don't tell anyone I was sent off." We didn't dare. But apart from Fergie's red card it was a good tour because it gave us the chance to bond. So from the start of the next season, 1976/77, we were well-placed to make a bid for promotion. Four of us were also involved in the Scotland Under-21 squad – Bobby Reid, Tony Fitzpatrick, Billy Stark and myself, which was quite a compliment for a club not in the top flight of Scottish football.

We hinted at what we were capable of by beating Rangers 2-0 in a pre-season friendly and I got the two goals. Fergie was certainly happy with my form and in November, when we had beaten Arbroath 3-0 to go top of the table, he told the press that I was the best forward in the First Division. We were still top of the table at the turn of the year and people really took notice when we beat Premier Division side Dundee United 4-1 in the third round of the Scottish Cup at Love Street in front of 19,000 fans. Fergie had captured the imagination of the Paisley public.

He was also becoming a dab hand at mind games. Before that game against Dundee United he had said to me that he had been talking to their manager Jim McLean, who thought I was hopeless. I swallowed it hook, line and sinker and I ran the Dundee United defence ragged.

When we were drawn against another Premier Division side in the next round, Motherwell at Fir Park, we took more than 10,000 fans with us. The game didn't turn out to be the classic that it had promised to be. I put all the blame on the Motherwell manager, Willie McLean, brother of Dundee United's Jim. Willie's tactics seemed to be simple and easy to understand – kick fuck out of the opposition. We limped out of Fir Park following a 2-1 defeat.

Fergie was raging about the tactics and complained so much to referee Ian Foote that he was reported to the Scottish FA. Fergie told me after the game that he wanted to see me at Love Street at 10am on the Sunday. I had scored the only goal at Fir Park, so as far as I was concerned he wouldn't be able to complain about my contribution in the game. I had heard that Arsenal and Ajax wanted to buy me, so I thought it might have something to do with that. Did I fancy London or Amsterdam? Maybe another team had come in for me. I even flirted with the possibility he was about to give me a rise.

The next day I went into Fergie's office and before I could get the pleasantries over with he said, "I've been told that you were drinking in the Waterloo Bar in Glasgow the night before the game." I was stunned. I hardly drank, and never before games. I told him that and also that my wife Pauline worked in the pub and that I had been there to pick her up. I then added that whoever had claimed to have seen me drunk was a liar and we started arguing.

Fergie picked up a set of keys from his desk and threw them at me, aiming to miss as usual. I pointed behind him and said, "If those keys had hit my head, you were out of that window." He screamed: "What, you'd put me out of the window?" He then came after me. I knew he would have battered me, so I bolted along the corridor and down the rickety old stairs. He stopped and I heard him shout, "Never come back here again." I shouted back, "I'll never play for you again anyway and don't bother phoning me either."

I had driven to Love Street contemplating the possibility of a move to London or the continent and returned home banned from the club and with the manager threatening not to let me play football again. He had obviously wanted to send a message to all the players that there was to be no drinking at the club because there were a few boozers in the St Mirren dressing room at the time. But he had picked on the wrong player. He phoned a few times and we eventually made up on the morning before a crucial home game against Clydebank the following week. They were one of our main challengers for the title and victory for us would virtually end their interest and put us on the way to the Division One championship. It wasn't the time to wrongly discipline your top scorer and Fergie knew it.

Promotion to the Premier Division meant a lot of money to St Mirren so Fergie was under pressure to get me back in, whether he wanted me or not. He said in his book that he could have put me out of the game at that juncture, which was nonsense. The club could have got £250,000 for me – they couldn't have got that for him. If St Mirren had missed out on promotion because Fergie had wanted to teach me a lesson then I know who would have been out of the door first. In the event we won 3-1 and I got plenty of plaudits for scoring the third goal. The win made us favourites for the title and after the game Fergie and I were cuddling!

The game that actually won us the First Division championship was against Dundee at Dens Park. We blew them away that night and I scored a hat-trick in a memorable 4-0 win, Billy Stark scoring the other one. Fergie was also pleased because Davie White, who was the Rangers manager when he was forced out of Ibrox, was the Dundee manager. St Mirren under Fergie were worthy Division One champions.

In the Premier Division in 1977/78 we struggled for most of the season, although my own form was good and an ever-increasing number of English clubs were beginning to take an interest in me. But I was enjoying life at St Mirren, especially with Fergie encouraging us to play football all the time instead of becoming more defensive.

Fergie told the press that he had knocked back four bids from English clubs for some of his players. Newcastle United were reportedly set to make a bid for me while Arsenal said that they would offer a record fee. Fergie dismissed the Gunners' interest, but he knew that he couldn't keep us all indefinitely. There were even rumours of my reported fee – £250,000 was being talked about – going towards building the Main Stand at Love Street.

After Christmas we struggled to steer clear of the relegation zone, even with the addition of new recruit Jimmy Bone, an experienced striker who turned out to be one of Fergie's last signings. We couldn't put a run of results together, but luckily enough for us Ayr United and Clydebank were struggling just as much as us.

We had to play at Ayr United in March and I managed to score the winning goal, which meant they couldn't overtake us. After the game Fergie was hugging Tony Fitzpatrick as if we had won the league instead of simply taking a step towards staying in it. When we got back to the dressing room we discovered that someone had broken in and stolen all the players' money.

Fergie took control right away, telling us that the club would reimburse us and asked Ayr to settle the bill later. He started taking note of how much we had lost, 'Tony Fitzpatrick, £2.75. Bobby Reid, £3.75'. When Fergie said, "Frank?" I quickly replied, "I've lost £95.50." Fergie almost choked and said, "What? Why the fuck did you have all that money on you?"

"I had a wee win at the bookies," I explained. He ended up giving me more money than all the rest of the players put together. We got a cheque from Ayr United a few days later for the amount we had all lost.

We ended up surviving our first season in the Premier League with a little to spare, finishing in eighth place, six points ahead of Ayr United and eleven ahead of Clydebank, both of whom were relegated. I had scored 19 goals for a team that hadn't challenged for honours. Nobody had to tell me my worth, although I knew that I had Fergie to thank for what I had achieved.

So it was like a death in the family when I found out that he had been sacked. We couldn't understand it. We had survived a tough opening season in the top flight and were set to make the next step up. All the players had ultimate confidence in the manager and I believe we would have ended up winning the Premier Division within two years if he had been allowed to keep all his players and bring in a bit more experience. None of the St Mirren directors gave us an explanation for their decision. We read about it in the papers and there was a lot of talk about problems over expenses and breaches of contract, but that turned out to be rubbish. Fergie made St Mirren a lot of money by taking them into the Premier Division and he had accumulated a set of young players worth a fortune to the club. But because of boardroom politics he was forced out.

It was simply a monumental mistake, probably one of the worst decisions ever made by the board of any football club.

2

'*I scored a penalty, although I had been so nervous walking up. I thought, 'miss this and you're a dead man'. As soon as I scored I stuck two fingers up at him. Luckily the players engulfed me in the celebrations so he didn't see my gesture!*'

Gordon Strachan, Aberdeen and
Manchester United player

Billy Stark

BILLY STARK can proudly proclaim that he was signed twice by Alex for St Mirren and his trophy-winning Aberdeen side. A creative midfielder, Billy also went on to play for Celtic before becoming the Bhoys' assistant boss. He also had a spell in charge of the Scotland national team. Since 2018 he has been head coach of Scotland Under 19s.

There was this wee scout called Archibald Lindsay – known as 'Baldy' – who was a taxi driver. Luckily for me he had a real liking for me as a player. I had been training with Rangers and Dumbarton and he was scouting for St Mirren. He was relentless in terms of his pursuit, so eventually I agreed to go to train with them and I also played against the Buddies for Anniesland Waverley, a juvenile team I was involved with. I don't know whether that game had been arranged for my benefit or to watch some other players as well.

On the back of that came an invitation to go down to Selkirk with St Mirren for a pre-season game in July 1975. It was in effect a trial, and one for which I missed a family wedding to play in. I didn't think, to be honest, it went very well in terms of my performance. As you can imagine, it was a difficult situation for a young boy of 19 having to play with established professionals. I was really nervous.

At the end of the game I thought I wouldn't be asked back. I couldn't have been more wrong because on the bus going back home Alex Ferguson produced the forms for me to sign. There wasn't much discussion. He just said, "Sign here." You learn when you go into coaching that the player you've gone to watch might not have a good game, but you can still see certain things in him. Everyone can have a poor day, but thankfully he must have liked something in my play.

So there I was, signing for St Mirren on the bus after some pretty straight negotiations. I think Anniesland Waverley got sixty quid and a couple of balls. But it was a great opportunity for me to get into professional football.

I knew all about Alex before I signed for St Mirren. He was a well-known character. He'd played for a few clubs and, of course, Rangers was the high-profile one. His goalscoring record at Ibrox was tremendous, but in football there are often scapegoats if you lose important games. Rangers lost the 1969 Scottish Cup final 4-0 to Celtic in front of 132,000 fans at Hampden Park and Fergie was blamed for Billy McNeill's opening goal after failing to pick him up from a corner. That was the end of him as a Rangers player.

Rangers had done the same thing in 1967 after losing a Scottish Cup tie 1-0 at Berwick Rangers, which is probably still the biggest Scottish Cup shock of all time. Two players who were involved in that game, Jim Forrest and his strike partner George McLean, never played for the club again. My father was a Rangers fan and for a time I went with him to Ibrox and saw Alex play. I always took to goalscorers, because for me they always had the hardest job and he was one of them. So I knew all about him as a player when I ended up at St Mirren, but not about him as a manager.

When Alex signed me in 1975 he had only been a manager for a year, having arrived from East Stirlingshire in October 1974. He was really in the embryonic stage and I think that benefited us. Certainly looking back it did, because in those days the manager had absolute total power over players. They could manage in whichever way they felt was right.

It's fair to describe the Alex Ferguson of that time as volatile, but I think we all noticed as players that it was an ambition, a drive to be successful. It was difficult to accept at the time, but it was never personal, certainly never so in my experience. Not that you felt that when you were in the firing line over certain things. He had an omnipresence. You always felt you were being watched by him.

He was only trying to get the absolute maximum out of you as a player. To be honest, I can say categorically that if he didn't have much to do with you in terms of criticism then you were in trouble, because he thought you were a lost cause. He was always testing you. You might get some bollockings, but at the same time you earned some respect because he was actually spending time dealing with you.

Even in later years, when I joined up with him again at Aberdeen in 1983, there was never total joy at half-time or following a game. There would always be some criticism coming somebody's way. From my experience of working with him, complacency is a word that could never be used or be associated with Alex Ferguson. That was behind his style of management. Once he got a group of players doing well there was no way anyone would be allowed to become complacent. He loved to shake things up. All of a sudden he would create a situation, a flashpoint out of the blue.

Coming in at half-time you couldn't predict how he was going to react to you. You might have thought to yourself that you'd done quite well so you'd be okay, but that was when he would be onto you. At other times you would think you'd had a nightmare and be ready for the hairdryer treatment, but he would leave you alone.

He had an uncanny knack of sensing the mood and knowing what needed to be done in terms of getting a reaction from his players. Not that Frank McGarvey appreciated being hauled off after just 20 minutes in a game at Love Street when we played Queen of the South. I was a substitute in that game and I soon had Frank sitting next to me. Frank was a colourful character, a really good player with a terrific workrate, but in his early days a pass from Frank was the last resort. That's how I learned to make decoy runs, when Frank was on the ball! But we did have a good partnership. Subbing him off after 20 minutes was proof that Alex wasn't afraid to make big decisions. He took me off on many occasions too, but thankfully not as early as his substituting of Frank that day.

No one could take that winning mentality away from Fergie. He wanted to impart that to his players and that's why some fell by the wayside, unable to meet his demands. Some players – the likes of Willie Miller, Roy Keane and Steve Bruce – are born with it, while others need cajoling to get the best out of them.

As a manager myself I've said to players, "Do you want to win this game?" And every hand will go up saying, "Of course we do." Then I've added, "Well are you going to do what needs to be done to win it?" That's what a winning mentality is all about – that you will go to the limits, but stay within the rules.

I'm in charge of Scotland Under 19s and with younger players this willingness to go the extra mile is inbuilt in some of them. But it is a different era now. When I was brought up there were more youngsters bred with this drive through a more difficult and demanding upbringing. We live in a different world now in terms of how children are brought up. Who's to say what is wrong and what is right? It was tough in our day and I think that's what bred players with real character. They had that resolute mentality – one almost of survival.

You now have to be more careful about how you manage young players, especially as an international manager because they are not your players. You are only borrowing them from the clubs, so you have to send them back in good shape and hope they have enjoyed the experience.

At St Mirren we had a young side under Alex and I didn't play any reserve team football. I was thrown straight into it, making my debut against Montrose in the League Cup in August '75. In my first season at Love Street I was either starting or on the bench. I was always involved and I was thrown in at the deep end. It was the same with Frank McGarvey, Tony Fitzpatrick, Bobby Reid – young boys like that.

Alex then played a masterstroke in his recruitment – and his recruitment over the years stands comparison with anybody – when he brought in Iain Munro, Jackie Copland and, shortly before he left for Aberdeen, Jimmy Bone. They were experienced professionals, but not only that they were the type of professionals who brought on young players as well.

We won promotion to the top-flight in 1976/77 and I contributed 11 goals, including the opener against Dundee on the day we won promotion at Dens Park. I also scored when we beat Dundee United, who were top of the Scottish Premier Division at the time, 4-1 in the Scottish Cup third round at Love Street. That team was nicknamed 'Fergie's Furies' by the *Daily Record* and we had promotion sewn up with two games to spare.

We were a good side and we certainly missed him when he

left St Mirren. Under him the crowds had increased phenomenally and he had done well to keep us in the Scottish Premier Division in 1977/78 with not much money to spend. He did a tremendous job at Love Street and there was real momentum.

It was disappointing when he left in the summer of 1978. Jim Clunie, who had some good success at St Mirren, succeeded him, but he was completely different to Alex. At times he had a short temper, but never in Alex's class.

Even then we all knew that the main man had gone and there would be a difference. We obviously didn't realise the greatness Alex would go on to achieve as a manager, but we enjoyed being on that bandwagon with him. It was a real jolt when he left. Normally managers leave when the club is struggling, but we had been doing well under him.

I must have done something right at St Mirren because Fergie signed me for Aberdeen as well. If I ever need a boost then I can come out with that fact – Alex Ferguson, someone who went on to become one of the best managers of all time, signed me twice. Not many can say that.

My contract was up at St Mirren in 1983, which was the first year of freedom of contract for players. I had been at Love Street for eight years and was now aged 27. Under the new rules you could move if your contract was up. I had made my mind up that I was keen to leave St Mirren and try to step up to a higher level. I wanted to win some trophies. Rangers and Dundee United were keen to sign me and Alex had also been on the phone telling me he wanted to bring me to Aberdeen. It was just before their European Cup Winners' Cup final against Real Madrid, which of course they ended up winning.

I think he was down at the Footballer of the Year dinner in

London. He had heard a rumour that I was signing for Rangers and was not pleased to say the least. He calmed down when I managed to reassure him that I was going to end up at Pittodrie.

I signed for Aberdeen a couple of weeks later and also watched on TV the Scottish Cup final at which he gave his players on-field rollockings even though they had just beaten Rangers 1-0. It was a reminder of what I would be letting myself in for again, but of course my time at St Mirren had prepared me for events like that. This one was stage-managed. He knew the points he wanted to get across to the players. As I've said before, complacency didn't have a place in his vocabulary, even when you won a trophy.

All my hopes at joining Aberdeen were quickly realised. It was a side packed with plenty of international players, which was a new experience for me. It was a big step up in terms of the quality of players like Alex McLeish, Willie Miller, Gordon Strachan and Mark McGhee. I wasn't frightened of the challenge even though I wouldn't call myself an ebullient, super confident person, but I knew the manager and what he expected, so I was ready to take it on. I think what relaxed me somewhat was that Alex had signed me for a second time.

At Aberdeen he had his moments with me and his psychology at trying to get the best out of me was always at the forefront. I missed a penalty at Celtic in a 2-1 defeat and in the next training session he came alongside me and whispered that he hoped my missed penalty hadn't cost Aberdeen the Scottish title. It wasn't done nastily, it was to drive me on for the next game to try and make up for that mistake.

In my early days at Aberdeen I had got into the team on a fairly regular basis, but from October 1983 I missed out through injury and didn't come back into the side until April 1984. It was a long spell to be out in my first season at the club.

I must have only played three or four games at the end of the season, but he put me in his 13-man squad for the Scottish Cup final against Celtic. That was a big boost. It was a tremendous gesture and I ended up getting my first Scottish Cup winners' medal. I came on as a substitute as we beat Celtic 2-1 in extra-time with Mark McGhee getting the winner to complete Aberdeen's first and only Scottish League and Cup double.

We also won the European Super Cup and reached the semi-finals of the Scottish League Cup and the European Cup Winners' Cup in 1983/84 – it was quite a season to be an Aberdeen player.

We won the title with five games to spare, Stewart McKimmie scoring the goal that clinched the championship with a 1-0 win against Hearts at Tynecastle, but the winners' medals were only given out following the last game of the season. I had a fight to get one off Alex. I had missed a lot of the season and his reluctance, at first, to hand a medal over to me was again another of his psychological ploys. He knew I would be determined to try to win the Scottish Premier Division the next season and be more worthy of a winners' medal.

Sure enough, we went on to win the title again in 1985 even though we had lost some big players in Strachan, McGhee and Doug Rougvie. Everything carried on as normal and we accumulated a record points total of 59 from a possible 72 under the old system of two points for a win.

Of course, we knew all the success Alex was having at Aberdeen was attracting interest from other clubs. I remember him being linked with Rangers and Tottenham.

There were a few times we thought he might be off. It prompted Aberdeen to hand him a new improved contract and I've got to admit it was a shock when Manchester United took him away in 1986.

We knew something was up when, during training, we noticed a lot of the top football writers had suddenly descended. It was a huge story – Alex Ferguson leaving Aberdeen for Old Trafford – and they had arrived to cover it. We were really disappointed that he was on his way, even though we often had to endure some biting criticism. We had total respect for Fergie.

He had also been incredibly loyal to me and the loyalty was mutual. I would have happily taken another bollocking if it meant he would still be my manager at Aberdeen.

He also had a tremendous sense of humour. Alex loved a laugh and loved to wind you up.

The trips on the coach to away games could be fun as well. He would sit and play cards with the players or organise quizzes. He was never a manager who would detach himself from everyone. One moment he would berate you, the next he would be sat with you having a laugh. He could always find the right words at the right time and his all round knowledge was exceptional. In quizzes he was the top man. He loved delving into the history of the game and knew his football.

I think he would have been successful in any other walk of life, whether it was politics – which he was keen on – or whatever else. He would have had the same galvanising effect as he enjoyed in football in whatever he turned his hand to.

When he left Aberdeen we all thought the same thing. How do you replace the irreplaceable?

Quite simply, you can't.

Pat Stanton

PAT STANTON is a Hibernian legend who played more than 400 games for the Hibees before becoming Alex's first assistant manager when he moved to Aberdeen in 1978. He played 16 times for Scotland and also returned to Easter Road to manage his hometown club in 1982.

I played against Alex a few times. He was an absolute nuisance on the park, a whole-hearted player who knew how to use his elbows to good effect. He was no stranger to a 'Glasgow kiss' either as I discovered when he was playing for Falkirk in 1972! But he was a real goalscorer, a real pain in the neck who never gave up, he always kept at you.

I got to know him on a coaching course at Largs, which has become famous for helping a number of big names on their way to a successful career, including Jim McLean and Alex. When the training was over at night we would go for a few drinks in town and that's when I discovered his personal side, one which I warmed to. He was also popular with some of the other lads because he was a great conversor on a variety of subjects.

You could also see the determination he had and maybe in the early days of his career it got him into trouble. He earned a reputation of being a bit of a hothead. When you got to see him at close quarters as a person he really wasn't like that at all, although he had his moments. But coming from his background in Govan, what would you expect?

He had learned from his boyhood in that environment that you had to be competitive to survive. He also came from a union background, which he was initially introduced into through his family, and was involved in helping set up the Scottish Players Union. I remember during my time as his number two at Aberdeen we would usually stay at the Glasgow Airport hotel if we were playing at Rangers or Celtic. The night before a game a couple of Alex's pals would normally join us for a chat. One night Jimmy Reid, the big Scottish trade unionist who had been prominent in the Upper Clyde shipbuilding strike, turned up to see Alex. But it wasn't the conversation you would expect – suddenly they started talking about music, singers they admired like Ella Fitzgerald! They waxed lyrical about various blues singers. This was a side of Alex that I hadn't seen before. He was so knowledgeable. It was really interesting listening in.

Alex was great company on coach trips. He would often start up chats about every subject under the sun and try to involve some of the players to help pass the time. But it never deflected from his prime concern, winning football matches. He generally had a good relationship with the players, although he knew you can't please all of them all of the time. The players understood what he was trying to achieve.

Asking me to become his assistant after he left St Mirren for Aberdeen in 1978 came out of the blue. I was with Celtic, having moved from Aberdeen, but had picked up an injury during a game against Dundee United. It was more wear and tear and I went to see the manager, Billy McNeill, who Alex had succeeded at Aberdeen, and admitted that I was taking longer and longer to get over injuries so maybe my time as a player was up.

Shortly after the news of my retirement was revealed to the newspapers I received a call from Alex about the Aberdeen assistant manager job. I met him in Edinburgh and I think the meeting only lasted around 10 minutes because he got straight into it and told me what he wanted and that was it. I was on my way to Aberdeen. I quickly rediscovered his will to win – even in training. There was no way he wanted to lose the seven-a-side games he would join in with. He had great enthusiasm, but sometimes it was too much and he would go racing away with the ball, ending up nowhere. So some of the players gave him a taste of his own medicine and wouldn't pass to him.

He would get irate and after he complained that he was making all these runs but no one was passing to him, one of the players shouted to him, "Why don't you run back to your mum and complain?" I don't know to this day whether he heard it properly because he didn't react.

Anyone passing by and seeing all the arguing and shouting would wonder what was going on. You'd think that Alex wasn't in control, but what he was doing was actually bringing everyone together at the club – manager and players. He just wanted his players to be as competitive and demanding as he was. Believe me, he was definitely in control.

He was a clever man who could handle the situations which arose when we went into big games. Some managers get really nervous and that can feed its way through to the players. That didn't happen with Alex. He was always positive and never dwelled on the opposition. He would tell his players it's what they do, not what the opposition does.

He knew that when going into a new club you have to get the players onside as quickly as possible. There were some experienced players at Pittodrie who would have played against him. Early on, a couple of results hadn't gone well and he was aware that maybe one or two were not on his wavelength, that they might have preferred playing under Billy McNeill. I said to him that it's not the chairman who sacks you, it's the players who get you the sack. If there are players in that dressing room not going along with you and things go wrong it's the manager who gets shown the door. So it's best for your future to show them the door first. He nipped it in the bud. He quickly fashioned a squad who were playing for him.

New managers are often judged by who they recruit. In the early days, Alex brought in a player called Dougie Bell, who had played for him during their time at St Mirren. I know a lot of the players were thinking, 'why has he come to the club?' after watching him at first in training. But he went on to become a superb player for Aberdeen, proving Alex's judgement right. Alex would listen to advice on players, but at the end of the day it was his decision whether to say yes or no to a player coming to Aberdeen. He would stand or fall by his own beliefs on a player and that didn't change over the years.

At first, Alex and I were in digs together with a chap called Charlie Rettie, who owned a guesthouse, and his family. We both got on well with Charlie and we would often eat our meals with the family. It was Charlie's tradition to be last up to bed, switching off the lights and saying goodnight to everyone. Alex and I would be in our rooms and once Charlie had wished us a good night's sleep Alex would invariably answer back, "Good-night John-Boy." John-Boy was a character from *The Waltons*, which Alex loved watching. It always gave Charlie a chuckle. "You cheeky so and so," he would answer back. Charlie loved having Alex around because his sense of humour made the guesthouse a great place to be. It was like we were the Waltons.

Until we went on a foreign trip to watch Marek Dimitrov – ahead of Aberdeen playing them in Europe – and were sharing a room together I didn't realise that Alex seemingly has a love of coat hangers. We were ready to leave the room and check out of the hotel when I noticed him busily helping himself to a collection of wooden coat hangers. He was stuffing as many as he could into his bag. I just stood there looking at him thinking, 'What's all this about?' He just shrugged his shoulders and got on with taking as many as he could with him. I couldn't believe it, but I grabbed one myself too!

Maybe he didn't have too many coat hangers at home or it was a Govan thing, but I think Aberdeen would have supplied him with as many coat hangers as he could wish for after we won the Scottish League title in 1980. We clinched it with a 5-0 victory against Hibernian at Easter Road. It was strange being crowned champions there against the club I had been at for many years. Ironically the same thing had happened when I was at Celtic. We won the Scottish League there as well.

I had played in some terrific sides at Hibs, but it hadn't quite happened for them in terms of the league title. So to go back there with Alex and clinch the title with Aberdeen was terrific. We expected the game against Hibs to be more difficult than how things turned out.

We had stayed overnight in a hotel next to Edinburgh Zoo and the night before, even knowing what was at stake, Alex was determined not to build the game up too much. He didn't want to create any apprehension. His team talk that evening involved telling the players they had worked so hard to get this far and it was up to them whether they wanted to take advantage of that. "Just go out and do your best." That was it, no great long speech. He would never lump any great pressure on you.

You see some teams before games and you would think they

were in a doctor's waiting room, white faces wondering what is going to happen next. That's the last thing you want your players to be feeling prior to a big game. Matches don't start the moment the referee blows his whistle – they begin a long way before that, something Alex knew only too well.

Alex would always listen to people and take from them things he could apply to his preparations for games. He took what he needed and didn't dismiss anybody who was willing to offer him advice. He gave them respect. Jock Stein was a big influence on him. He learned a lot from Jock, who he had admired from an early age.

Winning the Scottish league title the first time around under him was great. He had achieved his biggest ambition – to smash the domination of Rangers and Celtic. Right from the start he told the Aberdeen players they would always be judged playing against the Old Firm, especially at Ibrox and Parkhead. If they were to be serious contenders for the title they had to go there and not crumble. It's where reputations are made.

He would always try to put bits into the papers prior to these games aimed at placing pressure on the officials, saying things like 'Aberdeen are looking for a fair deal from the referee' and 'I hope the ref won't bow to the pressure of the home crowd'. He felt the media was biased towards the Old Firm as well. I think he was taking after Jock Stein, who would throw things into the mix for a bit of mischief, stirring things up with the officials.

Yes, I saw the hairdryer turned on a few times, but on balance he was really good with everyone around the club. He would know the names of everyone – the guy who handed out his training kit, the lady who made him a cup of tea. He would go and have a chat with the groundsman. All this was very important to him. He wanted everyone to be involved, no one was left out. He made certain that any new signing was looked after and was made welcome. He was aware of individuals as well as the team. He was the boss, although I don't remember him liking that title.

He was a bit surprised when I told him I was leaving in 1980, although he understood that I wanted to be a manager in my own right and Cowdenbeath had come in for me. I didn't want to stay there and just bask in his fame and success, remaining in the background. I felt I had learned enough to go my own way. I think he knew that one day the time would come for us to go our separate ways.

I actually told him that I would be leaving at the end of the season, shortly before we won the league. I was very open with him and he didn't try to persuade me to change my mind because he could see that my mind was made up. I wanted to see if I could do it as a manager.

We've remained on good terms ever since. I still send him Christmas cards and he sends them too – but without a stamp. Only joking Alex! I'm delighted he has done so well. In fact he told me off for not phoning him enough. I never wanted to bother him, feeling he was far too busy – especially when he was at Manchester United. He still wanted to have a chat though, and that's the type of man he is. He has never forgotten his past and those people he has been associated with over the years. He would never say no to a request for a signed shirt or something like that for a charity.

I couldn't wait to phone him after he won his first trophy in England, the 1990 FA Cup. I was so happy for him. I'm just pleased I was able to share some enjoyable times with him.

Gordon Strachan

*GORDON STRACHAN played under Alex twice in an out-
standing career which also included 50 Scotland caps at
Aberdeen and Manchester United. He went on to manage
his country in addition to being in charge at Coventry City,
Southampton, Celtic and Middlesbrough.*

Until Alex Ferguson's arrival at Aberdeen in 1978 my
career was going nowhere. In the early days he was the
manager who gave me the strongest platform for my
ability with the standard of the team he built at Aberdeen and his
discipline and organisation. His confrontational methods helped
me develop my mental strength. If I could handle Fergie then, as
a player or manager, I felt I could handle almost anything.

I'd never met Alex before he came to Aberdeen, but I knew all
about his St Mirren team. When I was at Dundee they used to
run us off the pitch. He knew I loved football and was interested
in anything to do with coaching and what made people tick.

I signed for Aberdeen six months or so before Alex came in
as manager and in the early days we would go to watch games
together. Like him, I couldn't get enough football. Rangers or
Celtic, Arbroath or Montrose – I didn't mind. We would go
anywhere in search of a game to watch and would be engrossed
discussing everything about it.

I used to be fascinated when, after 15 minutes, he'd analyse a
game and explain the differences between the ways the teams
were playing. After a year or two, Archie Knox became his assistant and took my place in the car. Anyway, we were playing so
much European football by then that opportunities were not so

frequent, but during our many trips in his car he would often play tapes of Bill Shankly talking. "Let's listen to Shankly," he'd say and shove a tape in. Mind you, that was far better than listening to some awful Glaswegian singer he liked – one who used to perform in pubs.

At first at Aberdeen we didn't see the full extent of his drive, the aggressive will to succeed. But when it emerged I'd never seen anything like it in my life. My dad had gotten angry, but it was nothing like I experienced under Alex.

After around 18 months of working under him we just seemed to explode and in 1980 we went on to win the Scottish league title, the club's first since 1955. I suffered from incredible nerves in the last few games of that season. I was always going to the toilet and people thought I was ill, but it was just the stress of realising we could win the league.

Even in the game which saw us crowned champions, a 5-0 win against Hibernian at Easter Road, he still managed to incur a touchline ban for raging at the referee. Nobody now needs to be reminded about his autocratic, abrasive style of management, the ferocity of his renowned 'hairdryer' verbal tirades. Don't forget it was a time when players didn't have the power they have now. Managers had the power in the dressing room.

His record and reputation probably makes him the British manager with the greatest charisma and presence, although over the years he might have modified his approach and been forced to become more mellow.

In recent years, more and more clubs have called in sports psychologists to help them get the best out of their players. I have worked with some of them myself. But for all their specialist knowledge I don't believe they can do a better job of motivating professional footballers than Fergie. For me, he is the game's motivational master.

He was a great believer in instilling a siege mentality within a club. He believed that players are at their best when they are angry and resentful. That's why in his team talks at both Aberdeen and Manchester United he would make comments that would make the players believe that everybody – referees, the media, the general public – were against them.

Because of Fergie's confrontational manner with his players it meant that any party or gathering attended by him wasn't the most relaxed of occasions. Half of the players didn't want to talk to him, some would no doubt have loved to have ripped his head off given the chance. But he was tough. It didn't bother him and no one can argue with the success this generated through his outstanding career. If a player couldn't handle his methods then he wouldn't last long.

At Aberdeen the dressing room was packed with strong characters, players who would stand up to him at times. It's no coincidence that a number of his players at both Aberdeen and Manchester United have gone on to become managers.

The Aberdeen captain at the time, Willie Miller, might have seemed a quiet, unobtrusive figure, but he would often go into battle against Fergie. As our captain he took his role very seriously. One row at half-time during a game in which Willie objected to Fergie's verbal attack on some of his team-mates led to Willie taking off his jersey and telling him, "You can stick this up your backside!" With that Willie stormed off for a shower meaning there was no way he was coming back out for the second half.

There were countless dressing room rants from Fergie. When

I was at Manchester United the ex-England winger Peter Barnes was very adept at always trying to get out of the firing line if he knew Fergie was ready to explode. In one game he hadn't played well and was substituted. Fearing the worst, Peter tried to hide in the bath area.

So true to form Fergie comes storming into the dressing room and yells "Where's that Barnes?" Someone replied: "He must be in the bath, boss." Fergie went off in pursuit, but drew a blank. "Where's the bastard?" he yelled.

With Peter out of sight it was the rest of us who took a verbal battering. Finally, when the tornado had blown itself out and the manager had disappeared, Peter suddenly appeared with a towel around his waist and water dripping everywhere. He admitted to everyone's amusement that he had ducked under the water when Fergie came looking for him. "I'm freezing. Has he gone?" he asked.

Long before that there was the infamous on-field berating of the Aberdeen players following our 1983 Scottish Cup final victory over Rangers. It wasn't the best performance, but we had won 1-0 and it did come 10 days after beating the mighty Real Madrid in the European Cup Winners' Cup final in Gothenburg. He initially got stuck into us in the post-match TV interview out on the pitch. It was my turn, once he reached the dressing room, for having the audacity, in his view, to suggest that it was time to open the bottles of champagne which had arrived.

The only players to escape his wrath were Willie Miller and Alex McLeish, who were both embarrassed at being spared. Willie even suggested that as defenders they had enjoyed an easier afternoon than the rest of us. It didn't make any difference and for the trip to St Andrews that evening for the post-match reception he banned the players' wives and girlfriends from travelling on the team coach. And just for good measure, he didn't allow us to have a single drink on the two and a half hour journey.

Poor John McMaster was nominated to go up to the front of the coach and ask Fergie to change his mind over the drinks. The conversation was one way with John getting a fearful ear battering. The mood at the reception was subdued to say the least. After a while I'd had enough and said to my wife Lesley that we were off. We spent the rest of the evening in a friend's pub. I was fined £250 for my walkout.

To be fair to him he later apologised to the players, admitting that he hadn't placed the Scottish Cup final performance into context of what had gone on before.

The season before, he hit the roof in Romania after a UEFA Cup tie against Arges Pitesti. We had beaten them 3-0 in the first leg. In the return game he changed the system and Mark McGhee was asked to play as the sole striker in front of Peter Weir on the left and myself on the right. It's a great system if you've got the right players, but it was kind of thrown at us. We had done just a day's training and it was my misfortune that, when it was all going wrong in the first half, I was on the side nearest to the manager.

He was on at me all the time yelling to spin and link with Mark and other things, but I honestly didn't know how to do it. Stuart Kennedy had always warned us to never be the one to shout back at him before half-time. So I knew I was in trouble when I told him to shut up, or said something about the tactics.

It was a long dark tunnel at Pitesti and I was walking alone.

We got into the dressing room and he had yet to arrive. In situations like this you would always keep your head down. He would always be wearing his black shiny shoes and sure enough they arrived. I could just see the shoes moving about the dressing room floor and then they stopped. They were pointing straight at me.

I could feel the boys on either side of me edging away. He came right up to me and slaughtered me. I stood up, but I wasn't being brave. I just had to come up for air. He turned away and with his hand accidentally knocked a row of cups of tea in the direction of Willie Miller and Alex McLeish. He saw me smirking and that made him knock over this huge tea urn. It was so hard that it must have hurt. It was also boiling hot.

We ended up drawing the game 2-2 and going through quite easily in the end. I scored a penalty, although I had been so nervous walking up to the spot. I thought 'miss this pen and you're a dead man,' but as soon as I scored – I couldn't help it – I stuck two fingers up at him. Luckily the Aberdeen players engulfed me in the goal celebrations so he didn't see my gesture!

Under Fergie at Aberdeen we had incredible professionalism – and imagination. At free-kicks we would pretend to bump into each other as we were about to take them. While we pretended to argue about what had just 'gone wrong', I would quickly turn around and chip the ball into the goalmouth knowing that Alex McLeish would be there. In the European Cup Winners' Cup quarter-final against Bayern Munich at Pittodrie in 1983 we tried that tactic and Alex scored from my cross to make it 2-2 before John Hewitt got the winner to put us through.

We used to make up loads of things like that. We all joined in and I don't think it's a coincidence that so many people from that team have gone on to become managers. At half-time we used to have 11 managers – but I can assure you there was only one real boss!

Although we had our moments, I do feel that I played a part in Fergie becoming Manchester United manager. I was already at Old Trafford after leaving Aberdeen in 1984, the same time as Mark McGhee – who went to Hamburg – and Doug Rougvie, who joined Chelsea. In fact Alex came with me when I signed for United. I'd never heard of a manager doing that.

Less than a year later he was my guest at Wembley for the 1985 FA Cup final when we beat Everton 1-0. He rang me on the morning of the match to encourage me and tell me that fortune favours the brave and all that. He even came to the United reception afterwards and Gary Bailey, the United keeper, thought he was my dad because he sat next to me all evening!

When United were looking for a new manager after Ron Atkinson left in 1986, Martin Edwards, the chairman, asked for my opinion on Fergie in the knowledge that I played under him at Aberdeen. I could only speak highly of him after everything he had achieved there. But I must admit, I had enjoyed playing for Ron at United. After being beaten with a big stick for so long at Aberdeen it was refreshing to have a manager who trusted me and appreciated me and treated me as an adult.

When Fergie moved to United I had to endure the big stick again. But I could understand it because as a newcomer to English football he had to quickly impose his authority on the dressing room and show everyone what was in store for them if they stepped out of line.

Our relationship started to deteriorate and I soon began to feel that I was living on borrowed time. The end of my

Manchester United career was marked by a 1-0 FA Cup quarter-final defeat against Nottingham Forest. Fergie was really critical of my performance when I was up against Stuart Pearce.

He said, "Strachan to me was like a trialist who had found himself completely out of his depth. He seemed to be intimidated by Pearce." The following day Fergie was knocking on my front door to tell me that he no longer wanted me and that the club had agreed a deal for me to go to Leeds United.

One of the mementos I have kept is a letter of congratulations he wrote to me after Leeds won the Second Division championship in 1990. It was a nice gesture and he even suggested that he might have made a mistake in allowing me to leave United when I did. I imagine he felt less kindly disposed to me when Leeds pipped Manchester United to the First Division title in 1992 though!

Alex McLeish

ALEX McLEISH was a leading light in Aberdeen's trophy-winning years, forming a long-lasting central defensive partnership with Wille Miller. He won 77 Scotland caps and went on to manage his country in two spells. His successful managerial career also included spells at Hibernian, Rangers, Birmingham City, Aston Villa and Nottingham Forest.

Ally MacLeod signed me for Aberdeen in 1976 before leaving a year later to take the Scottish manager's job, leading the country to the 1978 World Cup finals. Billy McNeill then took over at Pittodrie having done a good job at

Clyde in just two months as a manager. In his 12 months at Aberdeen we were runners-up in the Scottish Premier Division and Scottish Cup, but when Celtic came calling after Jock Stein stepped down it was a job he couldn't resist after his success as a player there.

It opened the door for Alex Ferguson to come in as Aberdeen manager and he was very different in terms of his characteristics. Billy went about his business in a quiet, supportive manner and was always ready to offer me some tips on playing as a centre-half, the position he had made his own.

It was Billy who gave me my Aberdeen debut thanks to a few players misbehaving on New Year's Eve. I had been named in the festive squad for the game against Dundee United on 2nd January 1978. No way did I think I would be playing. I said 'happy new year' to the boss and he replied, "happy new year yourself son, you're playing." We ended up winning 1-0.

I played at centre-half, but when Alex came in he had his favoured central defensive pairing of Willie Miller and Willie Garner. So at first under him I was used in midfield, but returned to centre-half when Willie Garner suffered an injury. It was in mid-season that I was switched to play alongside Willie Miller, a partnership and journey which went on for something like 500 games.

My first game there was against Celtic and Alex told me that he wanted me to be a scarf around Tommy Burns' neck, which meant try to play Tommy out of the game, don't give him a sniff. At least playing in midfield had given my game a different dimension, which came in useful when I was bringing the ball out of defence.

At times Alex could be hard on me, but in those days if a

manager shouted at you, you accepted it. There were other tough managers like Jim McLean at Dundee United, but it was an era when players didn't have a problem with their bosses being hard. I didn't go away moaning that I had been shouted at. I had the attitude that I wanted to show the gaffer that I could do better. That was the thing with Alex, you wanted to prove yourself. It was bringing the best out of you.

I suppose over the years under Alex, Willie Miller was shouted at the least and to be fair I wouldn't have been too far behind, although he still had his moments. In one game, according to him, I hadn't been tight enough and my opponent – Davie Dodds of Dundee United – had got in a shot which, although it had gone wide, had got the crowd going. I stood my ground and thought I had done enough because there had been no danger to our goal, but I sensed the gaffer would be waiting for me at half-time.

His memory was incredible and even though this piece of play would have passed many people by, he hadn't forgotten. "Why didn't you get fucking tight on him? Don't let him do it again. You are letting the centre-forward come off you all the time," he told me in no uncertain terms.

I told him that Davie had only done that once and hadn't scored so what was the problem? That only made him more angry. "He's been doing it all through the fucking half," he replied.

In the end I realised it was being drummed into me to get tight all the time, even if I thought he was exaggerating the whole situation. Sometimes I wondered what he was going on about because an incident had long gone out of my mind. But it was this incessant attention to detail which set him apart. It was part of his incredible powers of motivation and look at the success he had through it all.

He would pick on the creative players more than the defenders. Wee Gordon Strachan probably suffered more and at times would give him a bit back, but I lost count of the number of times Gordon would end up as man of the match after a half-time grilling. It was in Gordon's makeup to respond, to try to shove those words back down Alex's throat.

He set fantastic standards and woe betide any of us if we dropped below them, but we sensed that something special was happening under Alex. We were developing into a good side with guys like Stuart Kennedy – an aggressive attacking full-back who was probably ahead of his time – a phenomenal athlete. Willie Miller was a brilliant reader of the game plus we had John McMaster, Dougie Rougvie and Jim Leighton in goal. It was a unit which would play together for a number of years, so we knew each other's games.

It all started to knit together and he added people to the squad like Mark McGhee. Mark struggled at first, which often happens when a player moves clubs, and we wondered if he would prove to be a good signing, but he eventually became an important member of the side. With his goals and running up front we could see why the gaffer had brought him in.

Gordon Strachan was never an out-and-out winger. He would always cause problems by moving inside – he was a superb footballer – and Peter Weir came in for a club-record fee from St Mirren, where he had played under Alex. He was a two-footed winger and someone I had played with at primary and secondary school levels. Peter was incredible to watch, even at primary school. He could take players on with ease, a bit of Brian Laudrup type of player with great technique. He was another piece of the jigsaw contributing to the success under Alex at Pittodrie.

It was a fantastic achievement winning the Scottish League in 1980, but we quickly discovered we had now become a target for the other clubs. We were there to be shot down. I'll never forget Celtic's Danny McGrain saying to me on a Scotland trip, "Well done on winning the league, Alex, it's an amazing feat for one of the clubs outside the Old Firm, but I'm telling you right now you will find it harder next year." We were one of the big boys, much to the annoyance of Celtic and Rangers, but Danny was right. We didn't win the league the next season, but we did win the Scottish Cup.

Winning it gave us the reassurance that this guy Alex Ferguson was something else. His demeanour as a winner was infectious. In fact if you didn't buy into it you didn't hang around too long.

There were a lot of guys in that Aberdeen squad who were winners anyway. He helped us to achieve great things and imbued many of us with his competitive spirit to never lose at anything. You saw that if we were playing table tennis, tennis or golf. All the lads would be devastated if they even lost a game of tiddlywinks.

He wanted players to have the same thought process as him. He made everyone better and if you couldn't take any criticism then there was no way you were going to last in the dressing room. We accepted it because we were excited about the journey we were on.

I'll always remember the time that myself and Willie Miller felt left out after missing out on a tirade of criticism even though we had won the 1983 Scottish Cup final against Rangers

FERGIE: UNDER THE HAIRDRYER

in the aftermath of beating Real Madrid in the European Cup Winners' Cup final. In an interview on the pitch, Alex famously ranted that it had been a disgraceful performance and that, "Miller and McLeish won the Cup for Aberdeen. Miller and McLeish played Rangers themselves."

I didn't know any of this had happened until quite a while after the game. I had milked the celebrations. The rest of the boys had disappeared back into the Hampden Park dressing room while I had gone over to the disabled section to celebrate with some of our fans. I had taken the trophy over for them to have a close look at it, to see all the famous names on it.

When I got back to the dressing room it was very strangely quiet. The boys were still sitting there and no one was talking. I asked what was going on, where was all the champagne? Wee Gordon spoke up saying the gaffer had blasted them all except for me and Willie. "Well, that's alright then," I joked.

I eventually saw the TV stuff and thought 'oh no!' Had I been that good, had Willie and I kept Rangers out? My head was in a spin, but it was embarrassing for us both to have been picked out from the other boys.

The gaffer though was as hard as nails and had a massive determination to win and to win in the right manner. If any player couldn't accept that then they would not be part of the process. I think on that day, having already won the European Cup Winners' Cup, he wanted us to play with a bit of style against Rangers and thrash them if we could. But after the exertions of the season, especially the victory over Real Madrid in Gothenburg 10 days earlier, there were some heavy legs at Hampden Park.

To be fair to him he got us all together in a hotel room the next day and admitted that he had jumped the gun a bit and I suppose that was as good an apology as we were ever likely to get! We didn't hear, "I'm sorry," very often after his outbursts. "I was a bit harsh on you," was just about it.

Anyway, it didn't do the team spirit any harm because we went on to further glories. The Cup Winners' Cup success was brilliant. We had also beaten Bayern Munich in the quarter-final and that had given us the absolute belief that nobody could beat us. A lot of that was down to Alex's attitude imbued into all of us.

If you look at all the modern parts of today's football, the sports science, the array of stats, algorithms – Alex in his own way had all that in his head. He didn't need a computer or a huge backroom staff. In many ways he was ahead of his time. They were his football pearls of wisdom. He had unique methods of motivation.

When we went to Celtic Park or Ibrox to play Celtic and Rangers his psychology was to tell us when the ball goes out for a throw-in, or if we win a free-kick, take them as quickly as possible. Someone said, "hang on boss, most teams try to waste time there because they're difficult places to win at."

Opponents would normally walk slowly to the ball for a throw-in or for a corner at Celtic Park and Ibrox, but he replied that by reacting quickly we would unnerve them and put them on the back foot. It was simple, but absolutely brilliant psychology. It worked too. We could see the Celtic and Rangers players getting worried, thinking that we couldn't wait to have another go at them – that we weren't afraid of playing in their arenas.

Anything new which came into the game he would be respectful of. What helped him, especially at Manchester United, was changing his assistant managers because they would bring in new ideas and help him continue to grow the team, ensuring that nothing stood still. It was all about marginal gains and keeping the players fresh.

Obviously it was a huge blow to lose him to Manchester United in 1986 after all the success and silverware he had brought to Aberdeen. There had been plenty of speculation that he was attracting interest from England and abroad. It was obvious that we wouldn't be able to hold on to him forever. So it wasn't a surprise when Manchester United came in for him. We knew it was the end of an era and it was a case of how do we keep this going? Inevitably, when someone like Alex leaves, there is bound to be some disintegration.

To be honest, I was half hoping for a call to join him at Old Trafford. A couple of years later United made a bid for me. In the end Aberdeen made it too difficult in terms of the asking price and Alex ended up signing Gary Pallister from Middlesbrough. I still wonder to this day how things would have turned out if I had rejoined him at Manchester United.

Pally had a shaky start, but ended up a legend there. That's the way it goes sometimes. Nowadays your agent can just go and kick the door down and you're on your way. That wasn't the case then and so I had to swallow my disappointment, although I enjoyed five more years with the Dons and we won a Scottish Cup and Scottish League Cup double in 1990 with myself and eight others scoring from the spot as we beat Cetic in the first-ever Scottish Cup final penalty shoot-out.

During my managerial career I've kept in touch with Alex. He has always been available for any advice at the other end of the phone. I never wanted to pester him, but he has always been fantastic to his ex-players who have gone into management. To be honest, he has so much knowledge that I would love to have phoned him every day. Hopefully our paths will cross again soon.

The last time I saw him was in February 2020 when Bruno Fernandes made his debut for Manchester United. I went to see The Boss in the room he uses at Old Trafford after games. It was like going back in time to when he was the manager there, telling tales and having a great chat. He really looked after a group of us. He's still got a great mind.

What a man – probably the best manager of his generation and someone who can certainly be compared with the greats of the past like Sir Matt Busby, Bill Shankly and Bob Paisley.

Mark McGhee

MARK McGHEE won three Scottish titles under Alex at Aberdeen and was part of the triumphant European Cup Winners' Cup side which eclipsed the mighty Real Madrid in 1983. He went on to manage Aberdeen plus a number of English sides including Leicester City, Wolves and Brighton.

Alex first tried to sign me for St Mirren when I was at Morton. The fact that he came back to me when I was at Newcastle, after he had moved on to Aberdeen, helped make up my mind to go to Pittodrie in 1979 even though I didn't know too much about him at the time and I had never been to Aberdeen, let alone played there.

He was also different from other managers in that I wasn't

asked any questions – I was told what he wanted from me. I almost signed a contract without even seeing it. While I was listening to him he slipped the pen into my hand. He was in total control. As a player, before joining Aberdeen, I had pretty much done things off the cuff and people allowed that because I was good at getting the ball and taking people on. But I wasn't great at the more fundamental aspects of being a centre-forward. Alex taught me straight away that, even if I wasn't playing well, I could make a contribution. That wasn't the case before.

If I wasn't playing brilliantly I was no use whatsoever. He showed me the middle ground where I could contribute by holding the ball up, winning headers and putting defenders under pressure. Then I could do all the stuff I liked doing and it would be more effective. It changed me from being a nearly player who could produce the spectacular from time to time – beating three men and scoring a goal – to a proper team player.

Dominating the Old Firm of Celtic and Rangers was what Alex really relished. Beating them was a massive thing for him. And for most of us having been brought up as either Celtic or Rangers fans – apart from Gordon Strachan who was a Hibs fan – we enjoyed it too.

We used to talk about 'first blood'. I was instructed, when the first ball went forward, to make contact with my opponent. We were told to be physical. After I later joined Celtic, Roy Aitken told me that when Aberdeen under Alex came to Parkhead and stood in the tunnel he used to think we were on something. We looked mental – that's what the big games meant to us.

I remember someone living in Germany sent us a newspaper cutting after we had played Bayern Munich in our European

Cup Winners' Cup winning season of 1982/83. There was a quote from their substitute keeper Jean-Marie Pfaff, which was translated, and said Bayern knew they were in for a hard game when they looked at us in the tunnel and noticed that hardly any of us had any teeth!

We were so fit that we would have been competitive in any era. Archie Knox, who was Alex's number two, was a very thorough coach. About 20 years later, when he came to work with me at Millwall, we decided to give the players a series of runs to build up stamina. We took their times and just out of interest compared them with those he had kept from our era at Aberdeen. My Millwall players were way behind us even though all those years had gone by and despite all the supposed general improvements in fitness.

I'm certain our fitness was one of the reasons we won the European Cup Winners' Cup against Real Madrid. Physically we were too much for Real. I was up against Jose Antonio Camacho – who won 81 Spanish caps – and beat him most of the night. We had a great battle, but eventually they took him off and someone else picked me up at a corner. He immediately punched me in the face. I had a lump on my jaw for about a year afterwards.

At least I could still lay on the winning goal in extra-time for John Hewitt with a cross. As soon as the final whistle went Alex slipped over in a puddle and got trampled on by Archie Knox as he tried to reach the players, which gave us all a chuckle.

It had all been a bit different a few years later when our introduction to the European Cup had been a disaster. We ended up getting thrashed 4-0 by Liverpool at Anfield in the second round, second leg, after losing at home 1-0. He came into the

Anfield dressing room after the final whistle and absolutely slaughtered us. I always remember the match was sponsored by KP, the snack foods company. They had put out a plastic bag on everybody's hook in the changing room containing all these various nuts and cheesy crackers. After the manager came in and had his go at us we were all looking down and then we got quietly changed and climbed onto the bus with our KP bags – nobody was leaving them behind – to go back to the team hotel.

Gordon Strachan broke the silence on the coach by asking if anyone would swap their chocolate dippers for salt and vinegar crisps? Alex wasn't amused and warned that if he heard anyone laugh then, or for the rest of the night, they would be fined a week's wages. So we had to try to suppress any laughter.

We left Anfield for the city centre and entered the hotel in our Aberdeen tracksuits, with all the other bits and pieces you take to a match plus our KP bags. Suddenly Graeme Souness, who had been in the Liverpool team that evening, arrived with his wife and another woman, probably his sister-in-law. He was wearing a long, light coloured raincoat with a fur collar draped over his shoulders. Souness had the style, swagger and two glamorous women – and we had our KP bags!

We sat down to dinner in the hotel restaurant and Souness just happened to be on the next table. He greeted us cheerfully, but we were too scared to have a laugh with him in case we got fined. He was popping the champagne corks and we were all sitting silently eating with Fergie glaring at us from time to time to see if anyone dared smile or laugh. It was quite a contrast.

You never knew when you were going to experience his wrath. I missed a simple chance in a 1983/84 European Cup Winners' Cup game against Ujpest Dozsa in Hungary. "That's the worst fucking miss I've ever seen," he spat in the dressing room after our 2-0 defeat. It wasn't so much a hairdryer, more like a volcano erupting. He was actually touching me as he roared. At least I shut him up in the return leg because I scored a hat-trick. He would no doubt put that down to excellent motivation.

We were once three or four nil up against Morton. I'd been tearing them to shreds, dribbling, beating people and laying on goals. Yet there he was calling me greedy and selfish, yelling, "Who do you think you are?"

Archie Knox told me it was all about not wanting me to think that I could only do it in the easy games. But I was still livid when I walked into the tea room at Pittodrie to meet my wife. She told me Fergie had just come up to her and Lesley Strachan and asked them out for a Chinese meal that night with Gordon, myself and another couple of people. So he would disarm you. He'd knock you down and pick you up again.

When I became a manager he would stay in touch. I remember when I was in charge at Leicester City and he was Manchester United manager. He rang me and simply asked, "Cole or Collymore?" I replied, "Collymore."

He wanted to sign a striker and had to decide between Andy Cole or Stan Collymore. In the end he went for Cole from Newcastle United instead of Nottingham Forest's Collymore. He eventually told me that if Manchester United had been a counter-attacking team he would have gone for Collymore, but that because they tended to spend a lot of time in and around the opposition's penalty area Cole was the better choice because he was a predator. Those were the sort of intimate conversations we would have and at one stage I felt he might have thought of me as a future Manchester United manager.

Willie Garner

WILLIE GARNER played under Ferguson at Aberdeen, making 20 appearances in his first title-winning season of 1979/80. He later returned as the Dons' assistant manager in 1984.

We were beaten by Dundee United 3-0 in the 1980 Scottish League Cup final replay at Dens Park and under our previous manager, Billy McNeill, we had lost in the 1978 Scottish Cup final to Rangers. Following the latest setback under Alex we arrived back at Pittodrie after the game to see that someone had spray painted 'YOU'VE LET US DOWN AGAIN' on one of the walls for everyone to see.

It riled the players, but more importantly it riled the manager, who said to us that this would never happen again. That League Cup final replay was played in December 1979 and in many ways it was the turning point in our fortunes under Alex Ferguson.

Celtic, the dominant side at the time, began to falter and we began picking up with belief coming into the camp, especially from the manager. The whole mood changed and Celtic weren't able to deal with the pressure. The defining games in what proved to be our Scottish title winning campaign were at Parkhead where, in a short space of time in April 1980, we beat them twice. For the first of the games the Celtic supporters were on the terraces with champagne bottles because if they beat us that day they thought the league was won – that it was theirs. It probably would have been, but we beat them 2-1. Later that month we were back and beat them again, this time 3-1. Celtic had probably had it by then and the momentum swung our way. We were on a fantastic run – winning 10 and drawing five of our last 15 games – and it culminated in us clinching our first Premier Division title under Alex at Easter Road against Hibernian.

By then I had fallen out of the team, not helped by breaking my leg the previous season. The manager switched Alex McLeish to centre-back, my position, from midfield. It soon became clear that McLeish was going to be Fergie's first choice to partner Willie Miller in our defence. I didn't really fancy spending most of my time in the reserves and I had seen that Fergie was very single minded, almost autocratic. It was clear that he wasn't going to take any nonsense from anyone. I felt my time was up and I had the chance of going to Barnsley or to Hearts. Then I got the call from Fergie telling me that Celtic wanted to sign me. He was very fair and knowing I wanted to play for Celtic he purposely didn't demand a big fee.

At the age of 27 I was offered the Alloa Athletic player-manager's job, after initially going there on loan, and became the youngest football boss in Britain. I phoned Fergie for advice and he told me to take it because the opportunity might never come up again. Two years later he rang me and asked me to become his assistant at Pittodrie. His previous assistant Archie Knox had left to take charge at Dundee.

Working alongside him was a brilliant football education. Together we won two Scottish Premier Division titles, two Scottish Cups and a League Cup, but it was hard to take when he returned from managing Scotland at World Cup '86 and informed me that Archie was coming back and I was out of a job. A few months later he and Archie went down to Manchester United. Football can be cruel and I ended up starting a new career in banking, which lasted for about as long as Fergie was at Old Trafford.

3

'He told us we would have to abide by his rules or we would be on our way. He quickly had spies everywhere. People were forever ringing him up and letting him know if they had seen someone with a drink in their hand'

Norman Whiteside, Manchester United player when Alex arrived at Old Trafford in 1986

Alan Nixon

ALAN NIXON, a respected football journalist who has broken big stories for a number of national newspapers during an outstanding career, enjoyed a special relationship with Alex Ferguson during the Aberdeen and early Manchester United days. But that often unique partnership between a high-profile media man and leading football manager later turned sour.

I was on my first week on the *Sunday Mirror* in Scotland and Aberdeen were playing Waterschei, a Belgian club, in the European Cup Winners' Cup semi-final. I wanted to cover the game at Pittodrie and the legendary Scottish football reporter Jim Rodger, who knew everyone, introduced me to Alex.

I enjoyed a very convivial chat with him, especially as it came after a very important European game which they won 5-1. It couldn't have gone any better. I obviously had great respect for everything he had already achieved and looked up to him, so to be able to talk to him at some length was fantastic.

The next Saturday, just three days later, let's say came the first bit of 'fun' with the great man. Rangers were playing Aberdeen and as you would expect he had a big thing about Rangers. He looked upon it as his club through his playing career there and his connections with Ibrox. Rangers ended up beating Aberdeen 2-1 and Fergie lost his rag.

I'd covered the game, but I had to rush back to the office because I was in charge of the pages with the deadlines approaching, a main story for the back being the main objective. I had left a guy called Jack Adams from the *Daily Record* to be in charge of the after-match quotes, which he would eventually forward to me so I could add them to my match report. He phoned with the quotes, which were brilliant. Even though Aberdeen had lost Ferguson still said it was the worst Rangers side he had ever seen! So there we go – an obvious back page lead story.

It couldn't have been a better first week for me – wow! A back page lead with Alex Ferguson the focus of the story. I couldn't have been more pleased...until the Monday morning when I quickly discovered that Alex was gunning for me.

He made contact and insisted in no uncertain terms that the quotes attributed to him were off the record. A little concerned, I contacted Jack who had supplied them and he maintained there was no way Fergie had implied they were off the record.

"Right Jack," I said. "That's all I need to know." So I phoned Fergie and said no one had told me they were off the record.

"That's no excuse, son," he replied. "You're no welcome here." It was my first experience of what would become the Fergie hairdryer. I thought to myself, suit yourself. I'll just have to get on with my job and leave him to his super self-importance. But the fall out was only temporary and a few weeks later I'm in Gothenburg watching them lift the European Cup Winners' Cup against Real Madrid.

Also in those days you could actually telephone managers for previews or stories and I was able to ring him every Friday without a problem. Aberdeen were playing Celtic in a Scottish Youth Cup game up at Pittodrie and I decided to drive up from Glasgow to watch it. I managed to sneak into the boardroom and sat at the back, minding my own business. Fergie came in, spotted me and asked what I was doing? I just said that I wanted to see his youth team because I had been told he had some very good young kids at the club. "Good on you son," he smiled.

A couple of weeks later someone told me that Fergie was raving about me – that I had taken the time to drive up to Aberdeen to take in a youth team game and that I obviously took my job seriously. So before the Scottish Cup final that season I received a letter from him and enclosed were two free tickets to watch the game. It was all because I had watched his youth team, which he obviously felt was beyond the line of my journalistic duties.

The relationship then grew and grew. We got on better and better. In 1985 I left Glasgow to go down to England to work and Fergie was still at Aberdeen. I stayed in touch because I was still keeping abreast of some of the Scottish football stories.

I've got to say he wasn't chasing a job in England at the time – I've got to stress that. He did though want to know about players in England who could maybe do a job for Aberdeen. I suggested one or two to start with, including Stuart McCall who was at Bradford City. I also told him that I knew a mate of his, Ronnie Glavin, who was at Barnsley had also recommended a kid they had in the youth team, David Hirst. But he felt David was picking up too many injuries so didn't take him even though, at the time, he could have had him for nothing. He mentioned that he was looking for a midfield player so I said he should take a peep at a player at Southampton who was being overlooked for a first-team place, Andy Townsend.

In the summer of 1986, just a few months before he came to Manchester United, he came back to me on Stuart McCall and asked me if I was in his shoes would I sign him? I said of course I would. "Right," he replied, "in that case I need to see him play."

Bradford City were due to play Halifax Town in the Yorkshire Cup, effectively a pre-season friendly. He said he would take me to the game along with himself and his newly-appointed number two Archie Knox. I picked the pair up from Manchester Airport and drove to West Yorkshire.

It was a great build up to the match, plenty of absorbing football stories complete with a Chinese meal in Halifax. It was superb for me as a football reporter too because Ferguson and Knox were always fully aware of what was going on in the football world. They were great company.

We went to the game and Stuart McCall was crap! I was now feeling like a ruddy idiot and drove them back to the airport in virtual silence. To be fair, Fergie piped up and said there was something in McCall that he liked, but there was no way he could buy him on the evidence of that game. Archie, who was sat in the back, was going on about signing Robert Connor – whom he had managed at Dundee and Fergie had given a Scottich international debut after stepping in as manager following the passing of Jock Stein – instead. A week later, that's what they did.

During the journey it was the first time Alex had ever talked about possible managerial jobs in England. He asked me what I felt about the Everton job? I said that would be a great job for somebody. He also wanted to know if there were any other appealing jobs in England coming up? I said the one big club that really needed sorting out was Manchester United, but I didn't hold out much hope for them selecting the right manager to go about transforming Old Trafford. Little did I know what was going to happen just a few months later – he got the Manchester United job, although I had nothing to do with it.

I joined the rest of the media at Old Trafford for his unveiling as Ron Atkinson's successor. He spotted me and immediately invited me into his office. I was the only one given that honour. One of the first things he asked me was what are the media like, the ones who cover Manchester United? He wanted a complete run down. I told him he would get a fair crack, but that he would be up against it if he didn't produce. The media in Manchester were very demanding because of the club's illustrious history and felt they should always be winning something. Many of them had also enjoyed a good relationship with Big Ron and had been sorry to see him go.

I knew Fergie deserved the job. He was already outstanding and was a 24/7 manager. He never rested and was always committed to whatever cause he undertook. To be honest, I hadn't thought that Manchester United would ever have the bottle to go after the manager of Aberdeen. I just thought they were a showbiz club and wouldn't go for someone like Alex.

In his early days, he fed me a number of stories because he had never forgotten the times north of the border. One week, in July 1987, I was in the Manchester office of the *Sunday Mirror*. It was a Monday, so a long time to go before our next edition. It's a Sunday newspaper man's worst nightmare, receiving a tip on a great story on the Monday as you've got to sweat on it not coming out anywhere else before you've had the chance to write it as a big exclusive. On this particular Monday a reliable source told me that Manchester United were signing Brian McClair from Celtic, a huge, huge story. The source told me it was so advanced that the two parties had already met each other. I had to try and hold this news for six days.

It still, thank goodness, hadn't come out and on the Friday I got a phone call from Alex telling me he had a great story for me – that he was going to watch Mark Hateley play for AC Milan. I could write it and it would be an exclusive because no one else had a clue about it, but I had to stay quiet about McClair because I knew he would be annoyed that I had gotten wind of it. So I now had two belting stories for the back page of the *Sunday Mirror* – United to sign McClair and they are also looking at Mark Hateley. Sure enough, the phone predictably goes within hours of the paper coming out and it's Alex swearing down it saying I had done him in after he had revealed his intentions over Hateley. I asked him if he would rather I had written that Manchester United had already met McClair and so in effect tapped him up? There was silence at the other end.

So the fall-outs were now beginning to gather speed. At the time, I was also doing some work with the local ITV station, Granada. One of his sons, Jason, had managed to get a job in the sports department through a big friend of Fergie's, Granada executive Paul Doherty. I got on with Jason like a house on fire from the first time we met. He was a great guy.

In 1995, Manchester United were struggling for players and Jason, who was becoming a good source of information, told me that Frank Clark, who was the manager of Nottingham Forest, wouldn't pick up the phone to his dad who wanted to sign Stan Collymore. So I said to him "what about Andy Cole at Newcastle United?" "We'd never get him, would we?" he replied. I said I would find out.

United ended up actually signing Cole for £7 million, but neither Alex or Jason let me know once it was happening, which really disappointed me. I felt let down after instigating the whole thing and never getting a sniff of an exclusive story which should have been the payback. It was a British record transfer, my idea, and there was no call. I was left out in the cold and that changed my feelings towards Alex. A couple of months later I'm at Old Trafford ready to join one of Fergie's press conferences when he came up to me and informed me that I was banned. "What am I banned for?" I enquired. He claimed that I had told my newsdesk about Lee Sharpe. I didn't know what he was talking about. Evidently Fergie had gone around to Sharpe's house to give him a dressing down over something and the newsdesk had gotten wind of it. Later that day I received a phone call of apology. He had got the wrong end of the stick and told me I was back in – there was no ban. Okay, fair enough.

Later on in 1995, three of us on the Manchester patch ran a story that Andrei Kanchelskis wanted to leave. Fergie wasn't happy. At the next press conference he comes in and says. "You (David) Maddock, (Matt) Dickinson – (who was almost in tears) – and you Dixon, you're all banned."

Giving someone the wrong name is a Scottish custom if you want to really call someone out and that's what he did to me. The ban lasted around a month, which I wasn't that concerned about to be honest. I just thought all these bans being handed out were becoming a bit of a joke.

Back in favour, I was at The Cliff training ground for another press conference fairly early one day in 1998. I noticed that Ryan Giggs was heading out with strapping around one of his hamstrings. I was going to ask Fergie about it as soon as he came into the room for his conference, but before I could utter a word he shouted that I was banned again. He explained that I had given some quotes to the *Daily Mail* from his brother Martin, who was then Manchester United's chief scout.

Evidently he had a thing about the *Daily Mail*, which I was unaware of. What had happened was in that midweek I had spoken to Martin about watching Monaco, who United had been drawn against in Europe. They were just some harmless words about Monaco's pitch, which is on top of a car park, and how bad it was. A nice enough story, but not one which was going to change the world.

I was at a game and Ken Lawrence, who was on the *Daily Mail*, said he was really struggling for a Manchester United preview for the next day's paper. I told him to take those quotes from Martin Ferguson, which weren't really good enough to save for my paper on the Sunday. Alex must have taken umbrage at seeing these quotes in the *Daily Mail* and had rung his brother up to discover where they had come from. Martin said he had spoken to me.

So I was banned again – and for what? I'd grown tired of this nonsense. Enough is enough, I thought to myself, I'm not going to bother with a relationship with this guy any more. I was angry because it was so pathetic.

The worst thing was that Alex seemingly turned Jason against me. I was supposed to be going to Jason's wedding, that's how close we had been. But Alex told Jason that I had been trying to buy a tape off Granada to use in the *Sunday Mirror* about Alan Shearer saying why he hadn't joined Manchester United. My relationship with Granada was such that I wouldn't have to buy anything, I would always be given the first opportunity to run something they had produced. I knew they had this interview and just asked, before they were about to broadcast it, if could I see it.

So I now had Jason turning against me as well. From then on I was hostile towards them in everything I did, which continued all the way until Alex left Manchester United in 2013. I didn't want to deal with him and I also knew others who had gone through the same experiences. I had done a fair bit for Fergie, but I feel he believes that he doesn't want to ever beholden to anyone, or that he ever owes anyone for anything. He's quite happy to fall out with people.

I had even tipped him off once about UEFA changing the rules on the quota of homegrown players which could have landed Manchester United in serious trouble. I had counted them up in the squad put forward by United and they were clearly breaking the rules. He thought that the changes weren't coming in for another year.

He phoned me back later and said I was right and if I wanted to write a story about him signing Paul Parker feel free. That was the sort of relationship we once had, but that sadly was in the past. I never expected a special relationship to continue forever, but I didn't expect what happened with all the bans and ridiculous fallouts. So it became an enjoyment to start making his life a misery. Anytime I got a Manchester United story – bang, in they went with no questions asked.

I never begrudged the outstanding success he had in the later years, but to be perfectly honest I didn't enjoy it either. I'm not going to deny that I wasn't exactly jumping up and down whenever he collected some silverware. Yes, he was a great manager, but there are also a lot of great managers who are also top people. I wouldn't put him in that category. You've got to be tough, you've got to be ruthless to get to the top, but there's also one or two times you've got to have a memory as well.

To be fair I've made a lot of money on stories about him so I can't complain about that too much.

Not dealing with him for those years hasn't hurt me – but it hasn't hurt him either!

Martin Edwards

MARTIN EDWARDS was Manchester United chairman for 23 years after being a director for the previous decade. He was instrumental in appointing Alex Ferguson as manager in 1986.

The season before Ron Atkinson went we had a tremendous start to the campaign, playing some exciting football and winning the first 10 league games. But at the end of it we played Watford away and after a 1-1 draw slipped down to fourth place. Ron approached me and said that he thought things were coming to an end. From his point of view the team had gone as far as it could under his management.

I didn't feel the same and persuaded him to stick with it and give it one more go the next season. It proved to be a terrible start to the 1986/87 season and by the time we decided to make the change in early November we were way down the league in 19th place. We had also played at Southampton in the League Cup and lost 4-1 in a replay. I was then thinking, 'maybe Ron should have gone at the end of the previous season after all'. It was definitely time to make a change.

To be fair to Ron, in the five years he was with us we played some tremendous football. We played with wingers and reached a couple of FA Cup finals, which we won. He was far from a failure, but we were starting to go backwards. We were desperate to win the championship and were fed up of seeing Liverpool win it nearly every season.

There was no shortlist to replace Ron, it was Alex Ferguson and no one else. I'd met him before when we were signing Gordon Strachan during Ron's reign. There was a problem bringing

Gordon in from Aberdeen because he had signed a contract to join Cologne. Aberdeen were also keen on him joining us because they would be getting a bigger transfer fee. With that in mind, Alex was keen for Gordon to join Manchester United.

He was helpful in making things happen so that Gordon was able to come to our club. I'd been impressed with Alex in our dealings and of course I was well aware of what he had achieved with Aberdeen. It was unbelievable breaking up the Celtic-Rangers dominance. The real highlight for me was Aberdeen beating Real Madrid in the European Cup Winners' Cup final. To come out on top against Real Madrid was incredible. The fact he could obviously do it on a European stage was also instrumental in wanting him as the successor to Ron. But to get him I couldn't just pick up a phone to Aberdeen to see if he would be interested in joining us. Imagine the secretary or anyone on the switchboard hearing that it was Martin Edwards, chairman of Manchester United, wishing to speak to Alex Ferguson!

It was Mike Edelson, one of our directors, who came up with the idea of getting on the phone with a Scottish accent pretending to be Gordon Strachan's agent or accountant wishing to speak to Alex. That's what he did. He managed to get through to Alex and then he put me on the phone. I just said, "is it worth coming up to see you for a chat?" He immediately gave us the right vibes and so we travelled up and met him that night.

All this was done in secret before sacking Ron because we didn't want a repeat of what had gone on when bringing Ron to the club. It had been a bit of an embarrassment. Originally we had Lawrie McMenemy lined up, only for that to fall through. I think his wife didn't want to uproot the family. Then we went for Bobby Robson, who wanted to stay loyal to Ipswich Town, and then Ron Saunders, which fell through as well. So Ron, who was at West Bromwich Albion, was in effect our fourth choice. We didn't want to be scrambling around again so we needed to confirm things with Alex.

Some people might have felt we had made the wrong choice when things didn't go too well in his first few years and there were fans telling us that Alex should be sacked. There was the odd banner in the Stretford End, some abuse aimed towards him at games and the letters calling for him to go were mounting up in my in-tray. What made us confident in him was seeing at first hand the hard work he had put in around the whole club, not just the first team. He was immediately aware that, in his opinion, the scouting network wasn't good enough. He felt Manchester City were signing the best local talent and wanted to know why. The youth team wasn't as successful as it had been, especially when you consider what had happened under Matt Busby.

So he revamped the scouting system and along with Archie Knox, the pair of them put hours into working with all the teams – the first team, the reserves, the 'A' team, the 'B' team and the youth sides. He was involved in the whole running of the club from top to bottom and brought in a load of new scouts. This, of course, would have gone unnoticed with most fans.

In the early months of the 1989/90 season when he won his first trophy, the FA Cup, we allowed him to bring in five new players – Mike Phelan, Neil Webb, Gary Pallister, Paul Ince and Danny Wallace. We knew we had to support him and were aware that players need time to gel. You can't expect them to always hit the ground running. Winning the FA Cup was a massive relief to all of us who had backed Alex though, particularly myself as chairman.

It's a reality that with new signings you often have to be patient. I remember Pallister coming in and he wasn't an immediate success. Patrice Evra and Nemanja Vidic, who later became fans favourites, struggled early on. It's hard for some of them to appreciate the size of the club, the expectation, the publicity which always surrounds it.

Okay, the results in the league suffered a little bit that year, but we were determined to give Alex time for those players to come through and show their true worth, and also to let him reap the rewards of his hard work all over the club. We never honestly lost faith in him. There was never any talk, either on the record or off the record, of sacking him.

Personally, I knew that time was running out as far as many of the fans were concerned. If we had got to the end of the season, having been knocked out of the FA Cup in addition to finishing 13th in the league, the pressure would have grown, which may have eventually forced our hand. You can't resist pressure from fans forever as many clubs over the years have discovered.

People often ask me could Alex have survived in today's era of little patience and plenty of sackings? With the way of the newspapers, TV, radio and social media, the pressure is undoubtedly much greater today on managers and boards of directors. There have been instances of managers being sacked after just a handful of games, so it is difficult to imagine that he would have survived in today's tempestuous times. Would he have lasted as long with Bayern Munich, Barcelona or Real Madrid? He might not have done so, because they seem to judge their managers on whether they can win the Champions League. League titles don't seem to be the be all and end all for these teams. They want to win the European Cup every year. We won it twice during Alex's time. Maybe that wouldn't have been enough to have kept him in a job at those other clubs.

We were glad we'd had the courage of our convictions when Alex took us to our first league title in 26 years in 1993. It was absolutely huge, so after that he then had a lot of credit in the bank. That credit never ran out with all the success that followed. We won the League and FA Cup double in 1994. We'd probably have won the double again the following season if Eric Cantona hadn't been suspended.

The trophies kept coming under Alex and we supported him by continually spending on the team. The Premier League also became huge – and we'd been the first winners of it. Sky came in when the Premier League started. Before that all 92 clubs had shared the same income from TV. We all got £25,000 each. It didn't matter how many times you appeared on TV, you got the same as say Rochdale. That wasn't right. Now the money generated by the Premier League went to the Premier League clubs. Football was the driver for Sky and they were prepared to invest a lot of money, which was good news for clubs like ours. The way the game was televised also sparked interest abroad and we became one of the biggest clubs worldwide. The money banked from foreign TV deals has gone up and up.

Also, through floating the club on the stock market in 1991, we raised the finances to rebuild the Stretford End, which didn't affect any team planning. Signing Eric Cantona is often described as a masterstroke, but in all honesty it was one which came right out of the blue. Bill Fotherby was the Leeds United chief executive. He rang me one day and just said that Howard Wilkinson, the Leeds manager, wanted to buy Denis Irwin. I said I would have a word with Alex, but I couldn't see him being willing to sell him. At the same time, I'd heard that Eric and Howard hadn't been getting on so I added, "would you be prepared to sell Eric?"

I spoke to Alex at the training ground and told him Leeds had been on about Denis Irwin. "No chance," he said. "Would you take Eric Cantona if I discovered he was available?" "Too right," he replied. The following day Bill Fotherby was back on the phone. I told him there was no way they could have Denis, but that we would take Eric off their hands. They were agreeable, but Bill pointed out that it would have to be done very quickly because the Leeds fans loved him and they would get lynched if they got wind of it.

So if we could agree on a price quickly then it was on. "What are you prepared to pay?" Bill asked. "£1 million," I replied. "No, we can't sell him for that," he said. "How about £1.6 million?"

We kept arguing and I kept insisting we were doing them a great favour taking a troublemaker off their hands. In the end he agreed to our original offer, but only on the proviso that it was reported as being a £1.6 million fee.

We didn't always get the players Alex wanted. For instance, he wanted to bring in Gabriel Batistuta. The transfer fee wasn't the problem, but I wasn't prepared to sign off the personal terms. It would have shattered our wage bill. We had some big players of our own at the time and once some of them had heard what he was earning they would have been demanding parity.

We were also still having to find considerable amounts of money to keep improving the stadium, so I had to say no to Alex's request. We were still doing well both in the Premier League and in Europe and so it wasn't as if we were desperate for a signing like this. Batistuta would have been a luxury.

We tried to sign Alan Shearer in 1996, but as everyone knows he went to Newcastle United instead. Jack Walker didn't help either. I think Jack, the Blackburn Rovers owner, was unhappy about losing Alan and the last club he wanted him to join was Manchester United so he pushed a few obstacles in the way.

Then there was an attempt to sign Paul Gascoigne, only for Tottenham to offer his family, let's say, a few last-minute expensive gifts. There was also the opportunity to sign Gary Lineker which didn't happen, but mostly Alex was successful with his transfer targets. While I hadn't been prepared to smash the wage ceiling for Batistuta, we did smash it for Roy Keane. But he was already at the club and we knew his importance. He was the captain and we were winning things.

Eric Cantona's departure was as sudden and surprising as his arrival. We got to the end of the 1996/97 season and he had helped us win the Premier League, but it was also the season when I felt we should have got to the final of the Champions League. We lost the semi-final against Borussia Dortmund. I think that also played on Eric's mind, thinking we should have done a lot better. He didn't look that interested when we received the Premier League trophy and medals because by then he had decided to retire at the age of 30. Even so, it was still a shock.

He actually came to see me first to reveal his decision and I had the job of telling Alex. I also had to tell Alex that there was no chance that he would be open to changing his mind. Eric had told me that he didn't want the announcement of his retirement to be made until he was on holiday. He was going away on a certain date and then we could reveal all because he didn't want to be around to handle all the fallout and fuss.

He told me his time at Manchester United had been the highlight of his life and how much he had enjoyed playing for the club before handing me a statement to be made public. There was no going back on what he had decided, but who could we get to replace him? It was an impossible task. Somehow, though, we managed to bring in Teddy Sheringham from Tottenham.

Two years earlier, when Eric had gone into the Selhurst Park crowd to kung-fu kick the Crystal Palace supporter, he told us he was leaving English football. Brian Kidd, who was Alex's assistant at the time, said to me if Eric didn't return we should be thinking about Teddy Sheringham as his replacement. Eric came back, but I hadn't forgotten Brian's advice and the next time I saw Alan Sugar, the Tottenham chairman, I said that if they were ever inclined to sell Teddy we would be interested. Alan agreed to give us first option.

Fast forward two years and Eric has gone and I'm in my office scratching my head on what to do when the phone goes. It was Alan Sugar. He asked me if I remembered that conversation about Teddy Sheringham? They now wanted to get rid of him. "How much?" I asked. "£3.5 million," he replied. "I'll have to come back to you because I haven't mentioned this to Alex."

I rang Alex and told him Spurs were prepared to sell Sheringham for £3.5 million. "What do you think?"

"Bloody hell, he can be Eric's replacement," replied Alex. So I rang Alan back and said yes, we are interested, but £3.5 million was a bit steep. He wasn't going to lower the price because he knew I was only trying it on, so we got him for that price.

Teddy played a huge part in our treble success of 1999 and contributed with a never to be forgotten goal against Bayern Munich in the Champions League final. He also won another two league titles after that, so it wasn't bad business.

There were a few players I was sorry to see leave. I felt Jaap Stam was let go too soon. At the time I felt he was still one of the best central defenders in Europe. He had an injury and Alex felt he was past his peak, but he went on to prove that wasn't the case with Lazio, AC Milan and Ajax. I think Alex has admitted he may have made the wrong judgement there.

I don't think we got the goalkeeping situation right either after Peter Schmeichel left in 1999 until we eventually signed Edwin van der Sar in 2005. If Edwin had come in straight away I believe we would have been more successful during that period. Instead, Alex went for Mark Bosnich and he was followed by other keepers like Fabien Barthez and Tim Howard, who never got close to hitting Schmeichel's heights. Both Alex and I agreed we should have gone for van der Sar a lot earlier than we did.

We almost said goodbye to Alex himself in 2002 when he tendered his resignation. We had to think of a replacement and our number one choice was Arsene Wenger. I was still chairman, but had stepped down as chief executive. Peter Kenyon was now in that role. We had a couple of meetings with Arsene. He showed some interest, but ended up saying no because he hadn't finished what he had set out to do at Arsenal. Peter then persuaded the PLC board that we should then go for Sven Goran Eriksson, the England manager. I was not overly impressed with the choice, but I was out-voted. Peter met him and they agreed terms, but Alex changed his mind and Sven was left a little hurt and embarrassed. Because of Alex's change of mind, the success thankfully continued at United for another 11 years. Under Alex we went on to win the Premier League 13 times, which is amazing after how long we had gone without any league titles before that first one in 1993.

David Walker

DAVID WALKER was one of a small band of Manchester-based football reporters who were part of Alex Ferguson's inner circle – except when, along with others, he was banned by the Old Trafford boss. He was there in the early years as Fergie struggled to establish himself and witnessed at first hand United's transition into Premier League and European champions. David also reveals for the first time the story behind Kevin Keegan's infamous outburst aimed at the Manchester United manager.

My first ever dealings with Alex came when he was the manager of Aberdeen in the summer of 1986. The phone went at home with a voice at the other end asking if I was David Walker?

"It's Alex Ferguson of Aberdeen here," he said. "Howard Wilkinson has given me your number. We've got Neale Cooper going to Aston Villa. We can't agree a fee and we're going to end up in a tribunal. Howard has suggested I talk to you. Can you give us some help over how we should play this because we would love to screw Doug Ellis (the Aston Villa chairman)."

We had a conversation and he ended up giving me his number and said if he could ever help me in the future, he would.

A couple of days later he rang me to say that he would be coming down the road to watch a pre-season game between Halifax and Bradford City. He wanted to run the rule over Bradford City's Stuart McCall. I was actually scheduled to cover the game so he said to make myself known to him and he would give me a card mark on whether they were going to sign him or not. Alex arrived with his number two Archie Knox and sure enough he gave me a steer, but in the end the answer was no. It would have been a better story if Aberdeen were going to take him. In the early days of covering Manchester United under Alex for the *Daily Mail*, when he hadn't won anything, he confided to me that it was becoming increasingly difficult for himself and Cathy, his wife, to have much of a social life. They were aware of things being said and the increasing criticism, which meant going out could be awkward.

All the time I could see he was desperately trying to turn things around. He always believed he would ultimately be successful at Old Trafford. He also knew that it was the Manchester United way to cooperate with the press – that was drummed into him by the board of directors. The main Manchester reporters had to be given his home number. It was part of the remit of being the Manchester United manager – although things eventually changed on that score. It led to some interesting times, ones which are left ingrained in my mind.

Roy Keane was sent off in the FA Cup semi-final replay between Manchester United and Crystal Palace at Villa Park in 1995 for stamping on Gareth Southgate. The next day the Manchester-based press troops went to see Alex at The Cliff training ground as arranged. In his early days at Old Trafford, Alex had a much warmer relationship with the press. By now he thought he could keep us at arm's length, so we often had to use tactics to get him talking so we could go away with the best stories.

Knowing that the Keane sending off was likely to be a raw topic as far as Alex was concerned despite United's 2-0 win, we agreed amongst ourselves not to raise the issue until much later. It was a case of getting as much on our tape recorders as we could in a 10-minute general chat before the Keane stamping would be raised because we knew the potential was there for him to go ballistic and end the conference.

We all agreed on the plan and went up to his office. John Bean was the *Daily Express* representative and was often picked out for a tongue lashing, or worse, by Alex who had Beano's paper delivered at home every day. Unluckily for Beano, the *Express* was the Fergusons' paper of choice.

Seated around him, Beano was the first to go into bat. "Alex matey, how can you defend a player like Roy Keane stamping on an opponent?" That opening gambit provoked an intake of air from the rest of us, who were dumbfounded at Beano ignoring the carefully constructed plan to keep Alex talking for a while before beginning the Keane interrogation. Alex clocked our looks of astonishment and asked us all what was going on?

I replied that we had all agreed not to talk about the Keane incident until much later in our chat, that we would warm him up before mentioning it. Alex looked at Beano and said, "Is that right John?" Beano said it was and added, "You know me Alex, I much prefer the hand grenade down the underpants approach!" To be fair, Fergie cracked up and started talking about the Roy Keane flashpoint.

There were some spectacular fall outs between Beano and Alex, who saw him as some sort of Pickwickian character – a throwback to the Dickensian era. He would often growl at him, but deep down had respect and affection for him.

Beano would often annoy Alex with late calls to his home, checking out a story that had broken in another newspaper, in the era when the Manchester regulars had Alex's home phone number. One night in 1988, the phone rang at the Ferguson household. It was getting on for 11pm and Alex was in bed.

Beano had been told by his office that there was a rumour that Fergie had met Mark Hughes at Manchester Airport that evening and picked him up in readiness to sign him from Bayern Munich. So Beano put the question to Alex.

A clearly irritated Fergie, who was about to drop off to sleep, replied, "Were you watching *Sportsnight* tonight?" Beano said he had watched it. Back comes Fergie. "Did you see Bayern Munich playing on it then?"

"Yes I did actually," replied Beano.

"Fucking Mark Hughes was playing for them!" Alex blasted back.

In later years, Beano unfortunately suffered a heart attack and decided to take a retirement package and slope off into deepest Staffordshire and enjoy the rest of his life at home in Leek. Alex had been informed of Beano's imminent retirement and asked me to come to see him at the training ground at 8am one morning. It was really a trip down memory lane as Fergie recalled some of the old stories.

In 2017, Beano sadly died at the age of 81. I thought I'd ring Alex and inform him of the sad news. He was away somewhere, so I managed to contact his long-serving secretary Lyn Laffin. I explained the situation and said I wasn't expecting Alex to do anything, but just to tell him that good old Beano had passed away. She said for me to let her know any funeral details and to forward Beano's address.

Sure enough, all the information was passed on including that the funeral was to be held in Leek, where Beano was domiciled. Alex wrote to Ann Bean, John's widow, to express his sympathy and a number of John's colleagues attended his funeral in deepest Staffordshire, as Beano would always dub it.

Just before the coffin arrived at the church, who walked in through a side door? Alex Ferguson. He went to see Ann afterwards and explained how he had to get away fairly sharply because he had to be at Manchester Airport. When we were at the reception, Ann said that their grandchildren couldn't believe it. They knew their granddad was a sports journalist, but not that he knew someone as famous as Alex Ferguson, who had just turned up at the funeral.

It meant so much to the family that they wanted to send a message of thanks. So the following week I rang Lyn and asked her to pass on the family's thank you message. It was only then that she revealed that on the night before the funeral, Alex had been at a function in London with Cathy. He got the train back to the north-west on the Friday morning, shot off home to put on his funeral outfit, went to Leek and then had to race back to catch a flight to New York, where he was lecturing at Harvard. Despite that incredible schedule he was still able to make it to John Bean's funeral.

Alex is a man of many contrasts. This was the charming, caring side of him. But as many people discovered, there was a hard – even ruthless – side to him. I remember him telling me that for his management style to work, he always had to have control of a club. It probably took him the best part of 10 years to achieve that at Manchester United.

After United had done the League and FA Cup double in 1996 he thought 'job done' in that respect. He would often tell us to look at the best clubs and that they were successful because the manager had complete control. We used to argue back that he would never be able to control the press because, even when you were winning things, you couldn't stop a newspaper columnist coming up with some criticism just for the sake of being argumentative and provoking a debate. There were always people in the media ready to take a pop at him. His answer to it all was to ban people. I was banned three times by Fergie and each time it was for writing stories that were correct. He reacted because he didn't want the news getting out in the public domain. He would go crazy because he would be paranoid about where the information was coming from. He was a control freak, but it could never extend to the media.

What you always needed to do to survive was to show him that you weren't inhibited and in those early days, when you didn't have all the press conferences of today, keep ringing him. You would be told that the manager wasn't speaking to you, that you were banned. So this would go on until he finally relented and let you back in.

Few people will realise until now that I was unknowingly the catalyst for Kevin Keegan's infamous TV rant aimed at Alex as Newcastle's Premier League title challenge blew up under Manchester United's incessant pressure in 1996. About two or three weeks before United were due to play Leeds United, Alex – who admired the Leeds manager Howard Wilkinson and also knew I enjoyed a close relationship with him – told me that he felt the Leeds players were going to get Howard the sack.

Leeds were struggling in the bottom half of the table. They had pipped Manchester United to the old First Division title in 1992 and Alex suggested that they should be a top four side and if the players put their minds to it they could still beat any of the sides in the Premier League.

He said also you can't have the attitude they had of continually under-performing. I said after our chat there was a good newspaper piece for me in what he had said and would he put what he had just told me on the record? He said he would, but not right now, to run it in a few weeks' time.

Two weeks later I wrote the piece and it had nothing to do with Manchester United playing Leeds in the run-in, or title-rivals Newcastle playing Leeds 12 days later. As far as I was concerned, it was just a matter-of-fact article in which Alex suggested that the Leeds players should be performing better than they were for his mate Howard. There were no mind games aimed at Newcastle. It had been my suggestion to run the story, not Alex's.

Both Manchester United and Newcastle United beat Leeds 1-0, but after seeing his side win at Elland Road Kevin Keegan came out with his infamous, "I will love it if we beat them," rant. He maintained that Alex was trying to undermine Newcastle by revving up Leeds to pull out all the stops against his side and that his suggestion that Leeds players weren't trying was despicable.

I was at the game against Leeds United that night when Kevin went ballistic and couldn't believe where he was coming from. Alex's words were purely in support of his mate Howard Wilkinson. Newcastle United didn't come into it. I honestly don't know what got into Kevin's head and I have to chuckle to myself that this incident has gone down in football history as one of football's greatest ever examples of mind games – when Alex Ferguson did over Kevin Keegan.

It was nothing of the sort, I can assure you. He was just protecting his mate by saying to the Leeds players, 'Lads, you're going to get your manager the sack if you carry on like this having achieved so much together'. You could argue he was proved right as five games into the following season, Leeds sacked Howard Wilkinson two days after they were – ironically – beaten 4-0 at home to Fergie's United side.

Alex's first trophy with Manchester United, of course, was the 1990 FA Cup after he dropped Jim Leighton for the replay against Crystal Palace, something which appeared to leave Jim a broken man. You have to remember that Jim used to babysit for Alex up at Aberdeen and I don't think they ever spoke again.

We were with the victorious Manchester United party returning home on the train from London after the Thursday night replay. It had been agreed that Alex would give the regular reporters a few minutes to discuss the game. A few drinks had been taken, but he sat down with us and he was pretty cogent. It was all about how United could now move on after his first trophy.

One of the press corps, Peter Fitton, asked him how difficult it had been to drop Jim Leighton for the replay after all the years he had known him? I will never forget the answer. "It was animal instinct," Alex said. "I just knew I had to do it." It was the equivalent of taking your pet dog to the vets and having it put down. It was the sort of action that Alex was prepared to take in pursuit of turning Manchester United around.

Norman Whiteside

NORMAN WHITESIDE was the boy wonder from Belfast whose career was cruelly cut short by injury at the age of 26. He was renowned as one of the Manchester United group of drinkers who tested new manager Alex Ferguson's patience. At the age of 17 years and 41 days he beat Pele's record to become the youngest player to appear in the World Cup finals when playing for Northern Ireland in Spain '82.

A hardcore of the boys would go out socialising at Manchester United before the arrival of Alex Ferguson. The press, though, gave us a hard time. I was being followed by a tabloid newspaper, Paul McGrath was being followed and so was Bryan Robson.

We never went out on a drinking session 48 hours before a game. On the Sunday after a game some of the boys would meet up and we would sit all day and drink Guinness. At the end of the night we'd do the usual – have a curry, have a sing song and have a few laughs.

When Fergie came in he tried to lay down the law. We were all told to report to the gym on his first day and it was straight to the point. He opened up with, "I'm Alex Ferguson. I'm the manager of Manchester United now. I don't care who you are, if you're Whiteside, Robson, McGrath or Strachan or whoever. I'm the manager of Manchester United from this day forward."

I think he was one of those believers who thought the more you put in, the more you get out. So drinking was out. You couldn't get away with anything. He was at the training ground from early morning to night. It came from his working-class ethic and we'd already had a bit of a heads up from Gordon Strachan, who had played under him at Aberdeen. He told us we would have to abide by his rules or we would be on our way.

He quickly had spies everywhere. People were forever ringing him up and letting him know if they had seen someone with a drink in their hand. I never tried to hide anything. I would go up to him and say, "Before anyone rings you, I was out last night."

He went berserk when Paul McGrath and I went on Granada TV one Friday night for a live interview. Paul was always nervous before interviews so I think he had a few shots before he went on to help calm the nerves. It may have looked like we were both drunk, but I can assure you I wasn't. The next time at training the manager had strong words with Paul. I think United were considering terminating his contract. They wanted to split us up.

What didn't help us was that the newspapers would exaggerate things. You might have been just sitting there having a pint – the next thing you're all over the papers accused of going on a bender. What's ironic now is that Fergie and I have become good friends and after I had finished playing he would often invite me into his office after games for some scampi and a glass of wine. I always joked with him that in the past he didn't want me to have any drink and now he was pouring it down my neck.

As a manager he was far more detailed than his United predecessor Ron Atkinson. With Ron you'd turn up for the game and as long as you were fine by 3pm you were on the team sheet. With Sir Alex there would be countless meetings in the build-up to games. You half expected to have a meeting to let you know when the next meeting was!

I think Fergie knew about my reputation as someone who liked a drink before he became Manchester United manager. In the summer of 1986, he had been in charge of Scotland at the World Cup finals in Mexico and I'd been there with Northern Ireland. By a coincidence, the two squads returned to Britain on the same flight. A few of us, including Charlie Nicholas, had a bit of a champagne party at the front of the plane. We had a few to be fair – and it was all observed by Fergie. One of the first things he said to me after becoming Manchester United manager was, "Did you enjoy the flight home from Mexico?"

It was obviously a little warning that he would now be keeping an eye on me, but I never really fell out with him because we were very honest with one another and he actually helped me get a pay rise when he sold me to Everton in 1989.

I was handed a lot of money to leave United because that had been written into my contract, but then Fergie told me what kind of wages top players were getting when they moved clubs. He told me what to ask Everton for and I ended up on four times the money I was on at Manchester United. I didn't have an agent at the time and so I half expected Fergie to ask for his percentage cut!

Bill Thornton

BILL THORNTON was a respected Manchester-based football writer during the Alex Ferguson era, firstly for the Sunday Mirror before joining the Daily Star. As part of the Old Trafford inner circle he witnessed the growth of the club under a manager driven to succeed.

I first met Alex when the club held a Christmas lunchtime get together for the press. It was staged a couple of years after Robert Maxwell's aborted attempt to buy Manchester United and Alex hadn't been at the club that long.

I was standing at the bar in one of Old Trafford's hospitality suites, where the lunch was taking place, when Fergie walked in and stood alongside me. It was the first chat I'd had with him and it seemed to go pretty well. I was on the *Sunday Mirror* in those days and Steve Millar, a colleague from the *Daily Mirror*, joined us and the three of us eventually sat down on the same table.

Fergie seemed amused as we both regaled him with interesting tales of Robert Maxwell, who owned the Mirror group of newspapers that we worked for. We revealed some of the crazy and outrageous things he had done over the years. At one stage he turned to Martin Edwards, the United chairman who had previously been involved in discussions with Maxwell over a possible sale, saying, "Hey chairman, you want to hear some of these stories about Robert Maxwell!"

It's never ever been just about Alex. He loves listening to stories and discovering things about people. He loves to share people's experiences – he has always taken things on board.

From that first meeting, especially during my days on the *Sunday Mirror* before moving to the *Daily Star*, I enjoyed some good journalistic experiences with him. He was very accommodating and would give me the odd exclusive story. One of them involved his signing of Andrei Kanchelskis from Shakhtar Donetsk. I was able to call in at The Cliff training ground and suggest a topic which he would be happy to talk about for my weekly pieces on Manchester United. I was blessed in those early days by the great man's patronage.

I was sitting in his office at The Cliff one day when he divulged that United were on the verge of signing someone who turned out to be Kanchelskis, but he couldn't remember his name. He picked up the phone to his number two, Archie Knox. "Archie, who's that guy we're signing? Andrei someone?" Thankfully Archie was aware of his name and away I went with an exclusive for Sunday.

Although in the early days the results didn't go his way and there were stories of his job being in jeopardy, I didn't think it ever was and I never wrote that he was close to the sack. It was inevitable, I suppose, that there was talk of him being under pressure because he was struggling initially to get the whole thing off the ground. There was speculation, but my information was that the United board weren't seriously looking at terminating his contract. I don't think, from my conversations with Alex during those early seasons, that he believed his job was ever under threat.

Of course the breakthrough eventually came in the 1990 FA Cup final which United won following a replay against Crystal Palace. I can still now clearly visualise bumping into him after the game. I sensed in his demeanour that he realised he had lifted a huge burden off himself as a manager. His team had finally delivered. He was buoyant, absolutely bubbling and insisted that I returned to Manchester on their train. Some of the daily paper boys had already been booked on it, but I was due to make my own way home. He told me to join them on the victory train out of London.

Although many of us – myself included in later years – were victims of the Fergie 'hairdryer', certainly amongst the Manchester press regulars there was a desire to see him succeed because we knew how hard he worked and what he was trying to achieve behind the scenes. I don't want to sound like an old stager, but back then we had better access and many of us were old school in the fact that we could have off the record discussions and wouldn't print everything we witnessed. That has proved impossible for the Manchester United followers of future generations and is a major reason why relationships with the manager and the media became strained over the years.

It became harder for me when I joined the daily circuit because there was an incessant demand for Manchester United news. I also started to become surrounded by younger reporters who had inbred in them a different attitude to the job. That's not a criticism, it's just the way it was and it has probably evolved even further these days.

There is no denying that I saw Alex's attitude to the media change as the years rolled by. On the football field though, he became more successful and because of the man he is he never felt obliged to court the media, although at the same time he was shrewd enough to use the press when it suited him.

Sitting in his press conferences as the years went by I sensed more and more his antipathy to the media. He regarded younger reporters as young whippersnappers who, in his opinion, weren't necessarily qualified to be quizzing him about his methods. He didn't like the modern trend of turning up to his press conferences in jeans with knees hanging out. He would give that look of disdain if one of the young reporters walked towards him dressed as if he was about to do some gardening. In the early days of his Manchester United reign he had been used to the majority of us turning up, if not always complete with a tie, at least in an open-necked shirt under a smart jacket and trousers.

On foreign trips – and I traipsed all over the world with United – it never ever crossed my mind not to be wearing a shirt and tie. It may have been dubbed old school, but it was really basic respect for who you were travelling with and Alex knew that. In later years the looks he gave to some of the younger guys when they arrived at the airport check-in dressed as if they had been to an all-night rave were disdainful. You can argue that these are superficial matters that shouldn't have counted, but they did – and especially for him.

Well dressed or not, I didn't escape the Fergie hairdryer. I was on the end of my fair share of rants from the great man. I walked into one or two stonkers, although at times I was left absolutely baffled by what he was on about.

One of them happened when, quite embarrassingly, his antipathy to the Manchester football reporters had become so bad that every now and again I'd get a phone call from his press secretary Diana Law to say that the manager didn't want to see the lot of us, but he would accept a call from me. Or I would have to go to the training ground and the contents of our chat could be passed around. He obviously felt that he wouldn't be able to control himself if things became heated with some of the younger reporters who he had taken a dislike to. It was tempting to keep some of the information to myself, but I was trusted to pass it on – which I always did. On one occasion, towards the end of another successful season, I was tested to the limit.

I made the phone call on behalf of everyone, although really there wasn't much to get stuck into. Everything had been done and dusted – United had won the league again – so I was struggling for a theme to get him talking so we got some decent quotes. He was very quiet during the conversation and I was beginning to wonder why was I bothering, I was getting nowhere. He was obviously in a mood where he didn't really want to cooperate.

Out of desperation I referred to something about the next season. To my astonishment his response was, "Aye, that's if I'm here next season." I nearly fell off my chair. I asked him if I had heard him right? He repeated his earlier sentiment, "I might not be here next season."

He wouldn't elaborate although I knew that for a few months he had been in talks with the club over a new contract. We would often ask him whether there had been any progress on it and he would say there had been no movement.

This was a hell of a story, except there wasn't any real meat on the bones. I dutifully passed it on to the rest of the troops and we were now all frantically trying to make sense of it all.

I made one or two phone calls to try to find out what was behind this sudden confession. Somebody said to me that Fergie becoming a future director of football at Manchester United, after finishing in management, might be the sticking point in any agreement over a new contract. To be fair to Fergie, he had always maintained that when he finally left Old Trafford that would be it – he wasn't after any other post.

I proceeded to write a 1,000-word eulogy about Fergie, saying how could the club allow things to get to this point over his contract? He had won loads of titles, what was the problem over handing him a new lucrative deal? It was a glowing piece in his support and only really as an afterthought – and to cover myself because I knew others might go down this road – I wrote a couple of sentences referring to the director of football position as a possible stumbling block. But I deliberately played it down. In terms of the actual coverage it was buried. Anyway, we ran it as a back page story with two pages inside analysing the whole Ferguson issue. It was, of course, huge news. I thought nothing more of it – job done and the next day I was going on holiday.

My wife Pauline and I were picking up a few things in the

market in Ashton-under-Lyne for our sunshine break in Greece when my mobile phone rang. I didn't recognise the number, but answered it and straight away I heard, "What the fucking hell was all that shite you wrote in your paper today? How dare you, it's complete shite." As you'll have gathered, it was Fergie.

I think the whole of the market could hear his effing and jeffing so I told Pauline to continue with the shopping because there was no stopping Alex. It was a non-stop tirade. There was no way I could get a word in edgeways. "Don't you ever dare ring me again. You've got a good reputation in this game, but you won't when I'm finished with you son!" He also accused me of going behind his back to the board, which I hadn't.

I was thinking, 'don't say I've misheard him about maybe not being at United next season, that he had told me he would be there for another 20 years'. I was also thinking, 'what's the matter with him?' Eventually the phone went dead and I stood there absolutely baffled. As soon as I got back home I wrote to him via his secretary Lyn. I said I felt I had accurately reported him and had indeed also written a glowing testimony to his achievements. I then went on holiday.

When I returned from Greece I eventually discovered that the sentence or two about the director of football role had been taken out of context. He hadn't actually seen the whole story. Instead, this bit of it had been read out to him, making him believe I had gone against his word. He had always told us that he never wanted the role and thought that I had made that the main angle of my story. In his mind it was an outrageous bit of reporting when really any phone call from him should have been 'thanks for writing a glowing testimony of my success'.

While covering The Open golf championship that July I

received a call from the office to tell me the following week that I was scheduled to do a piece with Alex at Mottram Hall, where he was promoting something and would be available for an interview. I told them that he wouldn't take my calls. I had already attempted to break the ice by getting in touch. I had phoned his secretary Lyn to be put through only to receive another volley of abuse from Alex.

I just about managed to tell him I had written a letter trying to explain that he had got it all wrong. "I never got any letter," he barked and slammed the phone down. I then rang Lyn back, who had weeks earlier passed on his address to me. She said the letter had obviously gone missing, maybe because the Ferguson home was undergoing extensive work, so my letter was probably buried under a ton of rubble. So I faxed her a copy of the letter and finally he received it.

When I turned up at Mottram Hall it was as if nothing had happened. Thankfully peace was reigning again. That was typical of him, but for all those flashpoints the good moments with him easily outweigh the negative ones. I feel privileged to have covered some great years and probably the greatest British manager of all time. The regulars who had been there in the early seasons knew just how much blood, sweat and tears he had put into the job of transforming Manchester United.

The memory of ringing him at home in 1992, after they had lost at Liverpool knowing victory could have kept them on the path to his first title, seems a long time ago now. I was aware he'd worked himself almost to a standstill and had come so close. That's why I made the call, telling him I could feel what he was going through. He was very gracious and that was the side of Fergie that sadly a lot of younger reporters never got to see.

4

'He would get everything off his chest after a game. Someone had advised him to let things ride and analyse it on the Monday. But I think his wife told him if he kept on bottling things up over the weekend, making him grumpy and morose, their marriage would be over'

Brian McClair, former Manchester United player

Bryan Robson

BRYAN ROBSON was Manchester United's Captain Marvel under Ron Atkinson and the England icon quickly adapted to Alex's methods to help 'the boss' end 26 barren years by winning the league in 1993. The former England skipper, who won 90 caps, now works at Old Trafford as a United ambassador.

When you look at Sir Alex's career you've got to say he's the greatest club manager there has ever been. What he did at Aberdeen with a young side – taking on and beating the mighty Glasgow giants Rangers and Celtic and collecting the trophies he did – was phenomenal. Then he came down to Manchester United and while it took a few years before he got things rolling, winning the title in 1992/93 helped the club go on to gain incredible success in the following years under him. It was a long wait for Manchester United to win the title, but it was well worth it.

It was a bit of a culture shock for us players when he arrived after the departure of Ron Atkinson in 1986. For instance, the first pre-match meal we had he got the waitresses to take away the butter and bring margarine. He wouldn't allow us to have any salt either. It was all for a reason, although there were some tough times in his early years.

We had a great presence about the team that eventually won the title. That dressing room could handle strong characters. We really believed that we could win the Premier League that year after narrowly missing out the previous season. By then the boys had loads of belief in themselves and when we did win it, achieving what the gaffer had set out to do when he first arrived,

I can still visualise Sir Matt Busby's smiling face in the stand at Old Trafford. He was just delighted that we had won it again after so many years.

I could always see what Alex was trying to do, especially with his onus on developing young players at the club – something Sir Matt had done with the Busby Babes. It was one of the reasons he brought in Brian Kidd as youth team coach in 1988 – it helped United in their mission to attract the best young players from the north west area.

In 1993/94, my last year at United, the boss said that because I wanted to become a manager – and because I always got in really early – I could go up and sit in the trainers' room and have a cup of tea or coffee. It was at one get together that I discovered the club were thinking of signing Roy Keane. The gaffer was interested in everyone's opinion after telling us what United would have to pay Nottingham Forest for him. He wanted to know whether he should go for him or not? I joined in the conversation and said, "Gaffer, I've played against him quite a few times and I'd definitely pay that price for him."

I think the boss had already made up his mind that he was going to sign Keane, but he wanted some back up from the rest of his staff. I knew he was ideal for United, but at first Roy was very quiet. On the training ground and in matches, though, he was really aggressive. In an experienced changing room you expect young new signings to be quiet. You don't expect them to be shouting their mouths off – unless they are Paul Ince!

With characters like that in the dressing room confidence oozed through the club, contributing to the array of silverware won by Sir Alex's teams. Without a doubt the boss laid the foundations for the club to move forward before that success arrived, even though that was difficult at times. In 1994 we won the Premier League and FA Cup double. It was United's first double and took the club to a different level. Then we had the youth development side under Sir Alex with Ryan Giggs, Paul Scholes, David Beckham, Gary Neville and many other lads coming through to form a great team that held the club in good stead for at least another 12 years.

One of Alex's greatest strengths is his man-management skills. I think the thing that people sometimes forget to mention is that he has a great football brain. His vision and his knack at looking at a player and thinking he can fit into his system was uncanny. Most of his signings turned out to be top players and through that he was able to keep changing Manchester United around and continue the success.

One team could be successful for six years, winning things, then all of a sudden the boss switched things around, bringing in younger players and a new cycle of success followed. You have got to have a really good football brain to be able to do that.

Another thing he was great at was delegation. For top people in any role being able to delegate is important because you've got to have trust in your staff that they can do the job. You've got to have the trust to let them get on with it and he wasn't afraid to use any methods he could think of to improve a player.

Alex and Mike Phelan thought that Paul Pogba needed toughening up during his first spell at United. Paul Scholes would kick lumps out of Pogba in training and you'd think something like that was going to get stopped, but the boss and Mike were letting it go on purpose after obviously having had a word with Scholesey. It was another aspect of his man-management which was always designed to get the best out of his players.

Chris Turner

CHRIS TURNER played in Alex Ferguson's first game for Manchester United, a 2-0 defeat at Oxford United on 8th November, 1986. The goalkeeper made 79 appearances for United before joining Sheffield Wednesday then Sunderland. Chris went on to manage the Owls along with Hartlepool United (twice), Leyton Orient and Stockport County. He became chief executive and later director of football at Chesterfield.

There were rumours in the summer of 1986 that big Ron Atkinson was under pressure. His job wasn't safe. We had finished fourth, which for Manchester United wasn't good enough, especially with what had become an obsession – chasing the elusive league championship, which had been out of reach for so many years. Once it looks like the title hopes have evaporated for another season then whoever is the United manager finds himself under pressure.

We had started the new season with a 1-0 defeat at Arsenal. Within a few weeks it appeared that the whole world had collapsed because we lost successive home games against West Ham and Charlton, drew at Leicester and found ourselves bottom. It seemed obvious that there was no chance the title was coming to Old Trafford for yet another season. We were on the back foot and the clamour for change was underway.

We knew it would need a huge turnaround if we were to keep Big Ron. The players loved him, they loved his training, his style of football, his friendship with the players. The run of bad results was certainly nothing to do with what you often hear, 'the players aren't playing for the manager.' Well we were, but not very well. He respected his players, and yes he might have turned his back on a few things that were happening, that there was a bit of a drinking culture, but that didn't affect things on the pitch. Everyone gave everything for him, but ultimately a sequence of bad results cost him his job.

There were some names bandied about over his replacement and despite a lack of success it was still a big job for someone. Gordon Strachan, a United team-mate and good friend, told me that he had heard from people he knew at his former club Aberdeen that Alex Ferguson was on his way to Old Trafford as our new boss.

Gordon spoke to us about him and how Alex had broken up the Rangers-Celtic duopoly. At the same time, I sensed a little trepidation from Gordon knowing he was going to work under Alex again. I knew there had been some animosity about him leaving Aberdeen and that seemed to continue on his former manager's arrival. I can still remember Alex telling Gordon he was leaving him out in a game against Nottingham Forest at the City Ground. He said he didn't think it would be his afternoon against Stuart Pearce. I don't think Gordon was too amused.

Aberdeen had succeeded against both powerhouses Rangers and Celtic and had also won a European trophy, the European Cup Winners' Cup. They had become a real force in Scottish football. He had done a magnificent job with Aberdeen. Martin Edwards, the Manchester United chairman, had noted that and thought he could replicate it south of the border.

The players wanted to know all about him, so Gordon was the man to go to. He had played under him for a number of years in what was mainly a young side – one that Ferguson had turned into winners. He knew what he was like and knew what he wanted. He also warned us about the side of him when things went wrong and how demanding he was.

Like when any new manager comes to the club everybody naturally wonders how it's going to work out for them as individuals. It's a period when players get their heads down and work that little bit harder. You've got to give that extra bit and try to impress the manager as quickly as you can. It's why you sometimes get a 'new manager bounce' where results initially improve. Often though, after a few weeks, players revert back to their norm and the new manager gets a truer indication of what has been happening before his arrival. It wasn't long before the inconsistencies that Big Ron suffered showed themselves again.

He arrived with his assistant Archie Knox and to be honest it was Archie who made the biggest impression in the first few weeks because he was a brilliant coach, one of the best I've ever seen or worked with. He was full of banter, but very professional in his job. He was a good go-between regarding the manager and the players. He could have a cup of tea with you and share a joke, but also be very serious about situations.

If you wanted to speak about how your game was going, Archie was always prepared to listen and offer advice. To a certain degree it was good cop, bad cop, although Archie wasn't weak. He was no shrinking violet. He would let you know if he didn't like something. He knew how the manager worked. So he knew when to step in and maybe defuse a situation and at other times to let Alex have his say. That said, the pair of them could sometimes be at it. They used to play each other at head tennis every Friday in the little gym at the training ground. These games were contested very strongly with no holds barred. They could, let's say, be very interesting and well worth watching.

We quickly began to get used to the new regime and away we went from the relegation zone, although we only managed to finish 11th. At one stage there appeared to be more chance of being involved in a relegation battle than challenging for that long anticipated league title.

I was in his first team away to Oxford United at the Manor Ground. We had a very good squad of players. Okay, some of the players did like a few drinks, but that just wasn't exclusive to Manchester United. It was common during those days through-out football. I do admit though that it was a different league at Old Trafford – there were some big boozers.

Liverpool and Arsenal had their share, but the difference was they were winning things. With Alex coming from Aberdeen and being successful with a group of young players I think it surprised him what he had walked into – a group of experi-enced internationals, but also some hardened drinkers.

There was no great opening speech of what he intended to do. He just set about trying to move the players he didn't want on with the minimum of fuss. He wanted to try and build a side without the recognised players.

Paul McGrath was one of the best players I've ever known, a Rolls-Royce of a defender, but he struggled with injuries and had too much spare time to try and kill. Norman Whiteside was the same. It was always touch and go whether Norman would be fit. Bryan Robson was also picking up injuries, while Frank Stapleton had probably enjoyed his best years. So Alex had inherited top class players, but ones who were being plagued with injuries which led to a downside in their lifestyles. He had to try and sort these situations out.

As players you are a close unit and you don't want to see

your mates leave, but at the same time you've been around long enough to know that a new manager usually wants to change things. At a club like Manchester United the minimum requirement is being around the top.

Even in that first season with Alex being appointed in November we still managed to pick up some notable victories despite only finishing 11th. We beat Liverpool 1-0 home and away, and we beat Manchester City 2-0 at Old Trafford. There were signs that we would eventually turn things around.

As players we were under tremendous pressure because the club had gone so long since winning the title. The last success had been way back in 1967. It became an obsession to end this barren run, an unacceptable drought. It can be compared now to Liverpool's own determination to end their 30-year run of not winning the league. If we lost a game we were immediately written off and reminded that another season was about to pass without the holy grail, the league title. At the beginning of the season you could feel the tension – would it be our year?

Strangely, Liverpool didn't always have the best starts. They were like a horse in the Grand National which comes good after the last fence. They would get stronger after Christmas, go on a run and win the league whereas at times we were non-runners.

Alex came with the mandate – 'we have to win the championship'. As a manager – and I've been one – you go into a club thinking you can change the situation very quickly. As we all know that is not often the case. At Manchester United, with a lot of established internationals, he sensed that things would take longer to gel once changes had been made.

He brought in players like Viv Anderson, Brian McClair and Steve Bruce and in 1987/88 we finished second, although the pressure was still on. Liverpool had once again won the league – something he had been brought in to avoid happening – and the following campaign Alex found himself under scrutiny from frustrated United fans after only finishing 11th. It was obvious that, having moved on established internationals, their successors hadn't been a resounding success. There were no trophies. The heat was on. But you could see he was a passionate man. Football and the will to succeed was like a drug. It was about winning. He didn't want to lose to anybody, even in head tennis.

We saw it in him every Saturday afternoon on matchdays. Not so much in training, because Archie took all the training. He would come to the training ground for 10 minutes or so, walk around and disappear, leaving Archie to it, whereas we had been used to Ron Atkinson joining in with us in training. Alex would just have a chat with one or two players and then he was gone. He never took a training session.

Archie's organisation was excellent. The manager's contribution was on match days. In many ways he was like Brian Clough, who used to come into the dressing room at ten to three, having been in his office for most of the time after giving his team talk at around 1pm. We all knew about the set-pieces. There were a few reminders of what was expected and that was it.

It could be very different at half-time or full-time if things hadn't gone well. The first player at United who received the full hairdryer treatment was John Sivebaek. We had just lost against Wimbledon 1-0 and Vinnie Jones scored his first goal in league football. The changing room at Plough Lane was tiny. There were wooden benches and wooden walls with a small bath. Peter Barnes was already in it after being substituted when Alex came in. There was silence, with everyone fearing

'He was all arms and elbows and didn't care where they ended up'... Many team-mates recall Ferguson's unique ability to use his body to protect the ball, as seen in action for Rangers against Arsenal in 1967

'After about 18 months at Aberdeen we just seemed to explode'... Arriving at Pittodrie *(right)* and setting his sights on the Old **Firm**

'I knew I was in trouble when I told him to shut up'... Winger Gordon Strachan enjoyed a tempestuous relationship with Ferguson throughout his time at Aberdeen and later Manchester United, with trophies and rows aplenty

'We were excited about the journey we were on'... November 1982, and Alex plots a path through Europe for his all-conquering Aberdeen side as they prepare to take the Cup Winners' Cup by storm

As soon as the final whistle went, Fergie slipped in a puddle and got trampled by Archie'... Ferguson picks himself up and dries himself down to celebrate with assistant Archie Knox *(top picture)* as Aberdeen topple Real Madrid to win the Cup Winners' Cup in 1983, with John Hewitt's goal *(above)* the difference in a dramatic final in Gothenburg

'There was no shortlist – it was Alex and no-one else'... Manchester United chairman Martin Edwards only had eyes for one manager with the club languishing close to the relegation zone in November 1986

'He quickly had spies everywhere'...
United were beaten in Fergie's first game
in charge, against Oxford United *(above)*,
but the Scot soon began to shake up the
club, starting with tackling a perceived
drinking culture within the squad

'e was running the club from top to bottom'... Journalists and chairman alike were aware of the
ard work going on behind the scenes, despite pressure building as Ferguson chased a first United
ophy in the lead up to the 1989/90 season

t was obvious he was testing my character'... Viv Anderson and Brian McClair were
arly signings, with the latter already having earned the Fergie seal of approval following
incident in Monte Carlo involving a casino and a large amount of willpower

'It was a bit of a culture shock when he arrived' ... Despite some early teething troubles, Bryan Robson became a key man for Ferguson, and helped him win his first trophy, the 1990 FA Cup

'He would have a go at my performances, my haircuts, my friends, my clothes, my car'... The much-maligned Lee Sharpe holds aloft the Cup Winners' Cup in May 1991 after beating Barcelona – the winger was often targeted by Ferguson due to his rock 'n' roll lifestyle at the time

'To this day I don't know who was Daisy and who was Dolly between me and Brucey'... Gary Pallister had a love-hate relationship with his manager, with some added confusion about Ferguson's nicknames for his long-standing central defensive partnership

'Mavericks need special treatment'... The arrival of Eric Cantona in November 1992 proved to be the final piece in Ferguson's early 90s United jigsaw, with team-mates recalling how the Frenchman was immune from the hairdryer treatment. A few months later, Steve's Bruce's late double against Sheffield Wednesday in April 1993 *(above right)* put the Reds on the brink of ending a 26-year wait for a league title, with the final assist provided by Dolly... or was it Daisy?

'**From the moment I walked into Old Trafford, I sensed the obsession to win the league**'... Alex and assistant Brian Kidd celebrate as a rapturous crowd toast the title after almost three decades

'**He wanted everyone to look smart – he thought it put you one step ahead of opponents**'... Paul Parker remembers the boss being obsessed with his United squad turning out properly – here's a rare example of a relaxation of the rules, in tribute to the club's Newton Heath heritage

what was to come. It was so quiet you could hear Peter splashing around. John Sivebaek was sat next to me. He's one of the quietest men you could ever meet in football. Suddenly the boss ripped into him big style. I looked directly across to the other players, daring not to look at Alex. Archie Knox was stood in the doorway, out of the way, knowing what was coming.

I honestly don't know why John copped it. There hadn't been anything obvious. He was the one who got it as the expletives tumbled out of a red-faced Alex. He was right up against John's face – there was no room for him to move. He had to take it both barrels. He didn't say a word back. The rest of us were just grateful he hadn't turned on us. In my time in football I had never seen anything like that before. And there was no way Peter Barnes was getting out of that bath anytime soon!

That was Alex's style at the time. I think he actually mellowed over the years, well that's what some people have claimed. It was all down to frustration. If you didn't deliver what he wanted then you could find yourself in the firing line. He had been like that at all his other clubs and wasn't going to change just because it was Manchester United.

Some players seemed to be exempt from the hairdryer treatment – for instance I never saw Bryan Robson get it. But that's how it was in those days. There was no rebellion. You just had to get on with it. It was his style and one that eventually worked as success came under him.

We were never scared, but you certainly didn't enjoy it if you were on the receiving end. I didn't escape. It came my way after we lost 6-0 at Hartlepool in a pre-season friendly in 1988. It was a strong side – Norman Whiteside, Paul McGrath, Viv Anderson, Mike Duxbury, Lee Sharpe. Hartlepool were unbelievable. It was only three days before the start of the season and a lot of the players must have felt they wouldn't be in the opening day side, otherwise they wouldn't have been risked in a friendly. Even so, we were thrashed – something which was often pointed out in later years when I became manager there.

With a new stand being built at the Victoria Ground we had to change in a temporary changing room. We went into the dressing room at the final whistle knowing that embarrassments don't come much bigger than losing 6-0 to Hartlepool. We could imagine the headlines.

McGrath and Whiteside had been injured and so they had played to get minutes under their belt. The manager came in and exploded, telling us that apart from those two the rest of us had been "fucking shite." I don't know why, but I found myself speaking up. "Boss, I can't believe you've said that. We've just lost 6-0 to Hartlepool. I can't see how two players have done alright and the rest of us are shite? We're all in it together and if one is shite we're all shite."

He absolutely ripped into me.

"Who the fucking hell do you think you are?" and so on. I got the full verbals. You could feel the changing room rocking. He walked away, took his jacket off and hung it up on a peg. He then came back towards me. I thought he was going to hit me. Instead it was another verbal blast. I just had to sit there and take it and I was thinking 'why did I open my big mouth?'

The next morning the kitman Norman Davies informed me at The Cliff that Alex wanted to see me in his office. I thought hell, here we go, ding dong round two. I went up the stairs to his office, knocked quietly on the door and walked in fearing the worst. Instead, he got out of his chair, leaned over and shook my hand saying I had been spot on. He agreed that it was a team game and we were in it all together. Everybody had been shite.

Over the years I enjoyed a very good relationship with Alex even though he left me out of the side a few times and then signed Jim Leighton from Aberdeen, which saw me move on to Sheffield Wednesday three weeks after that Hartlepool game. When I became a manager I could always pick up the phone to speak to him for advice. I remember being at a sportsman's dinner in Manchester and Alex was on the top table. He found out where I was sitting and came over to say hello. It was a real sign of a genuine man.

Regarding the goalkeeping situation at United, although Gary Bailey had retired in 1987 before returning to South Africa, there was also Gary Walsh – a great young prospect. Alex gave him a chance, then put me back in so the two of us were competing for the number one spot. But in the summer of 1988 the rumours that Jim Leighton was going to follow Alex from Aberdeen to Manchester United came true, which wasn't a problem for me. If that was his decision then fair enough.

I was almost 30 and I didn't want to be stuck in the reserves. I was offered another year's contract, but I didn't want to sign it knowing the majority of the time would be spent as Jim Leighton's number two. I wanted to play. If it was today I would have probably sat on my arse and taken the money, as they often do nowadays, and stayed until I was 40. But I wanted to play and not to be sat in the stand. There wasn't even a goalkeeper on the bench in those days.

I told Alex it was nothing against him or the club, I just wanted to play regularly. I had nothing against Jim either. I had met him a couple of years before in Tenerife, he's a smashing lad. He was also Scotland's number one and so off I went to Sheffield Wednesday. Three years later we faced Manchester United in the League Cup final at Wembley and beat them 1-0. Who was the first person to come across the pitch and congratulate me? The manager, Alex Ferguson. That's the greatness of him. You can have a fall-out, a disagreement, a heated discussion, but it is never held against you. Also, Alex would never go in the papers or media and criticise you – he would say it to your face. Things were kept in-house.

As I said, when I became a manager he was a great supporter. After being placed in charge of Sheffield Wednesday I picked up an edition of the local paper to see two pages about me from Alex. He had given me a glowing report and praised my work as Hartlepool manager. He said I had deserved this chance and he also kept a special eye on his former players and looked on with special interest when they became managers. For many years after leaving the club I would also get a Christmas card from Alex and his wife Cathy.

Would he have had the same success at Manchester United if he was managing today in a cut-throat football world? I don't know because patience is in short supply in the modern game. Martin Edwards deserves great credit. Firstly for bringing him to the club, and secondly for standing by him when there were banners at Old Trafford calling for him to go.

The club have reaped the benefits of continuing with a man who Martin trusted and respected. He knew about the extra hours Alex put in. At the same time as running the first team he took a huge interest in young players coming into the club. He knew the families. It was part of the great pride he had in managing Manchester United. He knew the greatness of the club, he sensed it. Alex could see the potential of the likes of Ryan Giggs, David Beckham, Paul Scholes and Gary Neville when they were 14, 15 and working under the youth coach Eric Harrison. Seeing them develop gave him great pleasure.

I remember talking to the Manchester United scout Tony Collins at The Cliff about how the manager took a great interest in young players coming through. He ended up promoting them as he had done with young players at Aberdeen. He certainly ridiculed that suggestion from Alan Hansen, following a defeat at Aston Villa at the start of the 1995/96 season, that you win nothing with kids. He would have looked at that on the Saturday night on *Match Of The Day* and thought, 'I'll ruddy show you'. And he did.

He also had such an influence on officials. At games at Old Trafford he would stand at the top of the tunnel. He would always have his eyes focussed on the officials and ignore the players coming off at half-time or at the final whistle. You could hear him shouting, "You're fucking anti-Man Utd!" He was so passionate. Officials coming to Old Trafford would know what to expect and psychologically it would sometimes work because in future they wouldn't want to upset him.

In later years you could see the fourth official visibly shaking if the added time on the illuminated board wasn't to Fergie's liking. He was a winner and he tried to influence people. He would always stand up for his club and deserved every bit of success that came his way.

That winning attitude was transferred to the group of mainly young players that he brought through. Look at the Class of '92 – they were all winners. They owe it to him. Football owes a lot to him.

Jim McGregor

JIM McGREGOR was Manchester United's physio when Alex Ferguson joined the club in 1986 and remained a valuable member of his backroom staff for eight years before leaving to concentrate on running his own practice after falling out with Brian Kidd.

I was very close to Ron Atkinson and was really sad to see him lose his job. It was a surprise because under him Manchester United had won the FA Cup and had some great runs in the League, but we were struggling at the start of the 1986/87 season. Things went from bad to worse and the end came after we had lost 4-1 to Southampton in the League Cup. The day after Ron brought me into his office and just said, "They've done me. I'm going." That was the last I saw of him for a year or so.

I felt shattered – I could hardly speak. His assistant Mick Brown, who I had also got on well with, was going too. It was a bad day – it was like dealing with a death in the family. I had worked with Ron for five years and really enjoyed those times. Ron was a laissez-faire type of guy, he just let you get on with your job and was content with what was going on around him.

That was the big difference I discovered when Alex Ferguson came in. Ron would allow me to have full control of everything to do with the medical side of the club and that included dealing with the press. If there was an injury, Ron would often leave it to me to inform the reporters about just what the injury was and how long the player would be out for. Where injuries were concerned he would just say to me it was my department and to deal with it. As far as I'm concerned, there was a fair bit of criticism that Ron wasn't interested in lots of departments of the club, like the reserves, the youth team and even the medical side. But he was. He just let the coaches, like the youth team's Eric Harrison, get on with things. He was able to delegate whereas I don't think Alex ever could. He demanded full control of everything, including my area of the club.

When Fergie arrived, straight away he wanted to be heavily involved in all aspects of the club. He wanted to know how things were done – nothing escaped his notice. I had to report to him probably every other day. We had numerous meetings about injuries and the fitness of players. He wanted to know all the ins and outs as he prepared for games. He also didn't want me speaking to the press – he told me that he would deal with any injury news, but only if he had to. He wasn't as free with information as Ron had been.

He took an intense interest in every department of the club, but that didn't detract from the fact that when he arrived he was really good fun, especially alongside his assistant Archie Knox who had arrived from Aberdeen as well. At times they were like a couple of naughty schoolboys. They loved their pranks – often on each other – and happily wound each other up.

In the gym they would almost come to blows with a version of head tennis where they had to keep the ball off the ground with whatever part of their body. They could knee it, shoulder it, head it, whatever. But honestly, they were ferocious at it, always arguing. No one would give in. It was life or death and you could have sold tickets for people to watch it.

I couldn't wait to spectate, but I remember them asking me to referee. I quickly replied, "Fuck off, I'm not getting involved with you two mad bastards." They were exactly that at head tennis and it provoked the odd fight between them – not that any bad feeling carried on. They were very close.

The first game of Alex's reign in 1986 was an away match against Oxford United and we stayed in a hotel the night before the game. The players had their evening meals first before Alex and the staff followed suit a little later. I'd made sure everything was okay with the players before they went up to their rooms to watch TV and then I joined the group. First of all we enjoyed a couple of drinks, before going in for dinner.

I noticed after a few minutes that Alex was coughing pretty frequently. I thought he had a problem so I said to him I would run up to my room, collect my medical bag and find something for his cough. He insisted that he didn't need anything. I persevered and advised him to take some medicine for it. "No, no, I don't want anything. This is just something I do," he maintained with a stern look. I thought to myself, 'Oh Christ, what have I done?' Later on I discovered this was his nervous cough.

It stopped later that evening and didn't start again until around 2.30 the next afternoon, 30 minutes before kick off. You could hear him walking along the dressing room corridor with this nervous cough. Here was a man on the outside seemingly brimming with confidence, but inwardly his body was giving him away. He was anxious.

So that was my introduction to him – recommending something for a nervous cough, which continued throughout his career. There was nothing for him to be ashamed of. Lots of the greats, in all walks of life, attempt to hide a nervousness. You can't stop your body reacting if that is the case. In many ways it's like a safety valve, but I can imagine many people reading this being surprised – even some of those who know him really well. I can also reveal that he started chewing gum during games on my advice. During matches I would be sitting on one side of him with Archie Knox on the other. The coughing would start during the game, so after a time I plucked up the courage to suggest he should take some chewing gum.

"What do I want fucking chewing gum for?" he retorted. He also liked the odd spit, so I thought chewing gum would kill two birds with one stone. Eventually he accepted some chewing gum and that became a tradition during future matches. As soon as he sat down in the dugout I'd hand him some chewing gum. It stopped his coughing.

He also ended our custom, started by Big Ron, of allowing the coach driver Derek Sutton to sit with us in the dugout at away games. Sooty, as he was known, plonked himself on a dugout seat at Oxford's Manor Ground to be met by a Fergie stare followed by, "Who the fuck are you?" Safe to say that was the last time Derek got anywhere near the dugout again.

The other thing Alex was determined to stop was the drinking that had been part and parcel of the club over the previous few years. The biggest drinkers when Fergie arrived were Paul McGrath and Norman Whiteside. There was also – to an extent – Bryan Robson, but he didn't have chronic injuries like the other two, which didn't help their drinking patterns.

McGrath and Whiteside both had chronic knee problems. They were knee conditions that definitely weren't going to get better. It was a real shame. I was told by an orthopedic surgeon that Paul's knee was completely done in and wouldn't last long.

To the surprise of many, he was able to prolong his career after leaving Manchester United for Aston Villa by managing the injury through just keeping fit on a static bicycle. A bit different to copious amounts of drink! He didn't do a lot of actual training, but the bike work kept him going.

At United the manager obviously felt that his excessive drinking was getting the better of him and he was allowed to leave. But there's no doubt in my mind that Paul McGrath is the best centre-half I ever worked with or saw live on a football pitch. I've never seen anybody with so much power as a central defender – he had the lot. It was a shame, but he went to Aston Villa and they looked after him.

If he hadn't been a big drinker then maybe Fergie would have persevered and kept him. Who knows? The same can be said for Norman Whiteside. The difference was that when he left United for Everton in 1989, Norman didn't last for very long as a top player. He retired long before he was 30. Fergie was very, very anti-drinking. It's not an excuse, but because of their injuries Paul and Norman felt drinking was the perfect opportunity to escape from their demons and they paid the price.

Now Robbo might have been the leader of the drinking pack but you can be certain that on a Monday morning at training he would run harder than anybody else. He could disguise his beer intake and he also had Fergie's respect. Also part of that drinking group was Kevin Moran, but he was never really brought to book. He was always in the group that would all meet on a Sunday morning at the Four Seasons Hotel in Hale. Kevin could handle his drink and never got any serious injuries so he flew under the radar as far as any drinking culture at United was concerned.

While Fergie was determined to put an end to the drinking at the club he never involved me in laying down the law. He and

Archie dealt with it. He knew who the culprits were – although as I say, he never suspected Kevin Moran. I was never going to let on. I didn't need to because Alex had his spies everywhere. He quickly knew the pubs they frequented. He really should have been a detective. I think he had become particularly worried about the Sunday tradition of the boys. They would meet up, have a few drinks and enjoy a meal with their respective partners who would then leave so that the drinking could continue. Sometimes it would go on until 3.30 on the Monday morning. There's no way that could happen nowadays. It would be impossible. But that's the sort of thing that went on and the football wasn't that bad either, was it?

Even though I missed Ron Atkinson at first, I enjoyed a really good relationship with Alex in his early years, but it started to disintegrate in my last couple of years there before I left in 1994. My Manchester United nemesis was Brian Kidd. He was promoted to assistant manager in 1991, following Archie Knox's return to Scotland to work with Rangers, and it led to my relationship with Fergie starting to fray.

With Fergie you know what you've got. He's a bully, but one that you can live with when you understand it's all about trying to get the best out of people. But with Brian it is an arm around your shoulders with a knife behind his back.

He purported to be the good cop, and he was with the players, but not so much with the staff. We didn't get on, which was a contrast to my relationship with his predecessor Archie, who was a sublime guy and great to be with. We had a laugh every day whereas Brian, to me, was a real complex character. You could take the mickey out of Archie, but that wasn't the case with Brian and don't forget he was Fergie's number two, so falling out with Brian was never going to do me any good. We had a lot of rows and the biggest one involved a big mate of Brian's, the physio Dave Fevre, who would eventually replace me at Manchester United. Brian had got to know Dave when he was with Wigan Rugby League Club. They were very successful and Brian was very interested in Wigan's training techniques, which was fair enough, and formed a close relationship with Dave.

Brian then arranged for a young player at Manchester United to go to see Dave Fevre for treatment. It was all done behind my back. I went absolutely berserk. I would always tell players that they would often not be happy with what I had to say or with the treatment, but if they continued to be unhappy then to be honest and tell me because there is nothing more humiliating for a physio to discover someone has gone behind your back for more treatment.

It still happens now. Look at the number of foreign players who insist on going abroad to see someone they know if they are injured instead of relying on the club physio. I honestly don't know why it's allowed. So when I found out about this Manchester United kid going to Dave Fevre at Wigan, organised by Brian Kidd, I went mad. I completely lost it.

I had a shouting match with Dave on the phone. I had a big row with Brian. It went all the way to Fergie, but he wouldn't back me so that was a big factor in me leaving a few months further down the line. I don't think an assistant manager would ever go before a physio.

The writing was on the wall as far as everyone was concerned and I had a very miserable last few months at Manchester United, but at least there were some really good years preceding it. It was a case of just concentrating on my own practice, which I had set up, but I was still devastated to leave.

Once I was out of the Old Trafford door I received an offer to join Kenny Dalglish, who was the manager of Blackburn Rovers at the time. By then I had started my practice and wanted to concentrate on building it up. So it was just my luck that Blackburn ended up winning the Premier League that year, beating Manchester United to the title on the final day of the season.

However, that joy would have been short lived for me because guess who eventually ended up as Blackburn manager in 1998? None other than Brian Kidd. Ironically, he took with him to Ewood Park the physio who had replaced me at Manchester United, Dave Fevre.

Football can be a strange world at times.

Brian Rose

BRIAN ROSE was the faithful Old Trafford car park manager during the Alex Ferguson era and one of the club's staff who was trusted by the manager. He is an example of the importance the Manchester United manager placed on all members of staff, not just the players, although for Brian it did prove costly at times!

Sometimes under Alex the players would train at Old Trafford. If that was about to happen I would get the call from Albert the kitman, "Rosey, go and get the gaffer's racing paper, *The Sporting Chronicle*."

"Yes, no problem," I would reply before walking to the newsagents at the top of the road to purchase his regular paper. I would return to the ground, search out the boss and hand him the paper. "Well done son," he would reply without ever dipping into his pockets for any money. So every time they turned up for a training session at Old Trafford I knew I would be having to pay up for his racing paper. There's me on a pittance and him on big wages, but that's the way it went and there's no way I would have asked him for the cash. He sort of had this hold over you and you didn't want to do anything to upset him – like ask for money. He's a Scot after all!

He more than made up for it in my eyes by the way he treated people, myself included. He had time for all the staff, it wasn't just about the players. He knew the names of everyone who worked for the club in all the different sections. I was really appreciative of him asking to see me when I decided to retire. I think he appreciated that I was always prepared to help out away from the car duties if needed.

Before Carrington – United's new training ground – was up and running, on Christmas nights they would report to Old Trafford. There was no real need for me to be there, but I felt I should show my face in case somebody needed something. I know he appreciated that and I would muck in with anything that needed doing. I would help out with things like taking the nets down. The boss appreciated things like that, as did Eric Cantona.

One Christmas after training Eric came over especially to thank me and to wish me a happy Christmas. Some of that was down to the boss who instilled into his players that everyone had a part to play at the club – that no one was any more important than anybody else. That was one of the secrets of the tremendous success we enjoyed under his management.

So when I decided to call time on what had been an enjoyable spell at Manchester United, especially under Sir Alex, he asked myself and my wife Sue to join him at training. While Sue went off with his secretary Lyn, the gaffer said, "Come on Brian, let's go and watch the lads train." So here I am standing next to him and he's giving me his opinion on some of the players and what they had achieved. I was having to pinch myself that he was giving me his time on a training day and making me feel part of what was going on around him. That's how he was. He treated everyone as an individual and made you feel special. I had a photograph taken with him which I have in my house.

Ryan Giggs then joined us. I'd known Ryan from his early days at United, having taken a special interest in him being a Salford lad. It was fantastic sharing the conversation between them. Then before I left he told me that as long as he was the manager I would be welcome to come down to the training ground and see him or the players any time I wished. It was like I was walking on air when I heard that because as everyone knows he wasn't too keen on people invading the privacy of the training ground, which was his workplace, but I was being handed the freedom to come and go.

It was strange that a few people seemed to live in fear of the boss, including the former groundsman Keith Kent, who later moved on to be in charge of maintaining the Twickenham surface. Amongst the staff we had a codeword to let everyone know if Alex was around. I'm showing my age now, but it was 'Max Jaffa on site'. Don't ask me why we used that, maybe it was because of the strange name of the famous violinist and band leader of the time, but that was the warning.

One day I was in an office at Carrington when word went

around – 'Max Jaffa on site'. Poor Keith, who was with me enjoying a cup of tea, suddenly became a bag of nerves. He almost spat his tea out and rushed out onto one of the pitches, grabbing a fork on the way, pretending to be working furiously. He kept shouting out to me, "Has he gone yet, Brian?"

I decided I was going to wind him up and tell him the gaffer was still around even though he'd come in and gone out again. So there's poor Kenty forking the pitch for ages, desperate to keep out of Alex's way. I think it was because the gaffer was often on his case demanding better playing surfaces, especially at Old Trafford.

That was the gaffer. He maintained high standards every-where in the club. But if you met them and were prepared to go the extra mile he would look after you.

Clayton Blackmore

Welsh international CLAYTON BLACKMORE started his career as a youth player at Manchester United and was handed his first team debut by Ron Atkinson. He enjoyed eight years under Fergie and was there at the start of the trophy spree, winning the FA Cup in 1990, European Cup Winners' Cup in 1991 and Premier League in 1993.

Things started to go pear-shaped under Ron Atkinson in 1986. Once it was all over for Big Ron, Gordon Strachan started talking to us all about Alex Ferguson and what he was like. He had played under him at Aberdeen and told us that it wouldn't be easy, that he had high demands and would get

'We had enough strength of character to go again'... United's players recall how one league title was never going to be enough for Ferguson – after winning again in 1994, Ferguson celebrates with Peter Schmeichel *(top picture)* and with senior pros Steve Bruce and Bryan Robson *(above)*

'A wonderful side – a team of his making'... Eric Cantona's penalty
helps United beat Chelsea to win the league and FA Cup double in
1994, with Ferguson's 1993/94 vintage *(below)* hailed by captain Steve
Bruce and others as among the finest in the club's illustrious history

'Alex became like a father to me...'
Cantona, his bond with Ferguson secure
after his long ban, helps United win the
league and scores the winner in the 1996
FA Cup final for another double

**'I never wanted a cup of tea and a
chit-chat'...** Roy Keane was determined to
maintain a professional distance from his
manager, with he and the likes of Paul Scholes,
David Beckham, Ryan Giggs, Ole Gunnar
Solskjaer and Andy Cole hugely influential as
further titles arrive in 1997 and 1999

'I was warming up and warming up, waiting to catch the manager's eye'... Ole Gunnar Solskjaer finally gets summoned from the bench and wins the 1999 European Cup for United in stoppage time, clinching the treble in the process

The game of snooker had just been a bit of fun and he'd been winding me up'... onathan Greening *(bottom row, third from left)* makes the Champions League final quad and gets his hands on the trophy, despite the manager's pre-match mind games

He gave me strength to get through the toughest period of my life'... David Beckham credits Ferguson with supporting him through the aftermath of his 1998 World Cup red card

'Do you know who these guys are? They're the Chilean miners who got trapped underground for almost a month'... Rio Ferdinand, pictured here signing for United in 2002 wearing a suit that earned some stick from Sir Alex, recalls the manager's sometimes unorthodox motivational gambits ahead of big games

He kept yelling at me to pass it... and I don't think he was too happy with my celebration'... Ryan Giggs has mixed memories of his famous FA Cup winner against Arsenal in 1999

'If you weren't pulling your weight, you'd be in for it'... Paul Scholes remembers a hard taskmaster who had huge faith in him as a young player coming through the ranks

'His relentless drive was enough to inspire us'... The United squad of 2008 certainly felt no let up in Ferguson's ambitions as he pushed them on to the league and European Cup double

'You could see the fourth official visibly shaking '... Everyone at Old Trafford was aware of the influence the manager could exert over officials on a matchday

'I wasn't easy to handle at times, but he knew how to get a reaction from me'... Wayne Rooney often felt the sharp edge of the manager's tongue, sometimes to help motivate his team-mates

'Manchester is a city with lots of energy – it's an inspiring place '... Thousands gather to celebrate United's 20th (and Sir Alex's 13th) title in May 2013, but the boss has just made a seismic announcement

'I had two mainstays in my life – my grandad and Alex Ferguson'... Ryan Giggs is among those to feel his world turned upside down as Ferguson takes the acclaim of the travelling United fans after his last game, a 5-5 draw with West Brom *(above)*. His departure creates a huge void at the club, with a road named after him and a statue in his honour *(below)* recognising his enduring contribution

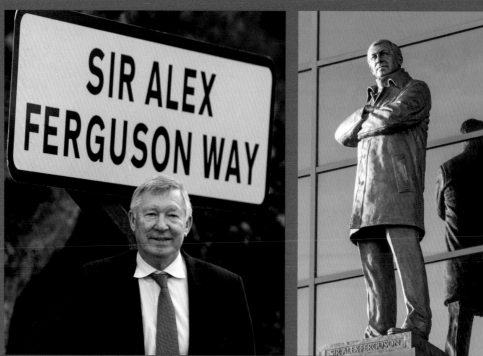

frustrated and let you know if you weren't delivering. We soon discovered that Strach was spot on when, in an early game, it was 0-0 at half-time and he went absolutely berserk at us. I had never seen anything like it before and I could see some of the players wondering what was going to happen next. But I quickly realised it was to get a reaction out of you. He pushed you and pushed you on the pitch and at times I felt if I was going to be physically sick. He expected you to run and run.

Straight away he also tried to stamp out the drinking culture, which wasn't just confined to our club – it was part of the times we were living in. In many ways he was ahead of his managerial and coaching counterparts. He knew, to operate at the highest level, you had to sacrifice many of the customs that surrounded football, like heavy drinking sessions.

Like many players at other clubs, most of us liked a drink and there would be some really boozy sessions. If you had any sense you didn't down too many on a Saturday night because he started bringing us in on a Sunday to get rid of the lactic acid in the body – something that had never been done before at Manchester United.

With few staff to help him, he even took to massaging our legs as part of the recovery programme. It would be the gaffer, his assistant Archie Knox and the physio Jim McGregor working on our legs. It's a wonder the kitman Norman Davies wasn't conscripted either, but he had too much other work to do. What Norman was doing at the time was unbelievable, having to wash the kit single-handedly, although sometimes the players would help if he was really snowed under with it. I think it's all a bit different now.

I didn't have the best of starts under Alex's management. I

got married and had organised to go away for the honeymoon in the summer of 1987. The problem was he was bringing the squad back for pre-season training a week earlier than had been originally arranged by Ron Atkinson, with pre-season dates given a year in advance. I had to go to see him and explain my situation, that I had already booked my honeymoon for that week. He told me to go and enjoy myself, there wasn't a problem. I did some running to stay fit because most of pre-season was all about running anyway. The only thing was when I came back he never spoke to me for a month and I only played reserve team games. He finally came up to me and all he said was, "You're playing against Spurs tomorrow."

Until then I thought my number was up at United. But to be back in the team was fantastic. The drinking days had also been banished. If we had a game on a Saturday then he didn't want you consuming any alcohol after Wednesday. It did make a difference. You weren't as tired, as dehydrated. Mind, it didn't stop the Welsh boys, myself included, having a good time away with the Wales international side. Quite often, if we had been playing abroad, I wouldn't get back for training with United until the Friday. What was interesting was looking at the merit marks in some of the newspapers after the next weekend's games. It was a mark out of 10 for your performance. I'd look at all the Welsh lads playing for their respective clubs and I would see a load of five out of 10s. There was no energy in our bodies, which was very unprofessional.

I enjoyed a good run in the United side although I was expected to play in a number of different positions. At times my head would go because I felt I was struggling in a certain position and not being able to do myself justice, although

I think he appreciated my versatility. The pitches weren't the best either which made it harder to control the ball, unlike the modern pristine surfaces.

I don't think it was any coincidence that the first time we won the Premier League under Alex the Old Trafford pitch had been re-turfed in mid season. It made a massive difference. When you are trying to break down a team a good surface can make all the difference. It means you can play your passing game.

Before then, with the pitch resembling a sand pit in most seasons, we were forced to play long and just knock it up to Brian McClair and Peter Davenport, who weren't the biggest. We knew they were struggling to win any headers, but we didn't have much option and we struggled to win games.

That was about to change and the breakthrough came in 1990 when we won the FA Cup. And I could have been the Wembley hero instead of Lee Martin, who got the only goal against Crystal Palace in the replay. In the original game, with the score at 3-3, I came off the bench – ironically to replace Lee – with just a few minutes to go. I hit one right at the end, a real beauty which just skimmed the bar. The keeper was beaten all ends up. It would have been the winner and it would have been me going down in United history instead of Lee, who did the business in the replay to give us a 1-0 win.

I had played at Wembley as a schoolboy at the age of 15 and it had always been my dream to return years later for an FA Cup final. It was great standing in the tunnel before the game. It could have been so much better going down it afterwards if we had won in the first game.

Crystal Palace weren't a bad side. They had beaten Liverpool in the semi-final and were very lively, especially Ian Wright who scored twice after coming on as a substitute. For the replay came the big decision by the gaffer to drop Jim Leighton. I thought he was right to do it and bring in Les Sealey, but it was a very brave decision and illustrated how ruthless he could be if he felt it benefited the team. You can imagine the criticism he would have received if it had all gone wrong and we had lost. What wasn't so obvious to the general public was I didn't get off the substitutes bench in the replay.

At least I'd had a taste of Wembley and was involved again at the start of the next season against Liverpool in the Charity Shield. I actually started and scored in a 1-1 draw, meaning we both shared the trophy.

Probably my best season under Alex was that 1990/91 campaign when we also won the European Cup Winners' Cup. I was playing regularly at left-back and also managed to score a few goals, including during this Cup Winners' Cup run. I always preferred playing further forward and Alex encouraged that. You always knew you had to get back and defend, but we were a fit side and were able to do that.

The Cup Winners' Cup success helped make up for losing the League Cup final against a Sheffield Wednesday side managed by our former boss Big Ron. But things were beginning to happen under Alex, proved by the FA Cup and Cup Winners' Cup victories. We were knocking on the door for more silverware. We were also starting to think that we were good enough to win the league – something the club was desperate to achieve after going 20 plus years without finishing on top, far too long for a club of United's history and stature.

European football seemed a lot easier than battling it out week in, week out in the league. You were given more time on the ball, which suited me because the best part of my game was the passing. I think one of the reasons English teams have been so successful in European competitions is because of the extra time you have to make big decisions, allied to the exceptional workrate our domestic teams often have.

In the 1991 Cup Winners' Cup final I don't think Barcelona had that many chances. We dominated because by then under Alex we all knew what was expected and no one could have questioned our work ethic. I'd enjoyed the whole run in the competition and probably scored one of my most important goals against Montpellier. They were a very good side and had drawn 1-1 at Old Trafford. We had our work cut out in the return leg of the quarter-final in France, but I made it 1-0 and Steve Bruce ensured a 2-0 victory with a penalty. It proved that we were now learning quickly because that was no mean feat to win over there against a side with the likes of Laurent Blanc and Carlos Valderrama in it. To be honest, I felt Montpellier gave us a bigger fight than Barcelona did in the final. I remember Paul Ince being taken out by one of the Montpellier players and suffering a seriously gashed leg. It was horrible. I'd been playing at left-back, but replaced him in midfield when he was forced to go off. I enjoyed it and felt I had a bigger impact on the game from there.

I probably enjoyed winning the Cup Winners' Cup in 1991 even more than the Premier League in 1993 because it felt like we had arrived as a team under Fergie. I know how important it was to end the barren years in the league, but personally I have better memories of the European success. We should have won the league in 1991/92, but Leeds United pipped us. I honestly think we were the better team, but they had Eric Cantona who

United fans would get to know well and worship. We always had a good team spirit and that went right through all the different levels of the club. Growing up through the ranks is special and that's why the so called Class of '92 were so successful. They were part of the Old Trafford fabric and were backed all the way by the gaffer who was never afraid to play young players.

Right from the start you had to be mentally tough because, even from a young age, there was always this desire to beat Manchester United. We were always a big scalp and so you were used to hard games where the opposition is trying harder than normal to beat you. Look at all those players from that successful 1992 FA Youth Cup winning side. They were all able to look after themselves and could handle the extra expectation.

I ended up suffering a few injuries and in 1994 Bryan Robson eventually took me to Middlesbrough, where he had become player-manager.

It was a massive wrench leaving United. I had been there 15, 16 years and I knew there were more trophies to come under Alex. But there was also a lot of young talent coming through so I knew I was struggling as far as a regular first-team place was concerned. It was a fantastic squad.

The gaffer never told me to leave, it was my decision, but I felt my time was up. He was fantastic and promised that he would look after me with a testimonial, which I was due. He always looks after his players and brought a United team up to Ayresome Park in August '94 with a near full-house turning up.

It was good at Middlesbrough under Robbo, but at times I can't help but look back and wonder. If only I had stayed a bit longer at Manchester United I would have more medals in my collection.

Viv Anderson

VIV ANDERSON was Alex's first signing for Manchester United after leaving Arsenal in 1987 and became the first black player to represent England in a full international match. He also played under Brian Clough at Nottingham Forest.

Every day in the lead up to our FA Cup third round game against my old club Nottingham Forest in 1990 we were picking up the papers and reading that the manager was facing the sack. All we read was that Alex Ferguson was facing his last game if United were knocked out.

The pressure was really growing, but that never came across from the manager. The members of the United board have since insisted that they were going to stick with Alex whatever the outcome of the game. Maybe he already knew that so he didn't allow any outside pressure to get to him.

There was no difference in his preparation for the game, there was no signs of desperation – that this was a must-win game or else.

Never in any of his team talks was any mention that this was a do or die mission.

But to be perfectly honest, even though the manager wasn't giving anything away we felt the whole country was watching us. For a start it was live on the BBC. Obviously the television cameras were there to capture the drama – that it could spell the end of his reign.

It was frustrating because we believed in the manager and what he was doing, but our results were inconsistent. One week we were good, the next we could be really bad.

I'd enjoyed success with Forest, winning the league and European Cup, and with Arsenal, winning the League Cup. I had joined United shortly after that League Cup final success against Liverpool to win trophies. I honestly thought we could do it with Fergie, but we all knew that at a club with the tradition that United enjoyed you were forever judged on how much silverware you can amass.

Under Alex it had been frustrating and we knew something had to change. That win at the City Ground seemed to inspire us. It was as if something had changed. You could feel the uplift in the atmosphere in the changing room after the game. We felt we had proved ourselves in difficult circumstances and we were on our way to winning something at last.

It was extra special for me that the successful FA Cup run started at Forest. It was the first time I had won there since leaving six years earlier. Before that win I had always hidden away somewhere in a bar trying not to be seen. But there was no hiding away after this win. I wanted to be seen! To this day I'm still proud to have been part of United's winning history under Sir Alex.

The reason I joined United was because of him. I had the chance to stay at Arsenal, but after meeting him I could see that he was driven and that he was determined to make United great again and to win things. I thought to myself that I want to be part of that.

He was the driving force, but also Kathy (Phipps) who was on reception when you walked in always made me feel very welcome.

She was fantastic and so the pair of them made me feel I had joined the right club.

Brian McClair

BRIAN McCLAIR was Alex's first big signing, Manchester United paying £850,000 for the Celtic striker in 1987. He helped transform the club, winning four league titles and becoming a cult hero with the United fans. He returned as the club's reserve team manager and later youth academy director.

As a Celtic player, and a little while before I joined Manchester United, I had spent a day with Alex in Monaco at the Adidas 'Golden Boot' award. There was no tapping up – in fact it was quite the opposite.

All I could think about when wandering around Monte Carlo was the 1960s spoof James Bond film *Casino Royale*, which was set in the famous casino there. I just wanted to go there. The Adidas event was brilliantly organised and with the dinner being fairly early I knew there would be plenty of time to make my visit to the Monte Carlo casino. I had £100 in my pocket and placed it with a money clip around it so I was all set to go.

In the hotel after the event Alex asked me what I was going to do for the rest of the night? I pointed to the beautiful casino and told him I was going there. All I had in my head was stacking the cash on red. It was a dream.

"No, you're not going there," he stated. I thought, 'what the hell is he on about?' "No, you're not going," he repeated. He wasn't even my manager, I was still a Celtic player.

I went back to my hotel room to get ready thinking, 'who does he think he is?' I was talking to myself in the mirror, but for some reason I got into bed and did what he said. I'm lying there without a book and with no TV on, on a wonderful summer's evening bored out of my brains wondering what the hell was I doing.

Even worse, after agreeing to his request, the next day I had to listen to what a good night he'd had in the casino! But when I look back it was obvious that he was testing my character. If I had ignored his advice then I would never have been a Manchester United player under him. He would have thought I wasn't the right character. I also kept my £100!

In the last year of my contract at Celtic in 1986/87 I was told there were some clubs interested in signing me. John Hollins, who was the Chelsea manager, came to a Glasgow awards dinner which I was also at and asked if he could have a word. He handed me a bit of paper with an offer on it. I said thanks, but I wouldn't be going to Chelsea. I wanted to join Manchester United. He wasn't pleased and told me they would finish above United the next season. Chelsea ended up getting relegated.

Tottenham were also interested, along with some clubs from abroad. They were all offering better terms than United, who had now come in for me, but I just wanted to play for United. It wasn't about money. Most Scottish kids would also follow an English team and mine was United. They were often on the highlights programme in Scotland. They prided themselves on their flamboyant football so if I was going to leave Celtic there was only one place I was going to – Old Trafford.

The transfer fee had to be settled by a tribunal. John Barnes had just joined Liverpool for £900,000 so I think they looked at that as guidance. United had offered £750,000 and the tribunal settled on £850,000. In my first season at United I scored 24 league goals. No one had scored 20 league goals at Old Trafford since George Best and I emulated that in my first season.

Alex's view was you had to be a special person to play for Manchester United. As a manager it was difficult to like him too much when he was screaming at you, telling you you're this and you're that. It would happen in training just as much as during games.

There's loads of football speak and one you hear quite often surrounding managers is, 'he's lost the dressing room'. Ex-players seem fond of coming out with this in their role as pundits – 'the manager has lost the dressing room so he has to go'. My experience of Alex Ferguson as a manager, and subsequently when I was coaching at Manchester United, was that he 'lost the dressing room' after every single game with his fierce outbursts. But a couple of days later you were ready to go to war with him again. That was part of the magic that he had.

He would just say what he wanted to get everything off his chest after a game. In his early days someone had advised him to let things ride on the Saturday and analyse everything on the Monday. So he did that at first, but I think his wife told him that if he kept on bottling things up over the weekend, making him grumpy and morose, then their marriage would be over.

He decided there and then to let loose after games, get rid of all his anger and frustration before he arrived back home so they could have a reasonable Saturday evening and a good Sunday. On a Monday he would wander around chatting to people, explaining what he had said on the Saturday and you would always come to an agreement that you had needed to do something different to improve your performance. By then you had also had an opportunity to reflect on yourself. But then he would build you up, making you feel 10 feet tall. "I need you for Wednesday. It could be your night." It worked.

There was lots of freedom in our play, but at the same time there was a lot of detailed preparation for games. There would be three or four match reports done on the opposition to his high standards. He was very thorough. There would be a 30-minute team talk with things like who was the key player for our opponents. 'Stop him and you'll win the game', he used to say.

You would have your own responsibilities at set-pieces and corners. Everyone knew their job. All his teams had a strong spine and within that he wanted a big domineering goalkeeper, an attacking centre-half next to a real defender, a box-to-box midfielder who could run up and down all day long, someone who could link with the forwards, a defensive minded right-back complementing a more attacking left-back, a midfield player who could go wide and on the other side an actual winger. That was his dream line up.

As a player he was an attacker and wanted his teams to be on the front foot. I remember when I signed he wanted me to be part of his rebuilding of a famous football club. I thought, yes, I will have a bit of that. He was determined to carry on the legacy from the Busby Babes and some of the exciting football he had enjoyed over the years. The whole idea was to score more goals than the opposition. It was brilliant to watch and great to play in. It was instilled into you as soon as you came into the club and to those young players coming through the youth system.

We were quite pleased when our opponents had a corner because Peter Schmeichel would always have a good chance of catching the ball and then bang, we were off. He'd clear the ball and we would be on a charge to the other penalty area. As soon as Peter grabbed the ball we were all away. But woe betide you if you weren't racing into your positions – the hairdryer would be waiting for you in the dressing room. Eric Cantona was always spared the treatment. Eric was quiet and respectful. I think he understood everything that was going on, the banter. He would join in and when he did it was always a classic. At one awards ceremony he started quoting William Shakespeare. He has stayed true to the morality and ethics of how he was brought up.

As footballers we've all had stick at various times, enough to want to do what Eric did at Crystal Palace when he jumped into the crowd, but you hold yourself back. During the game he had become angry and been in the red zone when he committed the foul that got him sent off. By the time he had walked off the pitch and that guy decided to give him the verbals I think Eric was in the purple zone.

I was on the pitch, but didn't actually see the incident. I heard a commotion and looked over to see Eric remonstrating with someone and Norman Davies the kitman holding onto him. After the game finished I was talking to Gary Walsh, who was the substitute keeper that evening. I asked him what had happened and he said that Eric had let fly with a kung-fu kick at some guy in the crowd. I thought that would have been impossible. My wife had recorded the game so when I got home I rewound the tape to that moment. It wasn't impossible after all.

Alex wasn't afraid to make big decisions. He made them swiftly and most of them he got right. He always picked a team he thought could win on the day and was able to separate himself from the emotions around him during the build up to games. The days leading up to the 1990 FA Cup final replay against Crystal Palace was a good example of that with Les Sealey coming in to replace Jim Leighton in goal. He made a call which he felt could help us win the game – and he was right.

Of course, when you win something it gives you the impetus to go on and do it again. That was the big thing for me.

I remember the very first day of pre-season training after we'd won the FA Cup he came into the dressing room and said, "I'm willing to climb back to the top of the mountain again. Anybody who wants to come with me is more than welcome. If you don't, come and tell me." It was a case of, 'we've done this, let's get to the next one'. Winning things definitely gives you a boost.

Football psychology is very important and the best at that was Alex Ferguson. He learned his psychology on the pavement. He learned from Bill Shankly, Jock Stein and Matt Busby. Anybody who played for those managers will tell you they were masters of psychology. Nowadays you can study it in a textbook, but these men developed their philosophies working down the mines. They transferred skills such as teamwork and simplicity to football to gain psychological advantages on the pitch.

In the early days at The Cliff training ground we had our cars cleaned by the Gallagher brothers, Noel and Liam, obviously before finding fame with Oasis. They worked for a car valeting company that was owned by a lad who came from the same part of Manchester as them. Even though they were all Manchester City fans they persuaded Alex to allow them to come to The Cliff to clean the Manchester United players' cars.

Noel would always love a Penguin biscuit with a cup of coffee. He would say thanks for the refreshments and that was about it, although one day I was handed an early Oasis demo tape. It was good, but there was no chance of knowing the impact they were going to make on the music world in years to come.

After finishing playing I coached the kids at the Manchester United Academy. Alex always promoted promising youngsters. His standards never slipped. I remember one day walking through the training ground after United had lost against Liverpool. All the staff appeared to be getting the hairdryer from the manager. The coaching staff, the kitchen staff, the laundry staff – they were all getting it. I decided to try and stay out of the way otherwise I'm certain he would have turned on me as well.

If he wasn't happy – and he hated losing to Liverpool – he would always pick on something. The chips were too cold or the cups and cutlery hadn't been put away. It was all about maintaining high standards through all parts of the club. He argued that the so-called little things could make a big difference.

He always felt Liverpool were the team to beat. For instance, the preparation for the trip to Anfield was different to when we travelled to Goodison Park to play Everton. We never stayed over when we played Everton, but we did for Liverpool. It was always the biggest fixture for him.

Something the boss never gets tired of mentioning is my cameo role on ITV's *Who Wants To Be A Millionaire?* For the Christmas 2004 charity show I was the phone-a-friend for Alex and big United fan Eamonn Holmes. And the pair got stuck on a question involving the BBC TV comedy *The Good Life*. What was the name of Tom and Barbara's famed cockerel?

There were four choices – Stalin, Lenin, Trotsky or Rasputin. I couldn't think straight and after my time ran out they came up with the wrong answer. I got the blame and I was met with a frosty stare at the training ground. Despite it being a charity event, Fergie was furious. He hated losing at anything. The competitive spirit was still raging inside him.

"Everyone knew the answer was Lenin," he kept reminding me for weeks on end.

5

'He knew everyone from the laundry lady to the kitman. He knew when their birthdays were. He knew everything about them. He's very good like that and it enabled the club to grow and become part of the United family'

Mark Hughes, Manchester United player who rejoined the club after spells at Barcelona and Bayern Munich

Steve Bruce

STEVE BRUCE was a mainstay of the Manchester United side that finally ended 26 barren years without the league title. His two late goals in a vital 2-1 win over Sheffield Wednesday has gone down in Old Trafford folklore. Bruce went on to manage 11 clubs including Birmingham City, Aston Villa, Sunderland and Newcastle United and has kept in regular touch with Alex.

I had agreed to sign for Manchester United from Norwich in 1987 and there waiting for me at Manchester Airport, after I had flown up with my wife Janet, was Alex Ferguson. He even carried Janet's bag. Wow, I thought, here is the manager of Manchester United picking me up and driving me in his car. How many managers do that? Especially at a huge club like United?

The transfer had been going on for weeks. I had spoken to him many times on the phone. Then he called me one morning and said: "Steve, I don't think we can wait any longer." That was the signal for me to go down to Carrow Road and try to force the move through. In the end it worked out well and Norwich finally allowed me to leave.

The humility of Alex Ferguson is something you never forget. It flows within him. It means as a manager it was not just his star centre-forward, like Eric Cantona, who got the special treatment. He was as good to Albert the kitman as he was to someone like Eric. Everyone talked about his hard work. His car was parked in the training ground car park before anyone else every morning. What made Alex great was this ability to work hard and a determination which bristled within him to succeed.

After doing this management job now for over 20 years, I

realise how difficult it is. For Alex to have the attitude and desire still burning after all his successes, I am just in awe. What he achieved as a manager was breathtaking.

From the moment I walked into Old Trafford I sensed the near obsession to win the league, to topple Liverpool after not having won it for so many years.

United always did well in the cups – and it was the FA Cup win against Crystal Palace in 1990 which set us on our way – but we were always aware it was the league title which really counted. The year before we actually won it, Leeds United came out on top. We bottled it, there's no other way of saying it. We had to play four games in seven days during the run-in, which was ridiculous, but having missed out again we knew the pressure was cranking up – we simply had to win it in 1992/93. As he famously said, knocking Liverpool off their perch was a goal that was pretty evident for everyone inside Manchester United at that time.

Eventually it happened because Alex had surrounded himself with people who sort of mirrored him, to an extent. He put together a real team and I still say that the 1993/94 side was the best I've ever played in.

We had the likes of Denis Irwin, Gary Pallister and others, many of whom went on to play for Manchester United for 10 years. This team had a bit of strength. It could play, it could fight. If you wanted a fight with us we'd fight you in the tunnel, fight you in the bathroom – we'd fight you any which way you wanted. All that stemmed from him.

It was Alex, with that relentless appetite of his, who put together the 1994 team. Paul Ince, Roy Keane, Andrei Kanchelskis, Ryan Giggs, Mark Hughes, Eric Cantona. A wonderful, wonderful side. A team of his making. He was great at handling players, even the mavericks like Eric. Look at that night at Selhurst Park in 1995 when Eric kung-fu kicked a Crystal Palace fan who had been shouting abuse at him. We're in the dressing room afterwards and Fergie is ranting and raving because we'd drawn the game.

We'd been playing for something like 25 minutes with 10 men after Eric decided to launch himself into the crowd. "We should beat this bloody lot with 10 men," he was yelling. He goes up to Lee Sharpe, who happens to be sitting next to Eric. "What the fuck are you playing at Sharpey, you never put a cross in?" He's screaming at him saying he hasn't done this, he hasn't done that.

Then he calmly just went up to Eric and said: "And I don't know what you were playing at, Eric!"

He then switched back into hairdryer mode and moved onto his next victim leaving Eric, who had probably committed one of the biggest sins we've ever seen on a football field, just sitting there seemingly without a care in the world.

The rest of us are thinking: "What the fuck is going on?" But we all loved Eric, who wouldn't have had him in their team? I think that was the difference with Eric being at Leeds and being with Manchester United. Fergie knew how to handle him.

You knew that one day Eric would want to be free to do what he wanted, to turn up late for training in his flip-flops. But the one thing we all knew was that when it came to practising, no one worked harder – which made the playing easier.

Fergie looked after him brilliantly and that comes out when Eric speaks about him in glowing terms. If Eric needed space to get away from things, Fergie gave it to him. Mavericks need special treatment. You do it because you know you will be rewarded on the pitch. I've got one of my own at Newcastle United, Alain Saint-Maximin. You know at times he is going to be late, you know my man is going to wear his headband the wrong way around. That's the way mavericks are, they want to be a little bit different. You have to manage that, and Fergie did with Eric. He's got many great strengths, but his man-management skills were absolutely fantastic.

And at long last the Premier League title came his way – the first of 13!

Everybody to this day remembers the win against Sheffield Wednesday in April 1993. It had been playing on our minds that, around the same time the previous season, Nottingham Forest had come to Old Trafford and beaten us 2-1. It left us with the realisation that we would almost certainly miss out on the title again and when we subsequently lost at West Ham and Liverpool, Leeds were champions.

At 1-0 down against Sheffield Wednesday we were fearing the same thing. Paul Ince had fouled Chris Waddle to give a penalty away which led them to scoring. John Sheridan was taking it and he was a mad keen Manchester United fan. I went up to John and asked him to do us a favour and put it past the post. Of course he didn't!

I headed an equaliser from Denis Irwin's corner in the 86th minute and got an even later headed goal to send us top when, with five minutes to play, it had looked like we would be beaten having been on a run of just one win in five games. Everyone seems to remember my winning goal in Fergie time – added on because the referee came off injured – in that 2-1 comeback success the most from that title run-in.

What summed it all up that it was finally going to be our

season was that Pally [Gary Pallister] delivered the cross for my winning goal. We had got back to 1-1 and it was that gamble to go for it which paid dividends. But what the hell was Pally doing on the right wing? And what was I doing in the middle of the goal to score? More than my header, it was the cross from Pally, flicked on by Sheffield Wednesday's Nigel Worthingon, that sticks in my mind.

I've been a manager for over 20 years, but people still mention it to me now and that day probably has to be the highlight of my nearly 10 years at Manchester United. To see Fergie and Brian Kidd celebrating on the pitch was marvellous. I love seeing people from time to time re-enacting their joy, Kiddo on his knees and Fergie jumping up and down, fantastic. It was the turning point for everything Fergie was trying to achieve. At last it looked like we were going to win the title after 26 years.

There were still five more games to go, but it felt like we had won the Premier League that day. It was like the roof had come off Old Trafford with all the wild celebrations.

Afterwards, the dressing room was full of emotion and great relief. You would have thought we had won the league there and then. For once we had to calm Fergie down.

By a coincidence, Chris Woods – who was in goal for Sheffield Wednesday that afternoon – was staying with me that weekend. He had been my next door neighbour when we played together at Norwich. We went out for a Chinese meal that night and, of course, I had to buy dinner for him and his family after what had happened that afternoon.

We still had work to do. Nobody talks about Denis Irwin's goal two days later at Coventry City. He blasted one in from 20 yards to give us a 1-0 win at Highfied Road, which was just as important, but that Sheffield Wednesday game sticks in people's minds more.

In the end we won the Premier League by 10 points, finishing ahead of Aston Villa. It was something that we had to do after the club had gone for so long without being champions. It's also remarkable to think that Alex ended up winning 13 league championships. That will never be repeated, but it's amazing to think now, after all of their success under Alex, that it was 2013 the last time Manchester United were champions. That's scary. Although maybe not as scary as getting the hairdryer treatment from him was!

I didn't escape the hairdryer treatment – few if any did. Archie Knox, Alex's number two at the time, would tip us off as we walked up the tunnel towards the dressing room. "Be ready for it," he would say.

Pally often walked into it, probably more than I did. Pally is a big lad, but he's laidback and Alex thought he could get the best out of my central defensive partner if he roared at him.

He was clever, he knew Pally wouldn't sulk. He would go round muttering: "I'll fucking show you, you horrible twat." It was that sort of mentality that Fergie thrived on. He always used to maintain there was nothing wrong in losing your temper as long as it was for the right reason. He could switch moods immediately. I've seen him bollock someone horrendously in the dressing room and turn around and give the rest of us a wink.

The time when he went for me was because, on occasions, I would bring the ball down on my chest to demonstrate a bit of skill. But one time I got caught and lost the ball. At half-time he went for me: "If I see you chesting the fucking ball down again near our goal line I will fucking drag you off." Two minutes into the second half I tried it again, lost the ball and they went through and scored. Alex went absolutely berserk. "You're a fucking clown," he yelled. I never dared do it again!

We had the hairdryer treatment all the time, but no one minded. It was always for a reason and on a Monday you could sit down and have a cup of tea with him and both have a chuckle over it. Yes, he was a fierce disciplinarian and he ruled us all with an iron fist, but that's the way he was. That's what made him a great manager, believe me.

I remember it was around Christmas time one year and Archie came up to me and said Alex wanted to see me, what had I been up to?

I said "what do you mean?"

Anyway, up I went to see him. The door of his office was always open. I could hear him coughing, which usually was a prelude to a bollocking. So I went in and he said: "What were you up to yesterday afternoon?"

I was trying to think.

"Nothing," I replied.

He said: "It's been reported to me that you were carrying beer across fucking Wilmslow High Street from a fucking off-licence. Carrying beer across a zebra crossing in full view of everyone. You're a Manchester United player. Now fucking don't do it again and get out!"

I told him that I hadn't drunk any of it, it was bought for the family. "I don't give a fuck, now fuck off," was his reply.

It was his high standards – a Manchester United player could not be seen carrying cases of beer and he certainly told me so.

I wondered who had actually seen me and told him. A little

while later I discovered that it had been Alex himself. He lives in Wilmslow and had spotted me. He went mad.

We might have enjoyed some great times together, but when he felt it was the right time to let a player go, no matter what he had achieved, he did it. I know from my experience as a manager it's one of the hardest parts of the job, but it's also one of his strengths that he can do it in spite of someone's history. It's never easy to say goodbye to someone who has served you well, but the club always comes first. That was certainly his thinking.

He left me out of the 1996 FA Cup final against Liverpool – and I've been in a huff with him over that for 25 years now. I'd been injured and although I was fit he didn't put me back into the side. We ended up winning it against Liverpool with a goal from Eric Cantona.

To be fair, he told me before he did it. You have to just accept it, even though you feel it's unfair. It had happened to Bryan Robson two years before against Chelsea, an FA Cup final we also won. I don't think I've got over it yet, to be brutally honest, but I can't speak highly enough of the fella for what he has achieved. To work for him for almost 10 years is something I will always treasure. It was fabulous.

Everyone in football has a Fergie story. No one can ever copy him. There are not enough hours in the day to replicate what he did. He's been quite remarkable.

Even now in 2021, when I was up against it at Newcastle United, he was on the phone. "Now remember when you are giving a team talk or making an entrance, stick your chest out and never show anything is getting to you. And before you go on the telly, make sure your tie is straight. Compose yourself."

Bloody hell, he never stops.

Rob McCaffrey

ROB McCAFFREY got to know Alex while working on Granada TV before going on to present a number of nationwide programmes for Sky Sports including 'Goals On Sunday' and 'Soccer Special'. He was also the host of football programmes for beIN sports in Qatar.

I had just started my job as a young researcher with Granada TV in the north west. I was to work on a football show called *Kick Off,* which first became famous in the seventies when it was hosted by Gerald Sinstadt and then Elton Welsby. It was also the show that had renowned commentators Clive Tyldesley and Rob Palmer on it.

For the first week of a new series in 1987 the producer Terry Smyth, a lovely Northern Irish guy who was mates with a number of Northern Ireland footballers, organised for George Best to be the first main guest. In hindsight, when you think of George's habits at the time, this was a massive mistake. True to form, George didn't show so the big *Kick Off* splash went down like a damp squib. There was plenty of negative publicity so the pressure was really ramped up for our second show.

I felt massively out of my depth because at the time I didn't have any experience and really I was just a big football fan. Here I was now in the midst of trying to salvage our reputation. So Terry pulled another Northern Irishman out of the bag, Norman Whiteside. The idea was to get big Norman and Paul McGrath, who were great mates at Manchester United, together on a live link for the second show straight from Old Trafford. These were the days when you might as well have had two tin cans and some string – today's technical genius was years away. My first real job was to go down to Old Trafford and make sure everything was okay. I was nervous as hell. If the link failed, what was I supposed to do? I would struggle to stick a plug in! I also had to make sure Norman and Paul were all set up for the live interview. It was a Friday night and these days you would struggle to get any footballers agreeing to do live interviews on the evening before a game.

This was also during the time at Manchester United when Alex was on the warpath, suspecting that there was a drinking culture at the club. It was fair to say both Norman and Paul were under suspicion as being leading members of it. I was just starry-eyed meeting them.

There had been surprise that Paul had agreed to do it as he was naturally very nervous over TV interviews, but Norman had managed to persuade him to do this one as a favour to Terry. All I was thinking about was are they in position? Was the equipment working? Was everything else fine? The last thing on my mind is whether they had both had a few drinks.

Thankfully we got it done. It wouldn't have been in the running for any BAFTA awards, but I was relieved and nothing to my knowledge had gone wrong. Paul giggled a bit at times, but Norman helped him through it. I went home feeling pretty pleased with myself and honestly didn't suspect that either of them had been on the booze. I had been in a state of panic so anything like that would have passed me by.

On the Monday morning I walked into the Granada TV office in Manchester to be confronted by our head of sport, Paul Doherty, who – believe me – made Fergie's 'hairdryer treatment' appear like a gentle breeze compared to his outbursts. He was the Alex Ferguson of TV, a colossus of the industry and a wonderful man, but to someone like me he was horrendously scary at the time. All I could hear as I entered the office was this booming voice, "McCaffrey!" I thought 'this can't be good'.

I went into his office and I sat down. He was sitting behind a huge table and I felt so insignificant compared to him. I wondered what was going to happen next. On the table was an outdated intercom system, one that you would now see in something like *Charlie's Angels*. I was already terrified, but that terror went up another notch when he told me that the manager of Manchester United wanted to speak to me.

I thought, 'is he going to come out of a wall or something? Where is he?' Suddenly out of this contraption a Scottish voice speaks. "Is that Rob McCaffrey?" I'm now shaking as Fergie is on this *Charlie's Angels* intercom. The next thing I hear is, "Were my players drunk on Friday night in your interview?"

I replied, "No, they weren't drinking," and added that I wouldn't have let them on the live show if I knew they were on the booze. But while I was saying that to him I was quickly wondering to myself whether they had actually had a few drinks beforehand.

"Are you sure?" he said. "Are you sure? Are you telling me they hadn't had a drink?" I replied, "Yes, I'm certain." The line then went dead.

Whenever I saw Paul McGrath after that he would give me a huge hug. I was covering a game between the Republic of Ireland and Northern Ireland and afterwards he came up to me and said, "Rob, thanks." I don't know how he knew I hadn't dropped them in it, but while I might have helped save them on that occasion it didn't stop Fergie eventually getting rid of them both a couple of years later. What happened on that Friday night was an example of Alex getting to grips with what he believed was affecting the club's progress, a nucleus of drinkers.

I loved being around Alex over the years and feel privileged to have witnessed the rebirth of the club under him. In the early years with Granada, if I went down to the Manchester United training ground there would often just be me there, no other members of the media. Sometimes Paul Doherty would come down with me and Paul would chat away, filling in his Pools coupon while having a cup of tea with Alex. You could see the pair of them really got on and I know Paul was very good when Fergie was under the cosh, offering advice which Alex often took on board.

If I was kept waiting to interview him this voice would come echoing down the stairs from his office, "McCaffrey!" The players would laugh, thinking I was in for it, but when I got up there he was always okay and ready for the interview. I would usually get a cup of tea, although that sometimes depended on what kind of mood he was in.

We did a video for Granada in which we took George Best and Ryan Giggs around Manchester in a stretch limo. It was basically George showing a young Ryan around some of his old haunts as a Manchester United player and included going to his famous nightclub, Slack Alice. When we returned the pair to Old Trafford, George happened to bump into Alex. It was a lovely scene witnessing the two of them together. Fergie was absolutely great with him, very respectful, acknowledging that he was in company of a football genius. That was Alex, he always recognised the greats of the game and went out of his way to make them feel comfortable in his presence.

We did Manchester United's official club videos for years and would often speak to his long-term secretary Lyn, to get some stories which we could tell. She told us that one day a little fat bloke turned up and had somehow managed to find his way to her office. He knocked on the door and in broken English demanded to see Alex. She asked him who he was and tore a strip off him for barging in unannounced.

The next minute Fergie came flying out of his adjoining office wondering what all the fuss was about. He suddenly hugged the 'intruder' and took him into his office. It was Ferenc Puskas, the famous Hungarian footballer. Fergie had no idea he was coming to see him, but the moment he realised who he was he treated him like royalty.

Alex was also very honest in interviews. In one I asked him if it was true that he didn't really have any interest in signing Eric Cantona – that it had been a stroke of good fortune. He admitted to me that the Leeds United manager Howard Wilkinson had rung up asking about signing Denis Irwin. There was no thought then of United bringing in Cantona. I had to admire his honesty. He wasn't prepared to claim that it was his idea to sign someone who helped transform the club.

Fergie was also one of the first to embrace the idea of having cameras following events at football clubs. With the advent of the Premier League and the big changes in the game, he was aware that there was huge interest – something that was ideal to be captured on film. At Granada we managed to persuade him to allow Steve Bruce to compile what was called *The Captain's Log*, which was essentially Brucey let loose with a video camera to record inside the dressing room and United's players travelling to away games on the coach.

There is even some film of Fergie's team talks, something I believe you can still find on YouTube.

At first, as you can imagine, he was sceptical of allowing access, but eventually he relented because some of the players insisted that having the camera inside the dressing room helped them focus more clearly.

I think he realised that it worked, although I'm certain no 'hairdryer' incidents made it to the final cut!

There we were in the early nineties doing a fly-on-the-wall programme with Alex Ferguson and Manchester United, long before documentaries on the likes of Tottenham, Manchester City and Sunderland could be downloaded or streamed. Alex and Steve Bruce led the way and it's there for all to see some of the build up to – and after they won – their first Premier League title under him in 1993.

A couple of years earlier it was great to be on the pitch with Alex when they won the European Cup Winners' Cup in Rotterdam in 1991. I was the only media man allowed onto the pitch to interview him straight after the game. I was delighted for him and have been ever since for all the success that has come his way, because he is a great and fascinating guy. He is inspirational, a one-off special person who always has time for everyone.

He is also very knowledgeable away from football. He loves his quizzes, but he has to win. He has such a competitive nature and would fight you for the lemons at half-time. He is a real winner and he also loves a sing-song.

In one of the early *Kick Off* programmes, he and George Graham were in the green room having a good old chat when they burst into song – fantastic memories of a fantastic guy.

Mark Hughes

MARK HUGHES, it is generally believed, was the first person to describe the verbal blasts from Alex as 'the hairdryer'. In between his own experiences of the enraged rollickings the Wales international helped him end 26 years of Old Trafford hurt by landing the 1993 Premier League title. Hughes went on to become a successful manager with Wales and clubs including Blackburn Rovers, Manchester City and Stoke City.

My time in Barcelona wasn't great. I had left Manchester United to move to Barca in 1986, but I wasn't really enjoying it and so I was looking for a different experience. I was made aware that Manchester United were interested in bringing me back. But I had a tax situation where I needed to be out of the country for a whole year otherwise I would have had to give back all the money I had earned.

I had the opportunity to go to Bayern Munich on loan in 1987, which was great for me. They are a fantastic club with real football people like Karl-Heinz Rummenigge around the place, whereas at Barcelona you were given your pay cheque and you had to sort yourself out. Bayern looked after you. They understood how players were thinking and what they needed to help them perform to their best ability.

The reality was if United hadn't come in for me I would have probably stayed with Bayern. At times I wasn't sure if it was going to happen or not, but thankfully it did.

At the time I wouldn't have gone anywhere else other than United and yes, I did find life under Alex a lot different from my previous spell under Ron Atkinson. It was a little more, shall we say, 'disciplined' the second time around. In fairness to Ron he wanted to relax you, believing that would bring the best out of you football wise. Obviously there has to be a balance between enjoying yourself and working hard. Some of the lads, myself included, took advantage of the enjoyment side too much. I don't think we were any better or worse socially than anyone else involved in football at the time. It was a different culture to what we have now.

There would be a few beers. It wasn't white water rafting in those days to forge any team bonding, it was a few beers! That's how it was. It was different and no worse for being different in my view. But I don't think Alex shared that view. He had clearly come in with his own ideas and was more of a disciplinarian. I know Gordon Strachan was quite taken aback when he discovered that Alex was about to become the new Manchester United manager because obviously he'd had experience of him before at Aberdeen. He was thinking it's going to be a bit different to life under Ron Atkinson. And it certainly was.

Of course I had an idea of what to expect after agreeing to rejoin the club in 1988, but I was coming to play for Manchester United again, not so much for Alex. I knew he was a strong character and life would be different, but I was also coming from Bayern Munich where everything was done correctly and I had enjoyed that part of it, more so than I would have thought.

I probably needed a bit more discipline and structure when I came back, and that's what I got. I was delighted to be back and I think I had become a better player through the experience of playing abroad, something that was acknowledged by my peers who twice voted me PFA player of the year during my second spell at United. That was very important to me and gave me more confidence as well. Early on there were all these stories about Alex supposedly being under pressure. Before we won the Premier League for the first time after so long there were stories every week about him being on the verge of losing his job. You would often see the image in a newspaper of a cracked Manchester United badge along the headline 'United In Turmoil'.

We'd turn up for training and have a laugh about it, "is it the cracked badge again?" someone would enquire with a smile. So we were used to all the media conjecture, but from a personal point of view I honestly never felt that pressure. We felt that the club was going to support him through whatever because they could see what he was doing behind the scenes.

He had reshaped the club, he had got the youth system in place. They could see progress. Probably, in this day and age, he wouldn't have kept his job because that's now the nature of the beast. He was able to have that time, two or three years, which you wouldn't get now and came through it. It's what all managers want, time to see all your plans come to fruition. United, of course, and everyone connected with the club will now be delighted that he was given the time.

Even during the so-called tough days he was very impressive. It wasn't just about the players. He knew everyone from the laundry lady to the kitman. He knew when their birthdays were. He knew everything about them. He's very good like that and it enabled the club to grow and become part of the United family.

I know it has been said that I came up with the term 'the hairdryer' over the blasts he would give the players. I honestly don't know. I think it first came up in something the former United correspondent for the *Manchester Evening News*, David

Meek, wrote in an interview with me. I must have mentioned it. Whether it was later embellished, I don't know. I had said at first it was like standing next to a blow torch. That then became a hairdryer. He would stand so close to you while he was giving you a bollocking and I would imagine the cartoon where the character's hair is standing on end from a blast of hot air. So yes, maybe I'm guilty of calling it 'the hairdryer'. It's certainly stuck.

He wasn't averse to giving me the hairdryer – I had a few blasts. I used to frustrate him because, on occasions, I was a bit loose with possession of the ball. I could hold onto it a bit too long and get dispossessed.

We were playing Leeds United in a FA Cup game at Elland Road in 1992 and I miscontrolled a throw-in about 10 minutes into the game. I've since seen a clip of it on the TV and he rushed to the side of the pitch and shouted at his assistant Brian Kidd to get me off. At the time I had been oblivious to all this.

Kiddo evidently placated him saying, 'there's only 10 minutes gone for goodness sake, calm down'. I actually scored the winning goal, but he still wasn't happy and I had to apologise for losing the ball. He could be hot or cold at times.

I think sometimes it was premeditated. He would think in his head, 'I'm going to nail you,' hoping for a reaction from his victim. You quickly learned not to be the person to lose possession just before half-time. If we were drawing or losing and you were the last one who had just lost the ball before the referee blew for the half-time whistle you were getting it because that would have been the last thing he would have remembered before coming into the dressing room. It got to the stage where nobody wanted the ball if you knew half-time was approaching.

Sometimes it didn't really matter. Even if we felt we had done well he would still nail us. If we were bad then we really got it. And if he had forgotten who had lost possession just before the break then it would be Gary Pallister who would be blasted because he was usually the first one into the dressing room.

I think Pally must have got 10 times more bollockings than anybody because he was first through the door. But it didn't bother him. He just went out with the attitude, 'I'll show you'. And that's the difference between then and now. Nowadays if a player gets a bit of stick from the manager they go straight to their agent saying, 'I can't play for this man. He doesn't like me. I need to move'. We just used to say, 'sod that, we'll show you we can play'. It was a different attitude.

We finally got things up and running at Old Trafford by winning the 1990 FA Cup. People always recall the third round game at Nottingham Forest. There was talk that if we lost then Alex would lose his job, but I never really felt that was the case on the day. We knew it was a big game and we wanted to get the job done as we were in the middle of a run of 11 games without a win in the league.

I'll never forget the United fans at the City Ground that day, they were brilliant. There had been, in previous weeks, a few dissenting voices against Alex, a few banners. But that day you sensed everyone was together because I think no one liked the mounting media campaign which seemed to be piling the pressure on the manager – that this was the one game he couldn't afford to lose. There was a feeling that the United fans were fed up with this and didn't want to be told what was happening, they would make up their own minds and it was a case of circling the wagons. They were brilliant that day and got behind us and we ended up winning 1-0.

We reached the final against Crystal Palace and it was a strange feeling. I scored twice in a 3-3 draw at Wembley, but we knew we just had to go again in the replay. There was still a job to be done. In fact we had very nearly lost that first game in extra-time and were probably grateful in many respects that we still had the opportunity to win it. Palace had been very aggressive in that first meeting and maybe overstepped the mark at times. That hadn't gone down too well so we were fired up for the replay and Lee Martin became the hero with the only goal. Palace had needed to win the first game because there was no way they were going to win the second one.

There was obvious relief for that group of players. You always need to learn to win in football, and learn to win together. The following season we won the European Cup Winners' Cup against my former club Barcelona.

It wasn't about gaining any revenge for me personally because they had still given me a great opportunity both through football and my personal life. I didn't really grasp it as much as I should have done. I wasn't married at the time, I was lonely out there. There were no player liaison officers to look after your needs like there is now. You were just left to your own devices, so I found it difficult – but not too many get to play for Barcelona.

Anyway, I ended up scoring both the goals in a 2-1 win in Rotterdam – sorry to Steve Bruce, but his header for the first goal wasn't over the line when I struck it into the net. I think once we had won our first trophy, the FA Cup, our confidence soared although it was always in the back of our minds that the club really wanted the league title.

We just missed out to Leeds the season before we did actually land the title in 1993 and I know Alex was really frustrated along with the rest of us. He could easily have ripped that team apart and started again. The fact that he didn't we were grateful for and understood that might not have been the case.

I think he knew he had a group of players containing strong characters who could go again and wouldn't be deflated by disappointments. We had enough strength of character to go again. We just needed a little bit of stardust from Eric Cantona who had joined us from Leeds. We weren't a bad team. We'd won the FA Cup, the European Cup Winners' Cup and in 1991/92 we won the European Super Cup and the League Cup, so we were close. We were a good team, but we just needed something else to get us over the line. Thankfully with Eric that happened.

He was something different. He was a different type of player to anyone I had played with before. Usually I would be playing alongside another striker because most teams were playing 4-4-2, two strikers up top, one coming short another going long. You worked the channels and tried to get your head on the end of crosses. That was the top and bottom of it really whereas Eric would start wandering off. I'd be looking around thinking where the hell has he gone now? He could be over on the left wing or somewhere. But all of a sudden he would pick the ball up and find pockets of space to attack from a deep position. He gave me a different perspective on the game. I think he made me a better player because he made me understand the game better. I think he had that effect on a lot of players in the group.

Of course there was no way Eric was ever going to get the hairdryer from the boss. He didn't even get it when he jumped into the crowd at Crystal Palace. I think he just received a blank stare. Eric was probably expecting a friendly tap on the shoulder from Alex and to hear him say, "unlucky Eric." At least that didn't happen. Eric was a special case, a different person, a different player. He was a maverick and mavericks are great as long as they keep producing for you. I've had a number during my management career. They are okay when they are playing well, but when they are not producing they are a liability.

You've got to treat them differently because if you don't you just don't get anything out of them. They are just detrimental to your team. Eric was never like that, but the first time the hair-dryer was turned on him it would have been au revoir. But that was the skill of Alex. He was able to get the best out of Eric, the absolute maximum from him week in, week out. That was all down to the way he was handled. That is credit to the boss.

Other players would respond well to criticism. Being auto-cratic and shouting and bawling was something that was preva-lent in those days and Alex led the way! The core of the dressing room was also British and you accepted that was the way you were managed. A dressing room with more foreign players might have reacted differently. We just got on with it if we got a bollocking. As time went on Alex needed to understand that dressing rooms were changing, becoming more diverse. You would have players of different races, different religions, different cultures. It's a different mix now and his skill over the years was to understand and develop that as he went on.

He would change his assistant managers as well which would help bring in some fresh ideas, never allowing the club to become stale. I don't think he was happy to lose Archie Knox in 1991, but after that he brought in others to keep things going. It gives you different eyes and a different voice. Given the length of time he was at United there was a danger that he was saying the same things to the same people. You have to instigate change at times.

Many people claim that the 1994 side, the one that won the Premier League and FA Cup double was the best of his era. I think the fact that we had got over the line to win the Premier League the year before was important. That group of players were strong mentally. We had to deal with the pressures of going another year without the title – the years were clocking up, something we were constantly reminded of. I think it reflected well on us. If we hadn't have got it done then I don't think we would have been Manchester United players for the length of time that we were.

They were more aggressive times in football. Games were more physical and we had to stand up and be counted in almost every game we played. It was a case of circling the wagons and defending our borders really. It was us against everyone else. Nobody was better than Alex at employing the siege mentality philosophy. We definitely had it that season. We wanted to be successful for ourselves and for Manchester United.

It all ended for myself, Paul Ince and Andrei Kanchelskis in the summer of 1995. It's still a bit of a mystery even today why we all were let go. In my case, maybe he still thought he could get a few quid for me. I think also in my own mind I felt I had been replaced when he went out and bought Andy Cole from Newcastle United in January 1995. I thought it was going to be Eric and Andy up front.

I did have the offer of a new two-year contract, but I felt I wouldn't be happy sitting in the stand at times. Then two weeks later Eric jumps into the crowd at Selhurst Park. I was thinking 'you shouldn't have done that Eric,' but in the back of my mind I was also thinking I might be able to stay now. I signed a new contract because I didn't think Eric was going to come back from that, to be perfectly honest. But the club and the manager tried really hard to get him back. He came back so I sensed I would be on my way and in the summer of 1995 I left for Chelsea. There was no attempt to keep me, no real conversations. My time was up. They obviously didn't want me to stay.

It was a huge call to sell the three of us at once, but to be fair to Alex he knew there was a young group of players coming through – the so-called Class of '92. As senior players we were aware of them because we were thinking 'Christ, they could replace us one day'. We kept an eye on the youth team games and we all knew there were five or six, the likes of David Beckham, Paul Scholes, Gary Neville and Nicky Butt coming through, who were excellent. For that amount of young players to be banging on the first-team door at once – with Ryan Giggs already established in the team – was unheard of really.

I still didn't think he was going to change things as radically as he did, but I could understand to an extent my situation because I was 31. With the likes of Incey and Andrei it was a bit different. I think there is probably more behind their departures than anyone is aware of.

When I became a manager, despite our past, he was always determined to beat me. No one would be surprised by that I imagine, but the reverse is also true – I desperately wanted to beat him. Manchester United fans might have misinterpreted how I was when I went up against United, thinking that I had fallen out with people and I didn't like Fergie anymore or the club. That was absolute rubbish. I loved playing for United and I love the club, but I also love competing against them.

I have always viewed Alex as the best manager at the best club with the best fans and I just wanted to go head-to-head and see how I went against them. It was about testing myself as a professional football manager. I didn't view myself as an ex-Manchester United player, I viewed myself as a professional football manager trying to beat the best.

Everyone connected with Manchester United must have wondered what I was doing managing Manchester City. It was about taking an opportunity, something Alex had done during his time in the game. I would have loved to have managed United, but this was 2008 and Fergie wasn't going anywhere. Arsene Wenger was going nowhere, he was staying at Arsenal. Chelsea never employed British managers. Liverpool was never going to happen. I had been at Blackburn Rovers for four years. My star was quite high so I knew I needed a move and I was given the opportunity of going to Manchester City.

It was a chance to manage head-to-head against Alex. I thought I could do something there and was told there was a few quid to spend – but there wasn't before Sheikh Mansour came in. Once the Abu Dhabi takeover happened I was on borrowed time. I think they were looking to sack me two or three times before they actually did. Khaldoon Al Mubarak, the chairman, flew in when we were playing Arsenal in September 2009, expecting us to get beaten.

But we won and he had to get back on the plane. He flew in again before a Chelsea game in early December, but we won that as well so he was back on his plane again. After that we drew at Bolton and lost at Spurs so he was going to do it after whatever happened in the following Saturday's game at home to Sunderland, which we won 4-3.

Everybody apart myself was told it was going to happen. But these things happen in football as Fergie knows only too well.

Ian Rush

IAN RUSH almost became a Manchester United player following a passionate phone call from Alex. Rush, Liverpool's legendary all-time leading goalscorer, had two spells at Anfield, spent a season in Italy with Juventus and won 73 caps for Wales. Now a Liverpool ambassador, he also represents UEFA.

The first person to ring me when it became apparent that Juventus were prepared to let me go after one season in Italy was Alex Ferguson. He was absolutely fantastic. The way he promoted Manchester United to me was different class.

He made it clear that he would love to sign me even though obviously he knew all about my Liverpool connections and my love for the club which had taken me from Chester in 1981. He told me that he recognised Liverpool as a great club, but so was Manchester United.

He said that with me in the side they could win more things, that I would be made to feel welcome and that the United fans would be right behind me, especially once I started scoring. If I hadn't played for Liverpool then I probably would have signed for him right there and then because he was so good at promoting his club. I felt honoured that the moment he had heard I might be available he was straight on the phone trying to convince me that Old Trafford should be my next destination.

At first I told him I didn't think Juventus were prepared to let me leave anyway, but that clearly wasn't the case because I soon had other managers ringing me. Next on the phone after Alex was Colin Harvey of Everton. After that Graeme Souness, who was in charge of Rangers, and Uli Hoeness from Bayern

Munich. Then came Kenny Dalglish, my former Liverpool striking partner and manager, who was still in charge of the club. As a football person I could only have the utmost respect for Alex and the fact that he wanted me in his team made me feel 10 feet tall. I must admit I was swayed to a certain extent until Kenny made his move. Then it was no contest – I was heading back to Liverpool.

Until he got in touch and I realised that my Italian adventure was coming to an end I didn't know if Liverpool were prepared to take me back. They had signed John Aldridge and also brought in John Barnes and Peter Beardsley to create a forward line that helped them run away with the title in 1987/88 while I was in Italy. But once it was plain that they did want me back I agreed to return to Liverpool without negotiating any personal terms. My love for Liverpool meant more to me than money.

Manchester United might have come up with more money and Alex had been very persuasive, but Liverpool was in my blood and that was the overriding factor in determining my future. Kenny obviously knew that because at the end of his phone call he told me I was already booked on a flight from Turin back to England for me to sign. Sure enough, I was straight onto a flight, ironically to Manchester, and he was there to pick me up – maybe making sure that Alex didn't get there first!

It was then announced that I was coming back to Liverpool so with everything completed in a whirlwind I didn't have time to phone Alex and personally deliver the bad news. To be fair, he has never held it against me that I rejected the opportunity to play for him. I see him regularly now when Liverpool play United. He is usually in a small United entourage that comes to Anfield and we always have a friendly chat.

It's great catching up. Not long after signing for Liverpool for the second time in 1989, Alex must have been tempted to run me over after he spotted me walking in Wilmslow, Cheshire, where he lives. I was just minding my own business on a leisurely stroll when someone sounded their car horn and made me almost jump out of my skin. It was Fergie, who was laughing his head off as he wound the window down shouting, "I wish I could have run you over!" That was some coincidence.

At Liverpool, in terms of the greatest, you have Sir Kenny Dalglish. At Manchester United it's Sir Alex Ferguson. What I also like about him is that he will speak to anyone. It can be a first team player, it can be a youngster, it can be any member of staff or a supporter. He is very humble. He has followed Sir Matt Busby, Bill Shankly and Bob Paisley in that respect. They were all the heart and soul of their football clubs and so is Alex.

That comes from their working class backgrounds, how they were brought up, never forgetting their roots. That's what makes them special. I hope it's the same with me – I believe it's about trying to help other people in the game, especially youngsters who will always make mistakes. You have to point them in the right direction and that's why Alex was so successful with his youth policy over the years at Manchester United.

In hindsight, despite Alex's charm and persuasion over the phone when I was in Italy, I'm glad that I didn't end up there because it would probably have affected my relationship with the Liverpool supporters, who have always been great to me.

I'm also now an ambassador for the club, which might not have been possible if I had played for Manchester United, but it doesn't dilute my admiration for Alex Ferguson and everything he has achieved.

Lee Sharpe

LEE SHARPE spent eight lively years under Alex after being signed from Torquay United in 1988 and became a cult hero to Manchester United fans. Living a rock star lifestyle, he often fell foul of the manager's temper. He won three Premier League titles and became renowned for his flamboyant goal celebrations, again to the disdain of his manager.

Ryan Giggs was always getting me into trouble, especially in our younger years under the manager. I'd bought a new-build house in Altrincham while Giggsy was still living at home with his mum. One day, we decided to have a party at my house that evening with a couple of the apprentices. After leaving training Giggsy rang me, "Let's go out in Stockport, it's Thursday night, we don't play until Sunday – we'll be fine," he said. I was like, "yeah, yeah, come down." It got to about 10pm and there was a knock at the door. We thought it must be the taxi driver. It wasn't. It was the manager.

Even worse, one of Giggsy's mates – who was in the house – answered the door holding two bottles of beer which had been left from a party the weekend before. One of the other lads ran up the stairs and said to me, "You'll never guess who's at the door – the manager." I'm thinking, no it can't be.

I was just finishing getting ready for the night out so I peered down the stairs and there he was. He was in a right agitated state – there was froth coming out of the sides of his mouth. I knew we were in serious trouble. He shouted to get rid of whoever was in the house telling me, "Get into the living room with Giggs. I want words with you."

In the meantime he threw everybody else out of the house, kicking them on their backsides, smacking them around the head. He then absolutely ripped into the pair of us. I got it first.

"You're finished at this club, you can't head it, you can't pass it, you can't run, you're letting your team-mates down, letting your mum and dad down, letting your family down."

Then he turned to Giggsy and started laying into him. "And you, you're letting your mum down, your family down, you're just not bothered."

While he was doing this he suddenly clocked a big set of drums that had virtually taken over my dining room. At the same time my big St Bernard dog was all over him. Pointing to my pride and joy he yelled, "What the fuck are they? I'll give you fucking drums!"

He was probably at his angriest that night in all the time I worked with him. He never let up – that was part of his make up. He was 100mph, full steam and no let up. Not in training, not in matches. He was always on your case trying to get the best from everyone. He was a workaholic, always trying to find out everything about the other team we were playing and how to get the better of them.

There was a different culture in football then. It was very British, very laddish. I suppose it was a sort of pub culture which he was desperate to put an end to. Personally, I had a difference of opinion to him about how to live your life. He wanted to win football matches. I just wanted to play well and win football matches, but maybe go about it in a different way. Either way, no one can argue with what we achieved at Manchester United.

For me, the European Cup Winners' Cup victory in 1991 was a special night as that was my first major trophy at United. We then went on to win the club's first Premier League title followed by two League and FA Cup doubles, which was amazing. Until I left United in 1996, I didn't actually believe that stadiums weren't always full because wherever we went people flocked to see us. "You've only come to see United," chanted our fans at away games.

We had some great trips, especially in the days before mobile phones were around to capture things that maybe you didn't want to be caught on camera. Talking of mobile phones, I got absolutely rinsed by the manager for having one of the first ones when they came out. I was 20, 21 and he tore me to bits, accusing me of being flash because I had a mobile phone. It was absolutely ridiculous. My nephew, who is seven, has one now. I don't know what the manager would say to him!

We had a great dressing room full of real characters and I used to sit next to Roy Keane. He was like the Roy Keane you see as a pundit on the telly now, there were no holds barred – always shooting from the hip. He could be pretty brutal and barbaric to some people. As soon as Paul Parker heard Roy Keane's voice echoing along the corridor he would rush out, pretending he was sitting on the toilet to get away from his barbs.

They were great times – it was real rock 'n' roll. The team had become successful, the music scene in Manchester was huge. The Hacienda was massive. You had Oasis, Take That, Happy Mondays, The Stone Roses – it was just an incredible time to be around Manchester, but I think at times we got confused as to whether we were sportsmen or rock stars. I'm not sure that it could have been any better, to be honest.

On the pitch, I think we learned a lot from missing out on the league title to Leeds United the season before we actually won the Premier League in 1993. The manager made some important decisions with the players he brought in. He trusted his senior players and listened to them. I think Roy Keane was signed after we won the first title on the recommendation of a few of the senior pros.

My relationship with the manager became difficult because he didn't think I took the game seriously enough. That wasn't true. There was no way I wanted to see myself with a four out of 10 in the newspaper merit marks. I always wanted to be the best player on the pitch.

He would have a go at my performances, my haircuts, my friends, my clothes, my car – pretty much anything you could imagine. Even if I had played well and scored the winning goal he would then criticise my goal celebration! In the end, I thought to myself that if he's having a go at me when I'm playing well what's the point in me listening? So up yours. I just decided to do whatever I wanted to do and if he wanted to have a go then so be it. We just cracked on like that.

One of my biggest rollickings came in a game against Liverpool at Anfield. A little while before I had plucked up the courage to ask him whether I could move out of my digs, where I had been living after signing for Manchester United, and to move into a house with my girlfriend. He said I was a bit too young, but seeing as I was in the first team he would allow it.

My girlfriend came up from Birmingham and we moved into the house and everything seemed fine. But then came the Liverpool game at Anfield. We'd had a terrible first half and at half-time he exploded. He picked on me and told me to sell my house, tell my girlfriend to go back to Birmingham and get out there in the second half and play. He could be ruthless, but it produced results. Away from the pitch, he didn't like his players going off to play golf. He thought it sapped the strength in your legs and could lead to problems with your back. After training or a game he would encourage us to go back home and sit on the couch and rest, which was frustrating. As young players you have energy to burn and so some of us would sneak off and play. I would team up with Gary Pallister. Paul Ince and Mark Hughes played quite a lot too. I think it was a good job Roy Keane didn't play because no doubt he would have sent the clubs flying everywhere after a bad shot.

As everyone from the team will tell you, the one player to escape the fiery Fergie treatment was Eric Cantona – even after his infamous kung-fu kick at Selhurst Park when he was sent off against Crystal Palace. I was in the team that night and we thought, for once, that Eric was surely going to get it in the dressing room. We couldn't believe what had happened, but when the final whistle went we thought that having only drawn the game, due to being reduced to 10 men, that Eric was finally going to be in his firing line. There was no way he could bollock us and not Eric this time.

Normally after a disappointing result like that 1-1 draw you would take your time getting back to the dressing room because you knew that the manager would be lying in wait, ready to combust. Not this time. There was almost a mad rush to see the fireworks explode around Eric's head.

We got back in there and it was a tradition to place your towel over your hung up clothes, just in case things went flying in the dressing room courtesy of the manager. You didn't make eye contact either or you would pay for it.

This time it was a case of keeping your head down and enjoying

Eric's first ever hairdryer blast. We were like schoolkids nudging each other, waiting for the show to begin. The manager walked in and true to form he was absolutely fuming.

The dressing room door was left just about still on its hinges, his jacket was off, his shirt sleeves were rolled up. There were sandwiches and cups of tea, which had been put on a bench in the middle of the floor, flying everywhere. But amazingly it wasn't Eric who copped it.

"You, fucking Pallister, you can't head it, you can't tackle. You, fucking Incey, you never laid a glove on anybody, where the fuck have you been? Sharpey, my fucking grandmother is quicker than you. What the fuck were you doing out there? None of you have passed to a black shirt all night. A performance like that, it's a fucking disgrace. You are all in at 9am in the morning. I'm not putting up with it."

Then, as calm as you like, he turned to Eric. "You can't go around doing things like that, son." And that was it.

We couldn't believe it. Eric had gotten away with it again, unlike the rest of us.

6

'*Eventually, with his ears pricked, the manager arrived at Brucey's jacket, pushed his hand into it and pulled out the mobile phone. Without a second thought he hurled it with force into a bin, completely smashing it*'

Paul Parker, former Manchester United player

Gary Pallister

GARY PALLISTER broke the British transfer record for a defender when he joined Manchester United from Middlesbrough for £2.3 million in 1989 and went on to play for England while helping Alex turn around United's fortunes. He collected four Premier League winners' medals, was in the victorious European Cup Winners' Cup side and also won the FA Cup three times.

I used to tell the lads that Alex seemed to practice 'the hairdryer' on me – I seemed to cop it more than the rest of them. I think myself, Lee Sharpe and Ryan Giggs were probably the ones most under threat if he was about to let fly.

No one was really exempt from it, apart from Eric Cantona. I can even remember Bryan Robson getting a little bit of one – half a 'hairdryer'. Others like Mark Hughes, Brian McClair and Paul Ince got it at times, but I think he picked on me because I was sort of a laidback, chilled type of character and so he felt he had to poke the hornet's nest now and again.

I suppose he felt I could take the bollockings – although that wasn't always the case.

During my second season at Manchester United we had a blazing row. Words were said during a game at half-time and I thought he had overstepped the mark, even for him. It got so heated I think we were both at the stage ready to throw a couple of punches before one or two of the players got between us.

He yelled that he had seen enough and told me to take my shirt off, he was substituting me. He kept on at me so once again I wasn't having that and we had to be pulled apart by Robbo and

Brian McClair before blows were struck. Even though I'm 6ft 4in he was clearly ready to go to war – there was no stopping him. I thought that was it, I'm heading for the showers – that's my day finished. I could hear his number two Archie Knox in the corner of the dressing room trying to reason with him. The gaffer wasn't having any of it at first.

I continued heading towards the showers only for him to shout, "Where the hell are you going?"

I said, "I'm getting showered."

He then said, "You're not getting off that easy, get your shirt back on and get back onto the pitch."

I told him he could sod off, I wouldn't be playing. I went into the showers only to be followed by Robbo and Choccy [McClair].

They said it was about the lads, about the team – not him and me – so forget about the argument with the gaffer, I couldn't let the rest of the team down. They reasoned with me so I put my strip back on, went out and we ended up winning the game. He still had to have another little chip at me when I came in to the dressing room at the end of the game, but I just shrugged it off. Deep down though, I thought there was no going back, that I was about to be placed on the transfer list.

I told my parents the next day that I didn't think I would be at the club much longer. He'd had a few pops at me and I felt after the latest one, which had gone over the top, I'd had enough as well. So the following day I made up my mind that I would go up to his office at the training ground following our session and get things off my chest. I had even worked out what I was going to say. He had tried chatting to me during training, but I deliberately blanked him. I was determined to let him know how I felt so I didn't want any distractions. As far as I was concerned I was going to give him both barrels, even if it ended up with him sacking me. I was going to have my say. I was getting changed, getting ready for the confrontation, when one of the lads told me the gaffer wanted to see me. 'Right', I thought, 'here we go' as I marched up the stairs towards his office. Normally you knocked on the door and waited until he told you to come in, but this time I knocked on the door and barged straight in. I was still full of hell. He had gotten me into such a state. I thought no matter what he says I'll be ready for him with an answer. "Take a seat, Pally," he said. I sat down and thought to myself, 'bring it on'.

"I've brought you in today about what happened the other night. I just want to apologise for what I said to you." It sucked everything I was about to say out of me. The last thing I expected to hear was an apology. I was in a daze, barely believing what I had heard. I just blurted out, "Okay." All the angst that had built up had suddenly disappeared. Here was Alex Ferguson actually apologising. He had taken the sting out of the situation. It takes a man to admit you are wrong and I respected him for that.

At Middlesbrough I had gone through a lot of stuff with the manager Bruce Rioch and if you had a fallout he wouldn't speak to you for weeks on end. But here was the gaffer putting his hand up and saying he had made a mistake. He grew so much in my estimation through that, but he did qualify it by adding that he couldn't have what happened – with me storming off into the showers at half-time – again when he had only so many minutes to address the team.

We shook hands and that was it.

On reflection, maybe he had been testing me, seeing how

far he could push me. But Archie Knox had even told him he shouldn't have said what he had said to me.

We all loved Eric Cantona, but at the same time we would have loved to have seen the gaffer turn the 'hairdryer' on him. It never happened. You never wanted to be the victim, although lads being lads we would have to suppress our giggles as someone was given the treatment. Luckily in our dressing room at Old Trafford there were a couple of pillars you could hide behind. So some of us would be pulling faces and smiling as the 'hairdryer' was on full throttle for some poor unfortunate. As we came off the pitch, Brian Kidd – his assistant after Archie Knox – would often warn one of us that we were in for it.

Obviously we expected Eric to get it at Crystal Palace after launching himself at a Palace fan in 1995. We were waiting for it all to kick off and manifest itself only for nothing to happen. It never did, even when he wasn't on his game and had struggled.

Alex made out to the media that he loved me and Steve Bruce, calling us 'Daisy and Dolly'. You wouldn't have thought so if you had witnessed some of the 'hairdryer' treatment, although to be fair he did look after his players. If you were prepared to go to war for him he was prepared to look after you, and that just wasn't about football things – it would be off the pitch as well. He would always help if you had a problem. That is inbuilt in him and we enjoyed some great times.

To this day I don't know who was Daisy and who was Dolly between me and Brucey. It was just a throwaway comment that the media picked up on and that was it – it stuck. Those names wouldn't exactly put the fear of God into opposition centre-forwards! 'Oh you're up against Daisy and Dolly today, it should be an absolute breeze then'.

The spirit and camaraderie we had amongst the lads was different class. I think Alex enjoyed that as well. It made his job a lot easier. It was all before social media and cameras on phones so we were able to enjoy ourselves more. I think the game was a lot easier to manage in those days. How times have changed.

On match days at Old Trafford after I first joined United I would just walk from the car park, through the forecourt and into the stadium. Nowadays the players drive up to the tunnel and have their cars parked for them so the fans really can't get anywhere near them. It was starting to change by the time I left in 1998. They were much simpler times although it wasn't very pleasant after we lost 5-1 at Manchester City in one of my first games for the club in 1989. Talk about 'Welcome to Manchester!' When we next reported for training we were met by, let's say, three burly gentlemen. There was no security back then at The Cliff so they had walked right up to the door leading to the changing rooms. All the players got stick and abuse. I was told by them, in no uncertain terms, that I couldn't lace Paul McGrath's boots. Emotions were still running high after the City spanking, but nothing was done – in fact I think some people at the club might have felt it was a good thing and might spur us on to do better.

There was pressure on all of us at the time, including the manager. I remember the banners – 'Time To Go Fergie' – and things like that. I was part of that, I was part of the reason why the team was failing and it was hard to swallow. We had brought in five players in 1989, myself, Paul Ince, Danny Wallace, Neil Webb and Micky Phelan for £7 million, which was huge money at the time. I cost them £2.3 million. United had paid over the odds for us at that time, although it all eventually worked out.

It was a huge gamble, particularly to sign me because I had only played one season in the top flight for Middlesbrough and we ended up getting relegated. So I'll be forever thankful to Alex for having enough faith in me to bring me to the club. The transfer fee did place a lot of pressure on my shoulders, but fortunately I had four other new signings who were also dealing with the expectations as well. We also had the likes of Sparky (Mark Hughes), Robbo and Choccy, who tried to help us as senior pros.

I was helped not just by them, but by the gaffer as well. He realised what was going on and the pressure we were under and tried to deflect a lot of the stick onto himself. But it was still hard when you had the likes of Tommy Docherty and the great George Best questioning your ability and asking why you were at Old Trafford.

So at first Manchester United was a hard place to be at, but in 1993 a whole 26 years of frustration ended when we won the Premier League title. The Easter Saturday win over Sheffield Wednesday at Old Trafford always gets mentioned, Brucey scoring those late headers after we had been 1-0 down with me providing the cross for his winning goal from the right wing. Giggsy had overhit a cross which had flown over me at the back stick. I was the last man on that side of the pitch so I had to sprint to collect the ball and put it back into the area, which I did, right onto Brucey's head with the aid of a little deflection. That goal was created and scored by Daisy and Dolly – or was it Dolly and Daisy?

The big significance about that game was a year before we lost to Nottingham Forest at home at a similar time of the season when we were battling with Leeds United in the title race. We had absolutely battered Forest, but they had two shots on target and beat us 2-1. It was Easter Monday and we came off the pitch feeling it was the deciding factor in that season's title race and that we were going to miss out again, which we did. If we had lost against Sheffield Wednesday, which for so long looked likely, then it would have probably been the same scenario, but conversely winning it in the manner that we did proved pivotal. We thought then that at last the league title could be coming our way. You saw that with the reaction of the gaffer and Brian Kidd celebrating wildly on the pitch following the winning goal.

In the dressing room after the game it felt like we had won the title and we knew our main rivals Aston Villa would have been in their dressing room, after a 0-0 draw at Coventry, hearing what had unfolded at Old Trafford. Two goals in stoppage time – that would be enough to deflate anyone. In the space of around six minutes we'd turned the season on its head. It was a massive game and three weeks later we were champions.

I also discovered during my time at Manchester United that you can get a bollocking from the manager even if you've scored two goals for the first time in your career to help your side win 3-1 against your bitter rivals Liverpool at Anfield. A former army general had written to the gaffer about how to use decoys at set-pieces, so he thought it would be a good idea to utilise this method when we took corners against Liverpool.

This was 1997 and until then we had not really ever worked that much on set-pieces. He had relied on the lads to be creative in games. So during training before the Liverpool game the gaffer presented his set-piece plans based on some players trying to fool the opposition by being decoys. We also had a vital Champions League semi-final second leg against

Borussia Dortmund coming up after our trip to Merseyside. We played Liverpool on the Saturday and deployed the decoy strategy on corners that we had worked on during the week. David Beckham took the corners and it worked brilliantly, enabling me to score twice at the Kop end. We won 3-1 to go five points clear of Liverpool with four games to play, so it set us on the way to the title. I was cock-a-hoop. Two goals for the first time in my professional career and when you win at Liverpool it's unbelievable. They were the yardstick we measured ourselves against. Everyone was buzzing and I got asked would I go and speak to the TV? Of course I would. I couldn't wait to get out there to tell everyone about my brace.

I was asked about my two headed goals and I just explained that it was something we had been working on in training and it had worked like an absolute dream.

I couldn't have been happier and when I returned to the dressing room I was still full of it. Suddenly the gaffer came up to me, after obviously watching my interview on the TV screen, and clipped me around the head. "What the hell were you doing? You have just told Borussia Dortmund that we have been working on set-pieces. I've just said in another TV interview that what happened was off the cuff!" I thought, 'Jesus Christ, I can't do anything right'.

"You're a bloody idiot son," he bawled and that was me somehow in his bad books after scoring two goals in a 3-1 win at Anfield!

To be honest, I still to this day feel very fortunate to have experienced what I did at a club like Manchester United and under a manager like him. I had come from non-league football and didn't start progressing until I was 19. I was made up to make it at my local club Middlesbrough and then I was playing for Manchester United and England. How did that happen? To go on that journey and win the things we did, with so many great players and great characters and under a great manager, I have to pinch myself. I'd love to live through those times again.

When the time came it was hard to leave Manchester United. To be honest, I didn't feel my time was up. Alex brought in Jaap Stam during the summer of 1998 and Wes Brown was coming through. There was also Ronny Johnsen, Henning Berg and David May at the club. I turned 33 that June, but I felt I'd had a decent season in 1997/98 even though we lost a 12-point lead in the Premier League as Arsenal became champions. So it was disappointing when he told me that Middlesbrough had made a bid and they had accepted it.

Once that has happened you have got to weigh things up. He told me he had no problem with me staying, but I couldn't be guaranteed a first team place week in, week out, which in reality at a club like Manchester United is always the case anyway. He also said there wouldn't be another contract after my current one finished because there were injury concerns regarding my back, but at the same time there was no way he would force me through the door.

With United having accepted a bid I thought the best thing to do was to have a conversation with Bryan Robson, who was now the Middlesbrough manager. If I wasn't in effect going home then I probably would have seen my final year out at Old Trafford, but it was Robbo, it was Middlesbrough and so after weighing things up I felt it was the right thing to do.

Great timing, wasn't it? The following season United went on to win the treble.

Mark Robins

MARK ROBINS is hailed as the man who saved Alex's Manchester United job with his headed winner in the FA Cup third round at Nottingham Forest when the Old Trafford boss was believed to be under increasing pressure. Robins went on to play for a number of sides including Norwich City and Leicester City before becoming a manager. He has twice been in charge of Coventry City.

Every time the FA Cup comes around I am reminded of THAT goal against Nottingham Forest in the FA Cup third round back in January 1990. I don't think Alex likes to dwell on it and it was never spoken about in the club at the time. I thought the goals I scored later in the Cup run were more important.

I scored the opener in the quarter-final victory against Newcastle United and the winning goal against my hometown club Oldham Athletic in the semi-final replay at Maine Road after coming on as a substitute. But honestly, I never thought that goal against Nottingham Forest would seemingly become so important in the history of Manchester United under Alex Ferguson.

If the manager, as the media seemed to suggest, was under intense pressure then we as players never felt it. He managed to keep outside pressures away from us. There was never any sign that he was feeling the strain, even when results were going against us. He always protected us and was a terrific manager in that respect.

Taking away what was supposedly at stake, the Forest game

was big in many respects. For me it was an opportunity to stake a claim for a first-team place because leading up to the game we had suffered a number of injuries. There was no Bryan Robson, Neil Webb, Paul Ince, Lee Sharpe or Danny Wallace. Also, I'd scored my first league goal the week before at Wimbledon so had been given another chance.

The game was live on TV and in addition to all the talk about Alex's future there was the sentimental stuff about how Brian Clough, the manager of Nottingham Forest, had never won the FA Cup. They would have been the favourites and had knocked us out a year earlier in the quarter-final at Old Trafford.

Although it was a long time ago, the memories of that Sunday afternoon in front of the TV cameras are still very vivid. To this day, people still talk about my winning goal – did it save Fergie's job? One of the newspaper headlines that morning had been 'D-day For Under Fire Fergie'.

I can still picture the ball being played out down the touchline for Lee Martin. Forest claimed the ball had gone over the line, but take a look at the goal on YouTube – it hadn't. Lee then passed to Mark Hughes, who released a sublime pass with the outside of his foot. The ball sat up nicely for me to run onto and head it into the corner of the net.

Alex has never thanked me for scoring that goal, which might have changed his life at Manchester United. Not only that, he wrote in his book that I only scored because Stuart Pearce pushed me onto the ball and it left me with no option but to place it in the corner whereas I could have gone for the other corner and missed.

Although we knew after the game that beating Forest had given the club a huge boost we couldn't have known we were on our way to winning the FA Cup – the first of an avalanche of trophies under Sir Alex.

From a personal point of view – I was only 20 – it was a step in the right direction of trying to establish myself at a huge club like United. I scored nine goals that season and came on in the FA Cup final against Crystal Palace as a substitute, but didn't get off the bench in the replay. I also regret that I later sold my winners' medals, which included the FA Cup one from 1990.

Paul Parker

PAUL PARKER, part of England's 1990 World Cup squad, joined Manchester United 12 months later and spent five years at Old Trafford being part of the 1994 Premier League and FA Cup double winning side. He was there during the emergence of the famous youthful Class of '92, eventually losing his first team place, after an injury absence, to Gary Neville.

I'll never forget the time Alex ended up smashing Steve Bruce's mobile phone, which happened to go off at half-time leaving the manager in a rage. Steve had left his phone on because his wife Janet was in hospital with a back problem and was waiting for an update on how she was doing.

The first half of a game hadn't gone too well and you could tell we were in for a rollicking because as soon as the boss came into the dressing room he slung off his jacket, which was an indication that he meant business. He started laying into some of us big time. He turned to Brucey: "You keep on going on about your wife having a bad back, well after seeing the first half I've got a fucking bad back watching you lot!" Suddenly a phone starts ringing and the first person he looks at is me because for some reason he always associated me with a mobile phone. Thankfully I wasn't guilty and so he started going along the line of players, staring at each one, trying to find where the sound was coming from. I was just relieved it wasn't mine because woe betide the person who owned it.

Eventually, with his ears pricked, he arrived at Brucey's jacket, pushed his hand into it and pulled out the mobile phone. Without a second thought he hurled it with force into a bin, completely smashing it. No one said a word. Even Steve, who knew it wouldn't have made any difference, kept quiet. You just had to get on with it and Steve knew there was a job to be done in the second half and any domestic worries had to be shoved to one side.

The boss had to be authoritative because it was an incredible dressing room with some strong characters. We all had our own personalities and he had to manage us in different ways. He knew he had to be hard on some of us. It might have been a façade, but it was necessary. There was no way he could manage us collectively. We understood that certain individuals had to be soft-soaped rather than blasted. There was no way he could have used the hairdryer on Eric Cantona, for instance.

We accepted that, we didn't think it was unfair. We were all in it together to win things and if treating people differently worked then so be it. We all loved Eric on and off the pitch. We knew he made a difference to the team so if things were going wrong Eric would be spared and instead the boss would look to hammer Paul Ince. Incey could take it.

He also loved to have a go at Choccy (Brian McClair). But it didn't bother Choccy because he was able to handle it in his own unique way. Every time Alex had a go at him he would simply reply: "You're right, boss." It used to wind the boss up because he ran out of insults as Choccy calmly accepted everything that was thrown at him. Alex loved a reaction, but he never got one from Choccy. He loved players to fight back and create a huge row. Choccy never flinched.

He wanted whoever had received the half-time treatment to go out in the second half and try to shove the insults down his throat. Then, if he got the right reaction, he would be waiting for you following the end of the game to give you a little slap around the back of the head with the acknowledgement: "I knew you could do it." He would also often shake your hand if you had delivered after a bollocking.

The boss didn't believe in holding grudges unless someone had really stepped out of line, such as going to the newspapers with a story about the club. But while I was there I can't think of anyone who would have done that because he created a spirit of us being together, ready to take on all comers. We just accepted things. As I have mentioned, there were some strong characters prepared to stand their ground like Roy Keane and Peter Schmeichel, but that didn't bother Alex. He was always having a go at Roy because with Roy the touchpaper was always smouldering. You never knew when he was going to blow up and I think Alex liked that in him.

Big Pete could sometimes go off on one and start screaming and shouting about something that he hadn't liked. We had players who couldn't hold things in – if they felt strongly about something then you would know about it. Alex led the way in that respect.

FERGIE: UNDER THE HAIRDRYER

At the end of the day we were a real team, something I quickly discovered because it was in contrast to my earlier time playing for London clubs like Fulham and QPR. At Manchester United we were living in each other's pockets. We were a close community, most of us having homes within 20 minutes or so of each other. When you play for London clubs you live all over the place so once you leave training you can't be bothered driving all over London to meet up.

As soon as I arrived at Manchester United I felt more attached and believed I was involved in something really special. I think that carries on after you have left. I was there for five years, but I don't think you ever disappear. It's like you end up renting a space there to continue to be involved and be part of the history of the club.

It's lovely to hear now that his side of 1993/94, which won the Premier League and FA Cup double, is often thought of as Alex's greatest Manchester United team. In all honesty, I didn't join United to win titles. I joined because of the huge tradition of a massive club. But within a few days I realised how the players had been primed to win things and you are then part of that winning culture. It emanated from one man, the manager.

He didn't have to say to me, 'we want to win this, we want to win that'. He could sense that I was already in awe of the football club. He didn't have to come out with any sales pitch that you were going to win things. I wanted to play for one of the biggest clubs in the world. It certainly wasn't about money because if it had been I would have signed for Terry Venables at Spurs, the team I supported as a kid. They were offering more money and I could have stayed in London. The best decision I made was to sign for Alex and Manchester United.

The club has played a big part in my life and still does because I've been able to do things off the back of Manchester United after finishing playing. While I was there I witnessed the development of probably the finest group of young players in many years. Of course, at the time you couldn't possibly have foreseen the impact the Class of '92 were going to have on the club and football. What we noticed was that these youngsters were in awe of the first team players. In fact I've never seen a group of apprentices so in awe of their seniors. It was probably due to some extent that they were nearly all United supporters, all coming from the Manchester area except for David Beckham. He was from London, but had been connected with United from being a young kid. David was originally a Tottenham fan, a Chingford lad. He quickly grew into Manchester United.

They were all good kids. They weren't outlandish. Their focus was on eventually breaking into the first team. You knew though that David was going to be a bit different to the rest. He was always going to be a bit more out there, if you like. Not in a way that you thought, 'Christ he needs to calm down', he was just a bit different.

Nicky Butt used to clean my boots. Even then I wouldn't have wanted to cross him. He was a proper lad brought up in Gorton. Once I began to understand about Manchester then I discovered all about Gorton. You never want to take liberties with anyone raised there, believe me! Nicky was straight, didn't ever bullshit, said it as it is. He wasn't afraid to call anyone out. He stood by what he believed in.

Alex was able to handle all these youngsters' different personalities. After coming into the club he had changed things around and one of his priorities was the youth side of

Manchester United. Some managers do that just to show the people upstairs 'look what I'm doing' as they try to secure their jobs. They want to show they understand the philosophy of the club, but are really just paying lip service to it. The boss was serious about using these kids in the first team.

He wanted to play them, it just wasn't cosmetic. He felt that good young players could make a difference. He knew it could help secure the future of the club. To help bring that many players through and to actually play them was fantastic and no group of young players have matched the Class of '92 since.

When I started out at Fulham in the early 1980s there were 11 of us as eager apprentices. Nine of us went on to play for the first team, but the difference was that few played many games whereas at Manchester United the players Alex brought through played hundreds of games between them and were part of magnificent trophy-winning sides. Alex made them into top class Premier League players. He made such a difference at that level.

There was no talk of taking them out of the side and resting them. If they were doing well he played them – it was as simple as that – because he knew if he took them out their confidence might suffer. Through his encouragement the likes of David Beckham, Gary Neville, Ryan Giggs, Paul Scholes and Nicky Butt became strong characters and you still see it now because they are involved at the forefront of the game in different roles. They were brought up with an old school philosophy. They weren't spared the shouting and screaming.

In their contracts, the rewards for making expected progress were all the same, no one was placed above or below anyone else. For instance, they all had to play a certain amount of games to be given a club car via a dealer called Ian Skelly. The car was a Honda Prelude. Alex worked out the games and found out that they were all due their cars around the same time. One day the big red gates opened at The Cliff training ground and there's Alex in his office, positioned purposely so he could see all the comings and goings, looking on. If he saw someone he didn't know or like then he would be out there finding out what they were doing there.

Anyway, the cars were all different colours but looked the same – except for one. It had different wheels and leather seats, a definite upgrade on the others. He saw this and his head was spinning all over the place like a scene from *The Exorcist*! The rest of us were all having lunch together. That wasn't an instruction, but we enjoyed doing it and it was good to show your face so the boss and the staff saw that you weren't in a mad rush to go home after training. So on this particular day we saw all the cars arriving and straight away we knew who the upgraded model was for. David Beckham. It had barely been parked up before it was sent back and the boss ordered the dealership to return with a car identical to the rest of the others. After that I can only assume Becks got a bollocking for secretly asking for a better car than the rest.

The boss would have none of that. He didn't like anyone thinking they were better or more important than the rest of us. I remember Clayton Blackmore putting ankle strapping around his football socks to show off his calves. He looked like a Palomino Horse. The boss went up to him and said, "We're a team and we all look the same in our kit." So off the strapping came.

I'll tell you now, the boss wouldn't let Jack Grealish wear those ankle socks which are completely different to those of his team-mates. He wanted everyone to be the same and used to get the raging hump when we travelled in our tracksuits on a Friday before an away game because some of the players would roll up the bottoms of them or tie the jacket around their waist.

He also hated the fact that we all had different sponsors and so were wearing different trainers. He wanted everyone to look smart – everyone to dress identically – because he thought that looking the part and being perfectly presented placed you one step ahead of your opponents psychologically.

Ryan Giggs

RYAN GIGGS made his debut for Manchester United in 1991 at the age of 17 and went on to become an Old Trafford great, winning 13 Premier League titles under Alex Ferguson, who became a father figure to the mercurial Welshman.

My dad left when I was 14. I had two mainstays in my life, my grandad and the manager, Alex Ferguson. We definitely had a father-son relationship.

Sometimes that was good, sometimes it was bad because he felt he could say whatever he wanted. Which was tough to take, especially when you're 18 or 19. Honestly, sometimes he would have fights with the players, or come close to it at other times. He would be right in your face screaming at you.

There was definitely fear, especially in my early days. He mellowed when he got older, but not a lot! He probably fined me a couple of weeks' wages six or seven times during my career under him at Manchester United after fierce rows. Sometimes I would try to have a go back, but there was only ever one winner. Away from football he was very perceptive. He would look out for you. If you looked a little down it would be, "Is everything alright at home?" Things like that. "You know you can always come and talk to me," he would add, which was very comforting. It meant that no matter how many arguments we had – if I wasn't playing well or he had dropped me – that I could still talk to him about all sorts of things. It wasn't about me as a footballer, it was about me as a human being.

In the early days I seemed to be never too far away from getting a telling off. There was a time Bryan Robson stitched me up and ended with the gaffer going berserk and looking as if he wanted to throw me through his office window.

I'd played between 20 to 25 games for the club when Robbo told me I should ask him for a new car as a reward for doing so well. All the other established players had top of the range new cars. So not knowing I had been set up by Robbo and the rest, I went up to Alex's office. "Listen boss, I've played 25 games now. I think I'm fairly established. How about a club car?" I said.

I had barely finished the sentence when I could see his face going red and looking ready to explode. "Club car? Aye, you won't even get a club bike. Now get out of this office before I throw you out," was the gist of his tirade. As I left the office Robbo and half the team were lined up outside trying to listen, knowing what was going to happen. I'd been set up.

In one of the Champions League games we played against Juventus in Turin I had spent the first half doing what I was all about, dribbling. But Antonio Conte was taking the ball off me, which put them on the attack. I knew I wasn't having a good game and at half-time the manager went for me straight away, telling me to stop dribbling with the ball in the midfield area. He kept on and on. He wouldn't listen to any counter-arguments when he was in that mood. We were handed cartons of a blackcurrant drink at half-time and I just threw mine right at the gaffer's feet. That was it, he pulled me out of the team. I was substituted and Brian McClair was sent on. He was always in control. You were never in any doubt about who was the boss.

He was even ready to tell me off before I scored that winning goal against Arsenal in the FA Cup semi-final at Villa Park in 1999. He kept yelling at me to pass it because we were trying to kill time, hoping to take the game to penalties because we were down to 10 men after Roy Keane got sent off. To be honest, until some reporters asked me after the game whether it had been my greatest goal for Manchester United I hadn't realised how spectacular it had looked. I thought my run had started a lot closer to the Arsenal goal than it had. Anyway, the manager was finally delighted with the goal although I don't think he was too happy with the goal celebration after I whipped my shirt off and whirled it around my head!

A few players were spared the hairdryer. He always treated Eric Cantona differently from any other player – something we accepted because Eric was a special talent, someone who could win games for us. I remember there was a black tie function. I walked in with the top button of my shirt undone. The manager went straight for me. "Get your top button done, you are representing Manchester United."

Two minutes later, while I'm sulking at being told off, Eric walks in wearing a white linen suit complete with garish Nike trainers on his feet. I'm rubbing my hands anticipating Eric receiving the treatment from the gaffer as well. I couldn't believe what happened next. The gaffer goes over to Eric, shakes his hand and turns to the rest of us saying, "Lads, that's style!"

Robbo, like Eric, seemed immune from the hairdryer treatment, but the gaffer was the master of psychology. He was a master at getting the best out of individuals. He knew who to put his arm around and who to give a rocket.

He would also plan well in advance for games. Three weeks before an important game against Chelsea he said he was going to use me in midfield, explaining that Michael Ballack didn't like players running at him. "You'll give him nightmares," he said. But I pointed out that there were five games before we faced Chelsea. "Forget about them, just get yourself ready for Chelsea," he insisted.

He seemed to pick out myself and David Beckham for regular rollockings in front of the other players. I think it was because he knew we wouldn't sulk for long and he would get a reaction on the pitch from the rest of the team, who would be desperate to save themselves from a similar blast. We always seemed to get it more than the rest. After one spat on a pre-season tour in the USA I pulled him to one side later because I felt it had been unfair. He told me it was a ploy for the younger players. If they knew I could receive a bollocking then no one was safe. Even though I moaned, looking back I do feel it made me play better on the pitch because I was determined to prove him wrong.

He also knew when it was the right time to move players on. For instance, he and Becks were arguing nearly all the time in the end. It was right for both parties to call an end to the relationship in 2003. To be honest, I was starting to think my time was up as well as Becks'. My form hadn't been great and it was when I'd started switching from being a flying winger to coming in a bit from the flanks. The gaffer thought I was losing my pace, but I turned my form around and finished the season strongly, which obviously saw me remain at Manchester United.

We became accustomed to having competition for places at Manchester United and I wanted that at Wales too after I became the manager. It makes a difference, even in training, when everyone steps up. The standards improve and that is carried into games. At Manchester United under the boss you were always looking over your shoulder wondering if someone was about to take your first team place.

With Wales and at Manchester United, it was also about having the right balance between youth and experience. Alex was the master of that. When that group of us came through at Manchester United we played without fear, but we also improved because we were suddenly next to senior stars who could see a pass and guide us in the right direction. Younger players can energise a whole group. The senior players know they have got to raise their games or they could be in trouble.

I saw this as a young player coming through and later as one of the older players in the Manchester United dressing room. For 10 years I was up against Gary Neville in training and you become familiar with one another's style. Then the manager brought in Rafael da Silva, a young Brazilian right-back. In training he was running at me non-stop, doing different things. My attitude and focus had to change. He forced me to step up my own game and that was how Alex was a master at getting more out of you.

As a manager I have learned that often the decisions I usually get right are the ones I have a gut feeling for. You often have to stick to your guns even though there could be criticism, especially from the media. That is something I learned from the boss. He was always so decisive. Often I would be in the dressing room wondering, 'Why is he doing this? Why is he doing that?' Of course, when it all works out you think what was all the fuss about? If you win games it's all forgotten. That's how you have to be as a manager – and I've seen the best in action.

Eric Cantona

ERIC CANTONA was the maverick who Alex Ferguson believes helped turn his nearly men into serial winners following the Frenchman's surprise move from Leeds United in 1992. Eric was one of the privileged few to be spared the hairdryer treatment – even after jumping into the crowd at Crystal Palace. None of his team-mates complained, although they all secretly hoped that one day the boss would give him the full treatment just to see the mercurial striker's reaction.

I had a very special relationship with Alex Ferguson. I think he is the one who understood me the best. His understanding helped me to improve myself as a person and as a player, and that translated into me helping improve Manchester United.

He made me feel comfortable and allowed me the freedom to be myself. And one of the most important things was to make the other players understand that they should give the ball to me! People ask why did I retire when I was only 30? It is simple. I wanted to try something else. Nothing can be compared to football, but acting is exciting in its own way. It is still about creating things, but in a different environment. It is another example of myself wanting the freedom to do what I want. If you put me in jail I will break everything to get out, even if I die in the process.

At Manchester United they said, "If you want to leave Eric, you can leave whenever you want." That made me want to stay because I never felt under pressure or imprisoned. The time eventually arrived when I wanted to go, but I always felt I was born to play for Manchester United.

We won the Premier League in 1993, my first season straight after helping Leeds United become champions the previous season. Alex was great for me, even after that game at Crystal Palace in 1995. I have been upset thousands of times and never reacted, but sometimes you are fragile and that time I reacted. I have one regret. I wish I had kicked him [Crystal Palace fan Matthew Simmons] harder!

When a manager does something like what Alex Ferguson did for me in always supporting me, then I am sure in return this player would have given his life to the manager, the club and the fans. After what happened at Crystal Palace some clubs may have sacked me. Manchester United offered me a new contract. That is the difference between them and the other ones. Winning the Premier League and FA Cup double when I returned from my suspension meant a lot, especially with a new generation of players in the side.

I left Manchester United in 1997. I told Alex that I had lost my passion for the game. With everything I do in my life, if I don't feel free I become crazy. He knew all the time exactly what I needed. It was more about psychology than being a manager. He is somebody who is strong enough to deal with any kind of personality.

When a man like Alex Ferguson gives you the freedom you need to express yourself you have to deserve it. You have to know how lucky you are to have this freedom. It is why I worked so hard and tried everything. I would give my life to him. He was, and still is, a great psychologist. Having that freedom at Manchester United was like a dream for me. It was the football I had always dreamt about. It was the first time in my life I felt that this was my place.

Manchester is a city with a lot of energy. It's an inspiring place. Many sportsmen have been inspired by this city. It reminds me of Marseille, where I grew up. I arrived not knowing much about Manchester, but straight away I felt this incredible energy. I felt the ghosts of the wonderful players who had played for Manchester United, great personalities like George Best and Bryan Robson. It is a club that has been built not just on success, but on tragedy as well.

Alex became like a father to me. As players we all respected him a lot and we loved him a lot. Those feelings still exist today. Manchester United needed me and I needed them. I was an outsider, but I was accepted.

We were told by the manager to be brave, to take our opportunities. We felt unbeatable. We felt unstoppable. And I saw the young players develop, which has always been so important going back to the days of Sir Matt Busby. If the players from your academy are good then they will ultimately be better than any other players because they are usually supporters of the club. They have the soul of the club. That is why young players like David Beckham, Paul Scholes and Ryan Giggs gave more to Manchester United.

I will always feel that Manchester United is a special club with a rich history and they possessed a special manager in Alex Ferguson. I will never ever forget, and will always appreciate, my time at Manchester United under Sir Alex.

Roy Keane

ROY KEANE left Brian Clough's Nottingham Forest in 1993 for Alex Ferguson's Manchester United – the best two managers he played for. He became Old Trafford captain, but was often outspoken and unafraid of confrontations. Keane left United under a cloud in 2005 following a critical interview on the club's MUTV channel, but has never lost his respect for the manager who brought him to Old Trafford.

I went to United at the right time. They had just won the Premier League and I joined a brilliant dressing room with great characters, huge expectation and huge pressure, but I suppose I loved Manchester United the minute I walked in.

With Alex Ferguson, in those years when we were winning things, I maintained a professional relationship and nothing more. I remember when we trained at The Cliff I noticed some of the senior players would go upstairs and have a cup of coffee with Alex and some of the coaching staff. There would be Bryan Robson, Steve Bruce and Gary Pallister all having a chit-chat.

I never really wanted that relationship with any manager I worked under. I never wanted to have a cup of tea and a bit of chit-chat, but I knew Alex wanted to do the best for Manchester United and there was huge respect between us.

Unfortunately that was probably lost at the end before I left, but ultimately I look back on my time at Manchester United and think of him as a brilliant manager. He was also brilliantly good to me, there's no getting away from that. Things happened towards the end, but that doesn't detract from the great times I had there under him.

Never at any stage did I feel I was in with him because I was captain. We weren't pals. I always kept it professional and this idea of having a cup of tea and a biscuit upstairs in the canteen – not for me.

Dressing rooms were always changing at United. Every summer one or two new players would come in, young players would come in and the dynamics changed. To be honest, when I was getting towards the end of my career I was looking around the dressing room at players like Wayne Rooney, Rio Ferdinand, Darren Fletcher, John O'Shea and all these lads. I would roll with the changes because if they were good players they would bring in different energy and help us win trophies, but towards the end I remember thinking, 'no I don't get some of these, I don't get their banter, their humour'. I didn't have that many conversations with them – the bigger picture was, would they be good players for Manchester United?

When I left there were a lot of players that I didn't miss one bit. The game was changing. After training a lot of the lads would be on their mobile phones. Whether I'm old school or a bit grumpy I don't know, but I didn't get it. I didn't get Wayne or Rio with the banter they stood for sometimes. Often when players came in later on I thought, personality wise, they weren't for me, although they might be very good players.

Both the manager and I loved winning. We both wanted the best for Manchester United. He was critical towards me in the end, saying I was running the dressing room. I was. Senior players run dressing rooms because managers are rarely in them. When I was at Nottingham Forest, Stuart Pearce and Des Walker would organise things. When I first went to Manchester United, Bryan Robson, Steve Bruce and Eric Cantona would be running things. Senior players ultimately run a dressing room so the role eventually fell on myself, Ryan Giggs and Gary Neville.

Most of the things we organised were trivial – the players' pool, Christmas functions, tickets for matches. It was part of my role, but I don't think I ever crossed that line where I felt I was more important than the other players. I was there to help people, not question what was going on. Did I make mistakes and get a few calls wrong? Probably yes, but at the same time I would like to think I got quite a few things right in trying to help motivate players, make sure they trained properly etc.

As a senior player you should be setting good examples. I hear stories that I was quite hard on some players. I think that has been exaggerated. I just wanted them to train properly and for people to be on time and to give their all for the club. Surely that's what you are supposed to do as a senior player?

I was there to win for Manchester United. I wasn't there to be pals with everyone. I didn't make big speeches, I tried to lead by example. Before some games I would just go, "Look lads, we're Manchester United and we're here to win." I knew I had to train properly and drive people on, to be focussed and not be distracted by off the field stuff. That's what I tried to pass on to the other players.

The brilliance of Alex Ferguson and Brian Clough, who I played under at Nottingham Forest, was that in big situations before games, or at half-time, I always felt they said the right things at the right time. It was just what a certain player might need. As I got older I would analyse more and think to myself 'what do the players need at this precise moment?' Both of them would get it spot on – they were both brilliant managers.

People talk about the Alex Ferguson hairdryer treatment. I never really had it for my performances on the pitch. I might have got it for something that had happened off the pitch. The players had huge respect for him, you didn't want to let him down. You wanted to give your all.

I had been really poor in the first 45 minutes of a home game against Aston Villa. There was no hairdryer, but it was the look of disappointment on his face as he just said, 'Roy'. It was a dagger through the heart. I had let my team-mates and the club down and the look galvanised me. It wasn't always the hairdryer, the look was often enough to motivate you.

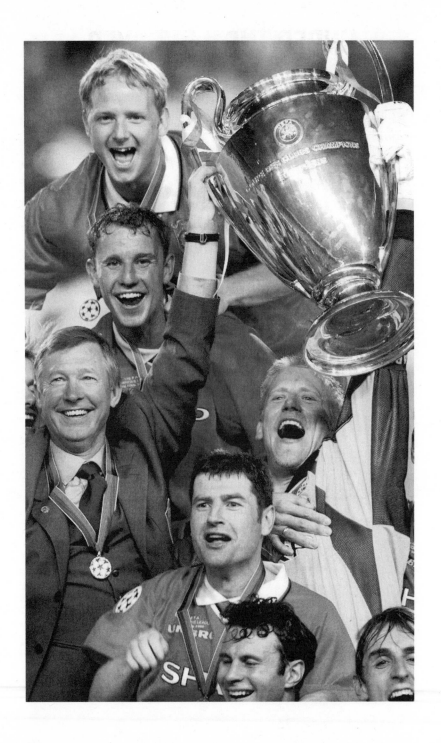

7

'There was a snooker table in the hotel and on the morning of the Champions League final Alex challenged me to a game. He said if he beat me, I wouldn't be in the squad at the Nou Camp – but if I won then I would be on the bench!'

Jonathan Greening, former Manchester United player

David Beckham

DAVID BECKHAM was part of the Class of '92 which helped Alex Ferguson's side dominate football for almost two decades. There were many fallouts over his lifestyle, but Becks still regards 'the boss' as the leading figure in his career. As well as making 115 England appearances, Beckham also went on to play for Real Madrid, LA Galaxy, AC Milan and Paris Saint-Germain.

I have said many times before that the boss wasn't just the greatest and best manager I ever played under, he was also a father figure to me from the moment I arrived at Manchester United at the age of 11 until the day I left. I am truly honoured to have been guided by the greatest manager and to have had a successful career under him. Without him I would never have achieved what I have done.

He knew all about me from an early age. He knew about every single boy he intended to bring to the club. He knew their parents, he knew their brothers and sisters. That seemed important to me, important for my future.

There were certain decisions that I made in the past which were the wrong ones and I can see now why the manager got so frustrated by certain things, but he protected the players at our club. We all knew that the success that he had was because if you were a Manchester United player you were treated like family, and that went right the way through to including your personal life.

The fear of the hairdryer was one of the reasons we all played well. He was also a manager you wanted to do well for, although there were times when I thought he went a bit too far, which caused a few issues. Before the 2000 Charity Shield at Wembley against Chelsea I decided to have a change of hairstyle. I went for a mohawk, which I knew wouldn't be to his taste. In the end I was too scared to let him see it so the day before the game I went into training with a beanie hat on, trained in the beanie, walked back into the hotel with the beanie on, kept it on during dinner and the next morning's breakfast and still had it on when we made the coach journey to Wembley.

Of course the moment was arriving in the dressing room when I would have to reveal my new hairstyle, which I knew would send him into a frenzy. Sure enough, within seconds of the unveiling, he yelled at me, "Go and shave it off!"

I thought he was joking. "No, I'm being serious, now go and shave the ruddy thing off!" So off I went to try to find a pair of clippers from somewhere and just before we're ready to go out for the warm-up I was in the Wembley tunnel shaving my mohawk off.

There was one occasion when Victoria was in Ireland. I had a day off so I flew over to see her. I didn't feel I needed to tell the manager what I was doing – it was my day off. He found out and when I came back he didn't talk to me for ages, so I knew I had upset him, but if you were in trouble he was always there for you.

He went out of his way to help me after the 1998 World Cup finals in France when I was made a scapegoat for being sent off against Argentina. He was on the phone backing me and telling me, "Son, get back to Manchester and you'll be fine." That gave me the strength to get through what became the toughest time of my life.

Everyone still goes on about the flying boot incident

following our FA Cup defeat against Arsenal in 2003, but that was blown up out of all proportion. I'd made a couple of mistakes during the game and he came into the dressing room and a few harsh words were exchanged.

He started to walk over to me and he kicked out at a pile of clothes on the floor. Out came this boot and then I quickly realised how accurate his kick had been as it struck me on the head, but there weren't any hard feelings. It was a complete freak accident. As far as we were concerned it was forgotten straight away within the club, but the incident made the papers which meant that people started to speculate about our relationship. But as far as the boss and I were concerned it was over, done and dusted.

At times he seemed to be harder on the likes of myself and some of the other players who had come through the youth ranks, but I think it was because he saw himself as some sort of father figure and didn't want us stepping out of line. We knew that he treated Eric Cantona differently, but no one had a problem with that.

Eric was really the first foreign star to come into our club. To see him walk around the corridors, to see him train… it was one of those moments when – as a youth team player – I just sat there in awe of everything Eric did. It was also the first time I saw a player being treated differently for a reason. That's what makes a great manager. He understood that to get the best out of Eric he needed to be treated in a different way.

There is not one player who would turn around and say it's unfair the way Eric was treated compared to the rest of us. He was different and as such deserved to be treated differently. As young players we just wanted to learn from him.

We had all come through the youth team. We had come through the reserve team. We were a very close family and eager to be part of the first team set-up.

A lot of us got that opportunity in 1995/96 and it was great to have Eric back early on that season following his suspension after jumping into the crowd at Selhurst Park. To see Eric back playing again gave us the momentum and an extra push that season to win the Premier League and FA Cup double. But his decision to quit the game a season later came as a huge shock. I didn't see Eric's retirement coming to be perfectly honest. I was devastated when I heard the news. It was really difficult to understand as a player and a team-mate, but once Eric makes his mind up no one can change it.

I was delighted when the manager offered me Eric's number seven shirt. I was nervous that I would have to live up to everything that he had achieved, just to come close would have been great. 1997/98 was a tough season because we didn't win anything. Whenever you are not successful, which means at Manchester United not winning the league or the FA Cup, then it's tough. That came from being a youth team player. It was drummed into us that having no success hurts. It did hurt us deeply. We knew we had to come back stronger and that was what the manager prepared us for.

There were a lot of doubters out there as we began the 1998/99 campaign. As a team we didn't want any repeat of the disappointment of the previous season. Little did we know we were on our way to winning an unprecedented treble of Premier League, FA Cup and Champions League. It was a frenetic climax to the season, but no one was tired. We were running on adrenaline. We knew it was all leading up to that final game in Barcelona.

Under Alex, the Premier League and FA Cup double had been completed twice already, but we'd never played in a Champions League final before.

To play at the Nou Camp against the mighty Bayern Munich in a Champions League final was probably one of the few games where I was nervous. Football has the power to change people's lives and it was an amazing night. There are many reasons why United were successful at that time – the boss bringing the youth team players through to combine them with those tried and trusted players before we came onto the scene was a big part of it. He also understood the history of the club, the city, the fans – and the need to give everything on the pitch.

Our goal was always to be successful in Europe. The manager always spoke about us as a team, and as individuals, being winners in Europe. In 1999 we were. Bayern went 1-0 up. They hit the bar, they hit the post, they had real chances. We knew we just needed that one opportunity – in the end we snatched two!

Paul Scholes

PAUL SCHOLES is the modest yet talismanic figure of some of Alex's most successful sides, but even a quiet and unobtrusive manner didn't safeguard him from a few verbal lashings from the boss. He made 66 appearances for England and is the second most decorated player in Manchester United's history.

Coming through with the likes of David Beckham, Nicky Butt, Gary and Phil Neville, we knew we were doing well because we were winning games regularly. Did we think that we would go on to play for Manchester United together for so many years? Probably not, but we did have a manager who believed in youth.

Alex Ferguson was watching us all the time and must have seen something in us that he liked. To accommodate us he had to clear the squad that won back-to-back Premier League titles in 1993 and 1994 out. It was a brave move to get rid of Mark Hughes, Andrei Kanchelskis and Paul Ince, but it enabled him to bring us into the team and give us our opportunities. It's always a proud moment to see a local lad get into the team, but it doesn't happen so much now with all the money everywhere.

When I was coming through the ranks at United it was a case of going from week to week, trying to prove myself. I never ever thought I was a first team player in those early days, I just wanted to keep improving so that the boss picked me the next week. Training was incredibly competitive. We would kick lumps out of each other every day because we were desperate to get into the team. I don't mean that I deliberately went out to injure someone, but it was lively. Nicky Butt and I would often come off the training pitch covered in bruises with blood streaming down our legs. That was the drive we had, a desire and will which came straight from the manager.

This competitive environment had also been created by our youth team coach, Eric Harrison, and it was continued by Alex Ferguson. Eric could see that there was talent, but he was on to us all the time – there was never a moment when we could relax, think we had made it and that we were first team players. We were never allowed to feel that way by either of them.

We were told by Alex that when we are on the pitch we must always be brave, we must be able to take the ball anywhere and feel comfortable. That just wasn't for midfield players, the message was directed at everybody. We were expected to move the ball forward because the mindset was always about going out to win games. Okay, we might concede a goal and no one would be happy with that, but it was always about scoring goals and winning games, being positive. We all loved being those kinds of players.

With the boss, you knew where you stood. If you weren't pulling your weight you'd be in for it. That was every single day, even when we were young players. It certainly worked for all of us, but you also have to have a manager willing to give young players a chance. He couldn't wait to give us a chance and I hope we paid him back.

At times he could be scary. If you stepped out of line he would have you. He never lost that fear factor – just his presence ensured you tried everything to stay onside with him. If I saw him coming down the corridor at the training ground I would try to look the other way because I didn't know what type of mood he might be in.

I had quite a few bollockings. We were playing Newcastle at St James' Park in 2001, the game in which Roy Keane was sent off following a bust-up with Alan Shearer. Newcastle were managed by Sir Bobby Robson and were a decent side at the time. Alex had put me on the bench and at 3-1 down, with around 30 minutes to go, he brought me on. Within five minutes we got back to 3-3 and without bragging, I made a difference and created one of the two goals. We sensed now that we could go on to win it, but around the halfway line I tried a bit of a fancy flick and gave the ball away, which led to their winning goal.

Roy had been sent off, but the boss didn't seem too bothered about that. He just went for me. He went absolutely ballistic. He was raging, warning that I would never play for the club again – every insult imaginable came my way. People like Giggsy would always answer back, Incey would have his say and also at times so would Becks. I would never say anything, but this time after every tirade I just went, "bollocks."

"You've had a fucking nightmare," he ranted back.

"Bollocks."

I was frightened to death of him, but I was shouting "bollocks" back at him all the time until it was over. On the coach journey back to Manchester I was thinking 'that's me finished, I'd better start looking for another club', but on the Monday he came over to me at training. I was thinking to myself, 'here we go, I'm going to be fined two weeks' wages'. Instead, I could hardly believe what I was hearing.

"I'm sorry," he said. "I realise you made a difference to the game and what happened towards the end and after the game was a bit of an over-reaction." Admitting he was wrong was the quality of the manager. The biggest thing to him was having desire and drive and I'm sure since he retired he will not have enjoyed some of Manchester United's performances. I'm certain the hairdryer would have been on full pelt after some performances in recent years. What did he hairdryer consist of? A lot of swear words, right in your face, and the odd flying boot.

He was also a good judge of a player and brought in some fantastic footballers. I'm certain some of the poor signings in the years after his departure at Manchester United wouldn't have happened under his watch and in some games he would have had kittens at the absence of the qualities that he expected as being the minimum requirement.

Sir John Hall

SIR JOHN HALL was the Newcastle United owner during the exciting Kevin Keegan era which came to an end with the former England captain's resignation in 1997. It was an ambitious target, but Alex Ferguson was the St James' Park board's first choice to become the Tyneside club's new manager.

K evin Keegan was a hard act to follow, but Alex Ferguson would have done nicely. He was the best in the business at the time and still was right until he decided to retire.

I wasn't directly involved in searching for Kevin's replacement in 1997. While I looked after the financial side of the club, much of the running of it was left to a fantastic team of Freddy Shepherd, Douglas Hall [board members] and Freddie Fletcher [chief executive].

I think Kevin had already threatened to resign three times before he actually did. By the fourth time we already had a resignation letter ready for him to sign. It was a real pity because they were interesting times, great times when you couldn't wait for the next match. Everything was buzzing. We had found Kevin and Kevin had found us. I don't know where we got the money from because we funded him well in the transfer market. It was all worth it. If we had won the Premier League it would have made all the difference and maybe those times would have lasted longer.

It would have stabilised the club because good players go to clubs that are winning. We had to win to get more players here. We couldn't rely on Kevin's charisma forever. We still managed to attract brilliant players like David Ginola, but the best buy was Robert Lee. Great times, we even had 3,000 people watching training at Maiden Castle in Durham with burger vans in attendance. Wonderful. We needed someone to keep up the momentum when Kevin left and the lads obviously felt they had a chance of snatching Alex from Manchester United, where he had already turned the club around to win plenty of trophies. Freddy Shepherd, who has since sadly passed away, revealed what happened a few years after our failed Ferguson coup.

"We had talks with Alex Ferguson's advisors about him coming to Newcastle after finding out that Alex was having problems over a new contract and could be vulnerable to leaving. Martin Edwards, the Manchester United chairman, had obviously got wind of what was going on. He rang me and said, "Have you got anything to tell me?" I said, "No." He then said, "What if I said Alex Ferguson. What would you say then?" I was on a boat at the time and I almost fell off it.

"We soon realised there was no way he was coming to Newcastle. He was just trying to get an increase in his salary. We felt we were being used, but Kevin had left so why not try for Fergie? You never know. We were ambitious and tried to get him because we had heard he wasn't happy at Manchester United."

If he used our interest to get a big pay rise then good luck to him. It proved what a shrewd character he was. I think he owes me a large drink if I bump into him again. I met him socially in the boardroom and found him easy to speak to. He was a tough fella who did brilliantly for himself. He won so many things it was almost unbelievable. I found him easy to get on with.

It would have been great if we had pulled it off and he came to manage Newcastle United, but we didn't do too badly. We managed to get Kenny Dalglish.

Jonathan Greening

JONATHAN GREENING is the answer to a football quiz question: Who gained a Champions League winners' medal for Manchester United in 1999 without playing a single minute in the competition? He also thought his place on the substitutes bench in Barcelona depended on a game of snooker with Alex Ferguson. Signed from York City in 1998, he spent three years at Old Trafford before moving to Middlesbrough.

I couldn't believe it when Manchester United asked York City if they could take me on trial for four days with a view to a surprise transfer in 1998. So there I was, at the age of 19, training with players I had only seen on the TV.

Brian Kidd, who was the United coach before taking over as Blackburn Rovers manager later that year, took us for a jog at first and while we were running I was struggling to get my head around what was happening. I could hardly believe I was being put through my paces at Manchester United. It was crazy, a mental four days. I was amongst players at the top of the game, but the rest of the squad treated me brilliantly. I was made to feel so welcome. Obviously I wasn't used to the high standard of the training. I was with a little club and had never really been coached. If you gave the ball away at York no one came down hard on you, for instance.

After the four days were up Alex came up to me and said they had been happy with me and to go back to York, which I did and played terribly. A week later the York manager Alan Little called me into his office and told me the club had agreed a deal with Manchester United.

I didn't know what to do. I didn't have an agent. I was on peanuts at York. I went home and told my parents that I needed to get to Old Trafford to sign. My dad was chilled out while my brothers were buzzing at the thought of me playing for Manchester United. But we didn't have a car. My dad called a mate to take us in his taxi. Luckily he was a mad keen United fan and offered to do it for free because he was going to Old Trafford with us and had a chance to see Alex Ferguson.

So he took myself, my mum and dad to Manchester to get everything sorted. Not having an agent, I just said yes straight away to a three-year contract with Alex. It wasn't great money – something like £450 a week. But it was still better than the £90 a week I'd been earning at York. That was it. Everything was done and dusted in no time and the taxi driver was happy because he had met Alex Ferguson.

Alex was brilliant to me, saying they had really liked me during my four-day trial and said they thought they could develop me. It was surreal. To be honest, not much was staying in my brain, I just wanted to get started. He also spent a lot of time talking to my mum and dad, reassuring them that I would settle okay after leaving home. He displayed a really caring side, which impressed my parents. He promised he would look after me.

I got a car, but it was a bit embarrassing turning up for training and matches in a little red Ford Fiesta 1.1 litre. Someone had stolen the petrol cap, so I had this green crappy push-in replacement in its place. At matches you would turn up and hand the keys over for someone to park your car. Here was my little red Fiesta parked up next to the Ferraris, huge Range Rovers and whatever else. I felt ashamed handing over my keys for someone to drive it off to park. After the game you would sign a few autographs and someone was assigned to collect your car. There was no rush to get my keys, believe me! I'd never had much money growing up, this was a different world.

I had a great three years with the club. Again, Alex was great when he gave me my debut. He told me an hour and a quarter before a League Cup game at home to Bury that I was playing. Not only that, he had let my mum and dad know in advance so they could be at the game. I don't honestly know how they got there – maybe by taxi again! I ended up playing up front with Ole Gunnar Solskjaer and we won the game 2-0 after extra-time. I got man of the match. It was a dream.

The manager also included me in the Champions League trips abroad even though I usually ended up making the teas and coffees. I'd be 19th or 20th man. I didn't care. I was visiting some incredible stadiums. I knew where I stood. I was a young kid from York City trying to make his way in the game. But when I was on the substitutes bench I'd get really nervous, hoping if I was brought on I wouldn't make a fool of myself or mess something up.

In my first season at Manchester United we won the Premier League and I was part of the squad for the FA Cup final. We beat Newcastle United 2-0 at Wembley. We also reached the Champions League final and even though I hadn't played a single minute in the Champions League, I was named in the party for the final in Barcelona against Bayern Munich.

Everyone was guessing who was going to make the bench out of the fringe players. We worked out that one of the places was between myself, John Curtis and Mark Wilson. I had been doing pretty well in the reserves, scoring a fair number of goals, so I thought I had a chance.

There was a snooker table in the team hotel and on the morning of the Champions League final Alex came up to me after breakfast and challenged me to a game. He then added that if he beat me, I wouldn't be in the squad in the Nou Camp – but if I won then I would be on the bench!

I thought to myself, 'this is great' because I was half decent with a cue in my hand. I used to play a lot with my dad in the working men's clubs. I thought I was going to smash him all over the place, but what I didn't know was that he had his own snooker table at home!

He absolutely spanked me and walked off after placing his arm on my shoulder and saying, "unlucky son." I went back to my room, put some depressing music on and felt ready to cry, believing I'd blown my chance of being involved in a Champions League final.

I got onto the team coach and went to the stadium feeling deflated. He still hadn't said anything else to me. I went into the Nou Camp dressing room and there was my shirt hanging on one of the pegs – it looked like I was on the bench. Then he read out the team and I was amongst the substitutes. Luckily for me the game of snooker had just been a bit of fun and he had been winding me up.

After seeing the shirt I opened my locker to discover that it belonged to the great Luis Figo, who played for Barcelona from 1995 to 2000. They had just won La Liga and there was an array of medals in there.

It was a big night, but I noticed how calm the manager was before the game. There was no massive team talk. I had goose-bumps. I could hardly believe what was happening. And of course it was an incredible ending to win 2-1, even though the game itself hadn't been the best. To be in the stadium and be part of it is something that will stay with me for the rest of my life. Watching it back now still sends shivers down my spine. I loved it even more because I was a Manchester United fan. I didn't play a minute in that Champions League campaign, but I was on the bench that night in Barcelona and nobody can take my winners' medal away from me. My family were all there. They all joined us at the after-match party back at the hotel. On arriving back in Manchester there were more celebrations and I ended up with a few of the players in a pub in Swinton. It was a really rough pub, but very enjoyable.

After three years at United I hadn't made many appearances and thought I wasn't making the progress I wanted to, so it was time to knock on the manager's door and tell him face to face. I walked down the corridor to his office, but turned around twice – I was so nervous about how he was going to react.

Finally I plucked up the courage to knock on his door. I was petrified. I was just mumbling, hardly getting my words out to tell him I felt it was time to move on. "No way, son," he said. "I want to give you a new contract." I told him I had only played a few games. He said that they really liked me and I still had a future at Manchester United, I was still young.

I was only 22. I had rehearsed my reasons for wanting to leave, but I just froze. I didn't want to upset him. There was a new four-year contract if I wanted to sign it. I'd gone in wanting to leave and now I had a new four-year contract on the table. What was all that about?

For a couple of weeks I didn't know what to do. It got to the end of the 2000/01 season and he said for me to go on holiday and we would talk again at the beginning of the next one. I went back to see him. Steve McClaren, his number two at Old Trafford, had just left to replace Bryan Robson as Middlesbrough manager and wanted to take myself and Mark Wilson with him. Again, Alex said he didn't want me to go.

A few weeks later United signed Ruud van Nistelrooy and Juan Sebastian Veron, which meant I was further down the pecking order. Finally after a few heated discussions I was on my way to Middlesbrough. I think they made a £4 million profit on myself and Mark Wilson. I loved it there, but I was desperate to play games.

In all honesty, I don't think I was good enough to be a regular starter at Manchester United, but it was a great experience under Sir Alex.

Steve McClaren

STEVE McCLAREN became Alex's number two in February 1999 and was instrumental in helping Manchester United win the unprecedented treble of Premier League, FA Cup and Champions League. He won another two titles at Old Trafford before becoming Middlesbrough manager in 2001 and went on to manage England and win the Dutch title with Twente.

A couple of weeks before there was any contact from Manchester United about becoming Alex Ferguson's assistant I was told by two sports journalists – Bob Cass and Joe Melling, who were close to Alex – that it was on for me to replace Brian Kidd. They said I would receive a phone call about the job. I told them that was ridiculous. There were all sorts of big names linked with the job. I was happy at Derby County alongside Jim Smith.

Cassy insisted I was going to be the chosen one. Sure enough, one Saturday evening the phone rang and it was Alex, "Do you want to come to Manchester United?" I didn't have to think twice. "Yes, Yes," I replied. The only problem was Derby were playing United at Old Trafford on the Tuesday night so he wanted me to keep it quiet until after the game. Once that was out of the way he would speak to Jim and try to clear it for me to join him at Manchester United. Hopefully, he added, he would see me then the next day.

Derby lost 1-0 at Old Trafford, which in hindsight was a good result because it was February 1999 and helped United ultimately win the Premier League as part of the famous treble of League, Champions League and FA Cup. When we got back to Pride Park Jim called me into his office. He said that I must know why I was being pulled in – that Alex had told him after the game that he wanted me as his new number two.

"Get yourself to Manchester tomorrow and get it done," said Jim. "Good luck." That was typical of Jim.

As I say, there were plenty of names linked with the position, which wasn't surprising at all as it's one of the biggest jobs in football. I was wondering how I had come up on his radar? We were doing a good job at Derby, Jim and I worked well together, so I actually asked Alex why he had chosen me? He explained that they had scouted potential replacements like they scout players. In the end it had been between myself and David Moyes, who was at Preston North End. I got the nod.

Jim had been very open-minded about me introducing a few different ideas into the club. While Jim was old school, he was prepared to encompass fresh ideas. He might have had old school values, but he wanted and encouraged innovation. I used to take lots of things to him – developments which he was happy to take on board – like sports science and sports analytics, which hadn't really been heard of. We were the first to try them. Massage chairs, recovery for the players, video analysis was all part of it. I was doing video analysis tapes, which are common now but were pretty much unheard of around this time. I have to thank Jim for embracing all that and it certainly got me noticed in football circles. I was able to take all that to Manchester United with Alex's blessing as well. I don't think he did psychology – he had his own version – but he allowed me to help develop the sports science part of the club.

So I was excited, but bloomin' heck I felt a bit of dread also because I was straight into the front line coaching some big players with big personalities. After having a good chat with him on the Thursday, the invitation from Alex came on the Friday, "Come and join the team in Nottingham." We met each other for dinner, which was a bit daunting, and then I was sat on the bench at Nottingham Forest the following day.

It was all a bit surreal really and everything had happened so quickly. It wasn't the worst of starts though – winning 8-1 with Ole Gunnar Solskjaer coming on to score four! But then it was about going in on the Monday morning wondering how to coach and what to do. In the end, I just asked him what he wanted. "Look son," he said, "I've brought you here to coach, now get out there and coach."

It was a fierce dressing room with many leaders, many winners. Every day was competitive, every day was a test. The key thing was that he trusted me to do the job. That was right from the first day, there was no 'you have to do this, you have to do that'. It was down to me. The key thing in my time with him was the trust. It was the same with everyone, if you couldn't do the job – whether you were a player or a member of staff – that he brought you in to do, you were out of the door very quickly.

For me it was a case of making training very competitive. Not over competitive and not too easy going – just getting the balance right. Sometimes it could become a bit over the top, but I could handle that. Once I was in there I felt part of the Manchester United family and Alex would protect me, look after me. There were one or two run-ins with the players where he backed me up. He always wanted control of things – he never wanted to lose that control. If you did the job you were part of the family.

By the time I was involved at Manchester United he obviously had full control of the club. I would have loved to have been there in the early days because he used to tell me some interesting stories. I know he inherited some right characters and had to stand his ground. He must have had to fight nearly every day to get control. When I was there everything ran smoothly because he had wrestled full control of all aspects of the football club. He didn't have to bark and bite a lot because one terse look at somebody was enough. I think we all know about that look!

Sometimes in training a certain player wouldn't conform or would refuse to do the little bits of punishment we would have if they did things wrong. That could cause arguments and the odd ruck. On the first occasion it happened he asked me if I was having trouble with a player. I said no, I could sort it. Anyway, it was nothing to do with me, but he didn't play that player in the next game. There were a few strong characters in the dressing room that you had to stand up to. In those first few months in 1999 I was being tested all the time. I would often be up well into the night planning the next day's coaching session, knowing it couldn't be anything less than perfect. If you didn't put the cones out straight there would be a quick wisecrack, usually from Teddy Sheringham, that I must have had a few too many wines the previous evening. I would often be questioned, 'Why are we doing this, why are we doing that?' But eventually my ideas were accepted because we were also winning football matches, which obviously helps.

Alex always backed me to the hilt. If the players were messing with me, they were also messing with him. I felt very fortunate to be coaching them because they were a fantastic squad. I hope I gave them what they needed at that time, which was intensity and a competitive spirit every day. It was the way you had to train to bring continual success and reinforced what I had always thought about top players – that they need to feel fresh and hungry. Boredom can be a dangerous thing.

I had a really enjoyable two and a half seasons at Manchester United with plenty of success. The key to it all? Competitiveness, even away from football. We used to have regular quizzes. The ones on European trips were legendary. John Peters the club photographer was the quizmaster and the timekeeper. He used to set the quizzes up. We would have a staff team taking on a players' team. The gaffer – surprise, surprise – never wanted to lose. At anything.

One evening there was a question about a famous painting. It was our question, but no one had any idea so it was passed over to the players. Alex was happily muttering, "Aye they've got no chance of answering this." Suddenly Nicky Butt put his hand up and answered something like "Rembrandt, 1645." Unbelievably, he was right.

Alex was beside himself. "How do you know that? John has told you, hasn't he? There's no chance you know the answer." A fork flew past John the quizmaster's head while Butty had to dodge a cutlery knife, which Alex had also thrown in anger. Nicky calmly answered back, "Gaffer, I've got the same painting hung up in my dining room!"

Roy Keane took these quizzes seriously as well. He would often storm off in a huff if things hadn't gone the players way. Believe me, they were always really competitive.

On the football front the trust he had in his players and in his staff was often borne out in the big games that went down to the wire. He never lost faith and you can see that if you watch closely images of our Champions League final victory against Bayern Munich in Barcelona. His experience in the game came to the fore when the odds seemed stacked against us, trailing 1-0 going into the final minutes.

His messages before and during games were always spot on. Whatever decision he made usually worked. At times I would think to myself, 'Oh my God, where has that come from? I would never have thought of that.' His messages weren't dominated by tactics, they were more about emotion, finding the right emotional trigger to get the players up for the task in hand. He certainly got it right in Barcelona and it is no coincidence that the two substitutes he sent on, Teddy and Ole, got the two stoppage-time goals.

He never, ever panicked. Even at 1-0 down in the last minute of a Champions League final. He might have come across sometimes as being in a fury, but his football brain was always calm and rational. He is a clear thinker and that is an incredible strength. To be thinking calmly amidst the unfolding chaos is a magnificent attribute to have. In chaos most of us become emotional. He did get emotional at times as well, but that was mostly for effect. The majority of times he was calm and collected in his thoughts.

He would always tell me that management is about getting seven things out of 10 right. "If I achieve that then I'm doing bloody well," he used to say. The majority of decisions he got right. Another key thing was he was prepared to take risks.

After the Champions League quarter-final against Inter Milan in 1999, people were criticising his tactics, saying they weren't right for European games, we were getting dominated in midfield, blah blah blah. It prompted him to give a very emotional speech to the players saying, "This is Manchester United, this is our history, our tradition and we won't veer away from that. We'll play our way – win, lose or draw. This is Manchester United."

He refused, at that time, to budge from his traditional 4-4-2. He did change in later years, but he didn't think he could change with the squad we had at the time. What we achieved in 1999 speaks for itself and our strength was the attacking quartet – two wide men and two strikers. Imagine having to pick just one striker from the four of Andy Cole, Dwight Yorke, Teddy Sheringham and Ole Gunnar Solskjaer if he switched to another system? It was hard enough choosing two of them.

He was always aware that he needed to try to keep players happy, even if they weren't in the team. He would plan for the next season as soon as the fixtures came out. He could pick out the periods which would prove crucial, when the team needed to step up. He managed the squad so well. My job on a Saturday was to pull those who weren't playing out of the players' lounge to go to see the gaffer, who would explain to them why they weren't being picked for that particular game. They were never dropped, they were always rested.

Before one game, Andy Cole didn't want to go down the corridor to the gaffer's office. "Coley, you've got to see him," I insisted, but he replied that he knew what it was all about – that he wouldn't be playing – so he wasn't going. I agreed that he was right, but said he still had to go to the office. "No Steve, you go and tell him to you know what," he replied.

I persisted and finally managed to persuade Coley to go down the corridor and walk through the manager's door. He just sat down on the nearest chair to the door and refused to go any further into the room, saying, "Just tell me, gaffer, and I'll be off." As usual, Alex came out with, "I'm just resting you for this game." Exit Andy, obviously not happy, but Alex didn't react, he didn't blow up. He knew how to handle these situations. He didn't want to lose a player. He had hard decisions to make and he stuck by them.

Alex could be ruthless in his decisions, but also very caring about delivering bad news. On the morning of the FA Cup final against Newcastle United in 1999 he went around every hotel room to see the players who hadn't been selected to tell them in person. He had to tell Dwight Yorke he wasn't playing, which left Yorkie devastated because everyone wants to play in an FA Cup final.

When Roy Keane got injured early on I thought here we go, Yorkie will get on now. He sent Teddy Sheringham on instead. Yorkie eventually replaced Andy Cole around the hour mark.

Players will never agree with a decision to leave them out, but under Alex Ferguson they always got it from the horse's mouth. That's how he managed to keep the whole squad together, but that ruthless streak was never far away from the surface.

After winning the treble in 1999 we had the celebrations in Manchester, the open-top bus ride through the city. It was fantastic, but I couldn't wait to go on holiday. I think we had all earned it. After the celebrations were over he said to all the staff, "We're all in tomorrow, see you at The Cliff." We turned up at 9am the next day all hungover, having tea, coffee and bacon butties while wondering why we were in. He arrived and said, "Here's your medals, now put them in the drawer. What are we going to do next season?" That summed him up.

The biggest shock came a couple of years later when he told me he was going to retire at the end of the 2001/02 season. I asked him what would happen to me in the case of him leaving? He said I had no chance of getting the Manchester United manager's job so advised me to look around because he felt I was ready to become a manager in my own right. "I'm off in a year so look after yourself," he advised.

That's why he gave me his blessing to become Middlesbrough manager in the summer of 2001. Otherwise I would never have left. So when he decided against retiring in February 2002 I was absolutely gutted because I had already left to take charge of Middlesbrough. If I had known he was going to change his mind I would have hopefully remained alongside him for a good many more years.

8

'If you play for Manchester United you have to play without fear and with courage. You go out there and show your skills. He used to say to us before games, "Go out and express yourself and be prepared to take risks"'

Ole Gunnar Solskjaer,
Manchester United manager

Ole Gunnar Solskjaer

OLE GUNNAR SOLSKJAER will be forever ingrained in Manchester United folklore for his dramatic late winning goal in the 1999 Champions League final. The Norwegian was Alex Ferguson's super sub during an 11-year playing career at Old Trafford. After seeing Alex as his mentor and making copious notes on his management techniques he has since followed him into the Manchester United managerial hotseat.

Sir Alex has influenced me in everything. The way he dealt with people, the way he was the manager of the club, how he kept 25 international players happy, hungry and wanting to improve. The way he dealt with all the staff of the club. I have learned from him and been moulded by him.

I had the best teacher there can be of man-management. I have taken a few tricks on board from him and taken his advice. At times I think, 'what would the gaffer have done in this situation?' I often look through the diaries I kept when I was a player and a coach at Manchester United, the notes I had made on observing different things from the gaffer. Some people must have thought I was a boring man doing all this, but it has helped me. There are notes on his team-talks, on his meetings, everything. I thought it might influence my own coaching and management career.

If you play for Manchester United you have to play without fear and with courage. You go out there and show your skills. He used to say to us before games, "Go out and express yourself and be prepared to take risks." I thought his last game as Manchester United manager – a 5-5 draw at West Brom in 2013

– summed it all up. Ideally you don't want to concede five goals, but it was fantastic, exciting football. It was the way he wanted football played. My management style has evolved from what I learned from him, but we are different characters.

I can't honestly remember what the gaffer said to me after that winning goal in the 1999 Champions League final against Bayern Munich. As a squad we just felt, after the dramatic FA Cup semi-final win over Arsenal, that something special was happening, that we could achieve something.

This was everything I had been preparing for and I've seen my treble-winning goal a million times. It's had a few mentions by other people as well, but funnily enough I've never watched back the whole game, just the last 15 minutes.

In 1999 the manager instilled this hunger, this humility to win. The culture came from him, but he let the players drive it. He made us accountable for our own performances. It was about workrate, discipline – like coming to training on time. It was about doing the extras that can give you those little per-centages that win you games. They are the things that are easy to do and also very easy not to do. Do we go all in or don't we?

If you want to play for Manchester United you have to have a personality. You have to be able to stand up for yourself against big boys. We were playing against the top players in the world. You can't always look around and ask for help.

At half-time in Barcelona, with us 1-0 down, the manager had a little chat with Teddy Sheringham to say that he was going to put him on early in the second half. I was just in the back-ground hoping he was going to come over to me, but he didn't. During the second half I was warming up and warming up, waiting and waiting to catch his eye. I was thinking 'why don't you put me on?' I had come on and scored against Liverpool in the FA Cup that season and got four in 18 minutes when I came on at Nottingham Forest, so I had a premonition I was going to do something that night.

As a substitute I would be very focussed on never sulking about not playing. My best ability was just being ready when I was called upon. Then I would be fit and my legs would be light. If you sulk and are on the bench when the gaffer calls you on, then you are not ready because there's something going on in your head.

I wasn't happy to often be on the bench, but if you are not one of the best players you have to be selfless. If you sulk and you are not the best player, forget it. I knew I wasn't the best player and I didn't sulk. If you want to win you have to have the best mentality as well. It was about creating an environment of world class, elite performances. We couldn't accept mediocrity.

Teddy scored the equaliser in the first minute of stoppage-time but instead of running towards him to celebrate I ran back to the halfway line ready for them to kick off. I was concentrating on the half hour of extra time that was coming up, thinking I was going to savour another 30 minutes playing in a Champions League final – but I ruined that by scoring! For the goal I was just doing my job as a striker by being in the right place at the right time.

I missed the start of the post-match celebrations because I was being interviewed about my winning goal. I also realised I had injured myself with my knee-sliding goal celebration. I tweaked my medial ligament and missed a couple of internationals for Norway, but it was definitely worth it.

Of course, like many of the other players, the gaffer had his moments with me, especially after a game against Newcastle United in 1998. I was sent off for chopping down Newcastle United's Robert Lee, who had a clear run to goal in the 89th minute. We were in the middle of a title race and the score was 1-1 so I thought I had done the right thing and would be praised for preventing what seemed like a certain winning goal. I was in for a shock. Sir Alex was far from happy.

He later called me into his office and lambasted me. "We don't win that way," he told me in no uncertain terms. That has remained with me ever since. As a football club Manchester United must always have its values. As their manager it's my duty not to go away from these values. We want to win in the right manner no matter who we are playing against and how important the game might be.

The only player who was never really told off was Eric Cantona, although no one had a problem with that. We were all sorry when he decided to leave the club and football. Strangely, only around 48 hours before his big announcement in 1997, I had been with Eric and our respective families celebrating winning another Premier League title.

After the last game of the season Eric had hired a local restaurant for a number of our families. We had a great night, a great time celebrating winning the league again. A few days later it was announced that he had retired and he had not mentioned one word about it to us. We were dancing, having fun until 4am – but there was not a single mention of his plan. That was Eric in a nutshell.

In 2007 it was time for me to retire through injury. As I was parking my car at the training ground ready to tell Sir Alex the news he came over to me and said, "How are you son?"

"Not great," I replied, "I need another operation. I'm not going to do it, I need to retire." He replied, "Well don't worry son, you've had a fantastic career, your family must be so proud. Why don't you coach the forwards? Go home for a few weeks and come back when you're ready."

I went away for three weeks, came back and was integrated into the first team set up where I coached Cristiano Ronaldo, Wayne Rooney and Carlos Tevez. So when any of them scored I would joke that I deserved some of the credit!

Really though, it was all down to one man – Sir Alex Ferguson. It always has been.

Gary Newbon

GARY NEWBON, in his role as ITV's roving sports reporter, interviewed Alex immediately after Manchester United's stunning 1999 Champions League triumph in Barcelona, where he uttered the famous remark, "Football, bloody hell!" Gary was involved in TV for 50 years and hosted numerous shows in addition to being Central TV's Controller of Sport.

On that incredible night in Barcelona I was the man designated to capture the post-match interviews. To be honest, the whole thing wasn't that well organised. Anyone who knows the Nou Camp will tell you there is very little room between the pitch and the fans. There's no running track, for instance, around the perimeter.

If you're involved with one of the teams that have reached the final, as ITV was as national broadcaster when Manchester

United got there, then at least you get preferential treatment in that you are allowed the first post-match interviews. Mine were to be conducted halfway down the Nou Camp tunnel, which must be one of the longest in football. It's even got a chapel in there where players can pray before a game if they want to.

Alex always refers to his interview with me, following that sensational late victory against Bayern Munich, as "gibberish." But what he hasn't taken into account is, during his obvious excitement at just witnessing an incredible turnaround in Manchester United's fortunes, that he probably came out with one of the most famous quotes in the game, "Football, bloody hell!" He also insisted that you should never give in, which was the apt title of a recent documentary about him that also told of his recovery from a brain haemorrhage. I have never reacted so much in my career compared to when those two late goals from Teddy Sheringham and Ole Gunnar Solskjaer went in. I jumped out of my seat in celebration, not realising that my headphones were still connected to the equipment, almost yanking my neck off in the process. Before that I had been thinking of the questions I would have to ask Alex as it looked like United's hopes of winning the treble had gone with them 1-0 down going into stoppage time. I was so disappointed for them.

Suddenly, the whole game was transformed and in the post-match interview it looked like Alex was still in a state of shock. I'd also got to him virtually straight away. He wasn't 100% 'with it' – he was in a daze. I think I had to repeat the first question because he was clearly not thinking straight. In the end it was just a simple question, "Alex, what's your reaction?"

Sometimes it is better to keep the question plain and simple, especially following such an amazing happening. He just blurted out, "Football, bloody hell!" After that he started really thinking about what had gone on and added, "We never give in, we never give in."

He kindly invited me to the victory banquet at the hotel that night and he would often ask me up for a drink at his office following games at Old Trafford. I sat down with Teddy Sheringham, who told me he had been furious at seeing the Bayern Munich players waving to their families just before the end of the game, obviously believing they had it won. Teddy told me he was determined to score after coming on as a substitute – which he did. I'll never forget our ITV commentator Clive Tyldesley saying with United 1-0 down and time running out, "Can Manchester United score? They always score." Then Sheringham pops one in and Solskjaer comes up with the winner. Incredible.

I had one disagreement with Alex as a TV interviewer – one that I have always regretted. He hadn't been at Manchester United that long and the rumour mill was at full pelt, saying he was going to be sacked. So the final question after one match was about his future, which evidently didn't go down too well.

A few weeks later we're at Carrow Road for Norwich against Manchester United, when ITV had *The Big Match* live. I went up to Alex before the start of the game just to confirm that he would be okay for an interview afterwards. He told me he wouldn't be doing it. I asked him why and he came back with, "Because you ask crap questions." To be fair to him he said he wouldn't stop his players talking to me, provided they wanted to, but he wouldn't be speaking. I was grateful because I would have looked like a right idiot if he had blanked me on live TV.

It was hurtful in some respects because during my career I have never stitched anyone up, as they say in the trade. Maybe, on reflection, I had been out of order with the question on his future when I hadn't given him any advance warning.

I was doing my boxing programme *Fight Night* and staying in the Midland Hotel in Manchester a few weeks later and there one morning, having breakfast on his own, was Alex. I went up to him and asked him if I could join him for breakfast? He said I could and so I collected my buffet breakfast and on my way back to the table I'm thinking what am I going to say?

I sat down, looked him straight in the face and said, "Alex, can I start again with you?" He asked me what I meant. I told him I felt I was bang out of order with the question which had upset him. I couldn't go back on it, but in the future if I ever had a curveball question he would know about it before I asked him. He said, "Okay, we'll give it a try." After that I developed such trust with him.

For the next 22 years we worked well together and he would be so helpful. He even became one of the first managers to speak at half-time in European games. I have always reserved the right to ask tough questions, but I've never deliberately tried to turn anyone over. You have to have a balance as a TV interviewer because you've got to get someone talking in front of the TV camera. You can't rely on getting quotes from any of your colleagues – it's down to you. Interviewing is an art. You don't have to look clever, but you must do your homework properly – then you can get respect from the interviewee. It's not about you, it's about the subject. Today's best TV interviewers in my opinion are ITV's Gabriel Clarke and Sky Sports' Geoff Shreeves. They get the best out of people.

Getting to know Alex over the years, one thing that stood out was that he never wanted anyone challenging his authority as the manager of Manchester United. You could talk to him, but you must never challenge his right to be the manager. His authority as manager was the most important thing for him. I suspect that was why some players were moved on. For instance, David Beckham became bigger than the club really. The man who ultimately replaced him, Cristiano Ronaldo, wasn't so bad either.

I spent 50 years in front of a camera on two big channels. The three most influential people in my career were Brian Clough, Alex Ferguson and Chris Eubank. I will always be grateful to the three of them. They had the greatest impact on me and I got them in their greatest moments as well. That was a privilege. It's also why that question to Alex on whether he could be sacked was the one I have always regretted. Thankfully I managed to resolve it with him over a traditional English breakfast. I'll never forget his kindness when I suffered a stroke shortly before I was due to cover the World Cup finals in Japan in 2002. Alex rang me three times during my recovery and I believe he was instrumental in me regaining my health and fitness, enabling me to travel to the Far East.

Later my wife Katie developed a brain tumour. He called me from the Manchester United team coach, which had just arrived at West Brom's ground for a game. He asked if I was going to The Hawthorns. I told him my wife was very ill. He said he had heard the sad news and that was the reason he was ringing. It was an hour and a half before kick off, so I asked him whether we should continue this conversation at a later date? "No, I want to know now," he replied. He had met Katie, who isn't really into football. She was very moved and that helped her recovery tremendously.

That's Alex's very caring side – one that really moves you.

When he found out that Joe Melling, a football reporter who he had been involved in a few battles with, was suffering from lung cancer he rang him up and told him, "You've got to fight this like you fight me." Joe was gobsmacked.

Alex is a seriously good guy. You have to take the professional side away from his personal side because the often abrasive way he behaved at Manchester United was the only way he was going to firstly survive, and secondly win things. It took me a while to understand that, but once I got to grips with that side of him I became very fond of the bloke.

So when he was taken ill in 2018 I wrote to him. My wife and I were so pleased that he made a fantastic recovery. We felt we owed him something. Many people do.

Neil Custis

NEIL CUSTIS has been The Sun's Manchester-based football reporter since 1999. He enjoyed and endured in equal parts Alex's Old Trafford reign for 14 years which encompassed seven bans – the price of being at the sharp end of covering the fortunes of one of the biggest clubs in the world with an iconic manager at the helm.

Alex agreed to go on a visit to The Christie cancer hospital in Manchester where my wife Alicia was head of communications. She arranged it in the knowledge that, with Alex's dad having died of cancer, he was very supportive of events surrounding the disease.

I'd helped her a little bit in setting it up by speaking to Di Law, the Manchester United press officer at the time. Unknown to both of us he had found out as much as he could about Alicia before meeting her. He discovered that she was half-Spanish, so when he arrived at the hospital and met her he immediately started talking to her about Spain, asking what part of Spain her family were from and things like that. I thought going into that sort of detail to discover something about the person who had arranged his visit was outstanding.

Going home after the event, Alicia said to me that she knew I'd had some problems with him over the years, but swore that he had simply been incredible from the moment he came in until the moment he left. At the start he had told her that he would be there as long as she wanted. He signed every autograph and posed for every photo. He did absolutely everything and made a wonderful speech in front of the staff. She was completely bowled over by him. I was delighted for her that things had gone so well, but normal service quickly resumed for me at the next Fergie press conference. Once it came to an end, and as he was about to leave, he shouted out to me, "Aye, there you go Custis, fuck off and get a proper job like your wife!"

The bans came thick and fast for many of the journalists covering Manchester United. One of mine arrived following a game against Bayern Munich in 2010 when United were knocked out of the Champions League. Rafael da Silva had been sent off. Alex blamed the Bayern players for getting him sent off, branding them "typical Germans."

That became the back page headline, which he wasn't too pleased about and he retaliated by refusing to do an extra few minutes for the newspapers, which was common practice once the TV and radio had completed their questions.

He argued that we had concentrated on his insult rather than on how well United had played despite them getting knocked out. I wasn't happy with his attitude so I started arguing with him, which he didn't like because the cameras were still rolling. He saw it as an insult and I ended up getting banned for 18 months, just one of seven bans during his time as manager!

I still went on a pre-season tour to the USA and he agreed to let me into the press conferences because it was a tour and I had made the effort to go on it. After one conference I went over and chatted with him. He was very pleasant and I don't think he could remember why he had banned me.

He told me that once we got back to England I would be welcomed back to the training ground, where the majority of his press conferences were held. So it was just my luck that for the first one of the new season my car got blocked due to some construction work going on around the Carrington training ground. It meant that I was late.

His conference had already started and I tried to sneak in without him noticing me. No chance of that. On spotting me he yelled out, "Aye, Custis, I let you back after all this time and you're late." I replied, "Yes, it's been so long I went to The Cliff [United's old training ground]." To be fair he laughed at that.

Despite the number of skirmishes I ended up making the speech on behalf of the press reporters when he retired. I presented him with a cake with a hairdryer on top of it. I made the point then that it hadn't been an easy ride for us, but we would be eternally grateful that we covered Manchester United during the time he was the manager. You would always have that churning feeling in your stomach wondering what kind of mood he would be in. Would you be in for a verbal blast? You were never quite sure what was going to come back. It was like he was judging you on a week's homework.

My brother Shaun was working for Express Newspapers at the time and one morning Alex had woken up to a headline in the *Daily Express* – the paper he had delivered to his home – about him signing an Italian player. He would often get the two of us mixed up. At times he would call me Shaun and vice versa. He hated these big transfer stories on the back pages, especially if they were right – that would annoy him even more. So when he arrived for the next press conference he didn't hold back. He launched straight into me.

"Absolute disgrace – that rubbish in your paper. You can get out, I'm not talking to you," he spat. I said, "Alex, you've got the wrong Custis. It's Shaun who has written the story, I'm Neil who works for *The Sun*."

His swift reply was, "Aye, there's too many Custises!" Richard Tanner, who was representing the *Express* that day, piped up: "Alex, I work for the *Express*. Should I go out?" So Alex ended up throwing Richard out, but he wasn't finished there. He also threw Matt Lawton out for writing in the *Daily Mail* that Alex could become the next chairman of Aberdeen. He physically got hold of Matt and threw him out of the door. For the rest of the conference he kept looking at me and saying: "Aye, sorry about that."

I don't think he was too enamoured with Richard, who was not helped of course because he wrote for the paper which was pushed through Alex's letter box every morning. On a pre-season tour in the USA, before a friendly between United and Celtic in 2003, Alex and Martin O'Neill, manager of Celtic, held a joint press conference. At the end, Richard – in his typical friendly way – had said to Martin that he had done so well during his managerial career that he was being mooted as Alex's eventual successor and had earned that right.

Alex doesn't do nicey, nicey talk. Martin came out with a diplomatic reply, saying they would be huge shoes to fill for whoever eventually succeeded the great man. Richard, on transcribing his tape – which had run on for a few minutes following the completion of the official conference – discovered that Alex had apologised to Martin over what he had felt had been an irregular question, adding, "That bloke asking it is an absolute prick."

I also remember how nonplussed he was when meeting, for the first time, a guy from new radio station XFM that had opened up in Manchester in 2006. It was a trendy indie station that everyone was encouraged to listen to with a big launch and they decided they wanted to encompass Fergie's United press conferences. This lad turned up at his conference with hair that was halfway across his face. He wore a pair of ripped jeans and a t-shirt. I swear that if someone had landed from Mars, Fergie would have been less in shock. He watched him all the way as he placed the recorder on the table and watched him all the way back to his seat. His mouth was wide open. He had never seen anything like it. Alex might have been in a club tracksuit, but he expected those attending his press conferences to be smartly turned out.

Certainly in the early days I would always wear a tie. Later you could get away with an open necked shirt. I would always say to anyone turning up looking scruffy that Alex was from a certain era where your appearance does make a difference. It was a sign of respect in how you dressed. I remember Paul Hayward, a journalist who helped him with one of his books, being told by

Alex that he thought I had always taken my job seriously and that I dressed smartly, which was really good to hear.

He also knew everyone's name after a time if they attended his press conferences regularly. He knew a bit about everyone. No manager since at Manchester United has really bothered about such detail. It's as if they don't really want to get to know you. All Jose Mourinho seemed bothered about was who was on his side and who was against him. Despite all the banning and furore which often surrounded his press conferences, to Alex's credit he knew who you were.

Alex is a huge golf fan and we were in Romania for Manchester United's Champions League match against CFR Cluj at the time of 'The Miracle Of Medinah,' when Europe launched a stunning last-day comeback against the USA to clinch the 2012 Ryder Cup. Two years earlier Alex had been in the dressing room where, under Colin Montgomery, they had won the Ryder Cup at the Celtic Manor so there was a huge link between Fergie and the Ryder Cup. We couldn't watch the drama unfold because Romanian TV wasn't covering it and the day after Europe's against-the-odds Medinha triumph there was a UEFA press conference in Cluj to preview this Champions League game.

James Cooper from Sky Sports weighed in with his final question. "Alex, I'm sure you will want to send your best wishes to the European team on what was a remarkable comeback?" James and the rest of us couldn't have predicted the response.

"What a stupid question. What the hell are you asking me that for? This is a serious Champions League press conference." James was visibly wilting in his chair wondering what he had done wrong.

Back in January 2000 we were in Brazil with Manchester

United, who had controversially ditched the FA Cup to play in the inaugural FIFA World Club Championship. They were getting loads of stick for pulling out of the FA Cup and relations with the media were at an all time low.

The other teams in the tournament had been doing great PR – visiting favelas, local schools, mixing with people on the famous Copacabana beach. United were doing nothing in the first week. They had planned to do it all later on, but they hadn't informed anyone of this. As a result United got hammered so Di Law, the United press officer, set up one of the journalists, the *Sunday People*'s Lee Clayton, to ask if United had any special events coming up? That would then be the opportunity to give the club some much-needed good publicity.

So in the press conference after a 1-1 draw against Mexican side Necaxa, in which David Beckham was sent off, we all asked questions about the game, including Lee. You were only supposed to ask one question because there were so many media in the room, but then Lee put up his hand ready to ask the pre-planned question. Before he could get a word out, Fergie snapped at him, "That's enough from you, you've already asked a question!" With that he was off and the message about United's forthcoming good deeds couldn't be relayed.

Another regular on the Manchester beat, the *Daily Mail*'s Ian Ladyman, was in the midst of a ban. Peace talks were arranged to try to bring him in from the cold. He was summoned to Alex's office at United's Carrington training ground. Again, I don't think Alex could remember what he had been banned for. While he was talking, Alex glanced out of the window and noticed Federico Macheda, one of his young players who, let's say, didn't lack confidence. He suddenly turned to Lado with the observation, "Aye, Macheda the wee cunt." So after banning Lado he was now taking him into his confidence. Covering all things Fergie was like visiting Fawlty Towers. It was never very comfortable, but you were never going to forget it.

Rio Ferdinand

RIO FERDINAND broke the British transfer record with his £30 million transfer from Leeds United to Manchester United in 2002. He went on to captain United and win 81 England caps. He was part of six United Premier League winning sides and also has a Champions League winners' medal.

Walking into the middle of the Old Trafford pitch with Alex for the official photographs after signing for Manchester United was the first time I had really met him. The only other brief meeting was when I was at West Ham after we had played United.

It was in the Upton Park car park and as I was going towards my car I nervously said, "Alright boss?" He went back, "Alright son, good luck," and got on the Manchester United team coach. Apparently he had tried to sign me when I was on loan at Bournemouth and Mel Machin, the Bournemouth manager, had to tell him I wasn't actually his to sell. Another time he called West Ham and Harry Redknapp, who was in charge of the Hammers at the time, said he would sell me in exchange for David Beckham plus cash!

Alex had an incredible presence about him and when I signed for United I was still in awe of him thinking, "Shit man, Alex

Ferguson's my new manager." He lightened the mood at the press conference when he looked at my suit and said, "Bloody hell, are you going out after?" It was a magnificent suit, white linen with a thin black pinstripe. I later found out that if anyone wore any dodgy gear the gaffer would rip into them.

I didn't know whether to laugh or cry because he had a reputation for blowing a fuse, but was charm itself. After the press conference was over he said, "Well done son." Even that gave me a buzz. I hadn't kicked a ball for United and yet he was praising me. I felt 10 feet tall. He told me I would love it at United and the fans were fantastic and to make sure I enjoyed it, although I wondered how I'd get into the team with the quality already at the club.

On my first day of training I got a bollocking from Roy Keane. I knew that going on a training pitch with players of the nature of Keane, David Beckham, Ryan Giggs, Gary and Phil Neville, Ruud van Nistelrooy and Paul Scholes was going to be a daunting prospect. And if you've just cost £30 million they are going to want to see what that buys. They want to know what you've got and will test you out.

Keane was never going to let me break in gently and after I'd played a square ball he went mental and barked, "Pass the fucking ball forward." His face was contorted. "It's fucking easy going sideways, pass it forward." He was the manager's voice on the field. He could read a game better than anyone and I realised United was going to be very different to anywhere I'd been before.

We won the Premier League in my first season there. It was my first winners' medal in senior football, but there had been a lot of talk during the season that David Beckham could be on his way out to either Barcelona or Real Madrid. Relations between him and the gaffer had become strained after an FA Cup defeat against Arsenal.

It was the day the gaffer kicked a boot and it struck Becks above an eyebrow. It would be fair to say the gaffer was steaming in the dressing room that day. He said something to Becks about how he'd let someone run through for one of their goals. Becks didn't agree and a few words were exchanged, but a dressing room argument after a defeat is not unusual. The manager says his piece and if someone doesn't agree they might challenge him. It happens all the time, but at Manchester United the boss always had the final word.

There was a pile of boots lying in the middle of the floor and the boss just kicked one of them in anger. It was like slow motion as this boot flew through the air and smacked Becks on the forehead. If the gaffer tried a hundred times to do it again he couldn't. The best player in the world could not have pulled it off deliberately. He hadn't lined it up or anything – he just swung his foot and bang, it whacked Becks. We could tell the manager was upset about what happened and he apologised to Becks as David went off to see the doctor.

The dressing room was silent for a few minutes, but feelings had been running high and we all knew it was just one of those things. Becks wasn't going to talk about it to anyone and the gaffer certainly wasn't. But the story came out in *The Sun* with the headline 'Fergie Decks Becks'.

That day Becks was pictured going to training with his hair pulled back under a hairband, so it was hard not to see the plasters. The world went mad. I'd never known so much commotion about a player with two butterfly stitches in his eyebrow. For the first time I began to wonder if Becks would still be at United the following season even though he loved Manchester. He knew loads of people there and was comfortable in his surroundings.

When the manager finally decided to let him go it was still a shock. There was a lot of talk about Ronaldinho coming in as a replacement. I remember walking onto the training pitch one day having seen a mention of it in the papers and asking the manager about it. He seemed quite confident that Ronaldinho would be coming and I was buzzing. But he went to Barcelona instead, who ironically had lost out on a bid for Becks, who ended up at Real Madrid.

There were also suggestions that Kieron Dyer might be coming from Newcastle, but later that summer the Portuguese winger Cristiano Ronaldo played against us for Sporting Club de Portugal in a pre-season friendly in Lisbon and he was unbelievable. John O'Shea, who was marking him, needed an oxygen mask at the end of the first half. At half-time Paul Scholes, Nicky Butt and I were going, "Forget anyone else, we've got to get his kid." After the game we said to the gaffer, "Are you going to get him or what?"

We were left sitting on the coach for ages and everyone was messing about, having a laugh, saying the gaffer was upstairs doing the deal for Ronaldo. As it happens he was and a week later he joined United for £12 million, a new record transfer fee for a teenager.

What I admired about Alex was the desire and dedication he had right to the end of his management career. He was still the first in and the last out of the training ground. There was always an incredible belief in what he was doing. His work ethic was incredible, but he didn't have to talk about it – you would just see it. Every day when I came into training his car was already parked there. It was something that rubbed off on me.

As a footballer you don't always have to be told what to do or preached to, sometimes just seeing what your manager does day in, day out, sets the example to follow. His relentless drive and energy was enough to inspire us at United. When he wasn't at a training session, which would only have been a handful of times in the 13 years I was there, the session would drop a little bit in terms of intensity and quality. When he was there, half the time he might be on his phone placing bets – not really taking any real notice of what was going on – but his presence was enough.

Sometimes he wouldn't talk about football to try to motivate you. We had a massive Monday night game against Arsenal at Old Trafford in December 2010 and we were on the bikes in the gym. We were watching the big screen, seeing all the stats coming through from training sessions and things like that when suddenly a stream of guys – loads of them – came into the gym, followed by the manager.

He said to us, "Do you know who these guys are? They're the Chilean miners who got locked underground for around a month and almost died." The gaffer, who is from a mining background himself, went on to explain how they had survived, how hard they had to work as a team – as a unit that believed in each other – to make sure they all stayed strong to the point where they managed to survive.

Later that day, just before the game, he came into the changing room and told us he had already done his team talk. "If you can't be committed. If you can't give it your all. If you can't work your hardest to get the win today, bearing in mind what you have seen and heard from those guys from Chile and what they went through, then you are not meant to be here." We went out there, beat Arsenal 1-0 and stayed top of the Premier League for the rest of the season.

He didn't always have to push our buttons by bawling and shouting all the time. He would bring different things to the table and you would just go 'wow'. He just knew how to manage you as individuals as well as the team. He would also delegate in other areas, but in terms of knowing the characters in the dressing room it was all him.

We were due to play Liverpool at Anfield in March 2011. I knew if I got a knock on my hotel door that morning there was something wrong and I probably would not be playing. On the morning of the Liverpool game my heart started pumping when, after answering the knock at my door, Alex was standing outside my room.

He came in and I was saying he had to play me, it was Liverpool away, there was no way I wanted to miss the game even though I had only just come back from injury after a month out. "Look, I want you fit for the Champions League quarter-final at Chelsea," he said. I was screaming at him, demanding to play against Liverpool. "Son, we've got Chelsea in the Champions League. That's when I need you. You are always brilliant there. Their fans hate you. You always thrive under that pressure. You'll get us a result."

By the time he left the room I was shaking his hand thinking 'this guy is the greatest'. That's the way he was – he could just cajole you. So in the changing room before the game at Anfield I was going around speaking to everyone, geeing them up, wishing them good luck whereas I might have walked in there depressed thinking it's a joke that I'm not playing and I hope they lose 2-0! We lost that game at Anfield 3-1, but sure enough he put me back into the side a month later when we played Chelsea in the Champions League at Stamford Bridge. We won 1-0 and then 2-1 at Old Trafford on our way to the final.

Of course he also had a ruthless streak and would use it if it meant the club benefited. I was shown around United's training facilities by Dwight Yorke after signing. Dwight had been part of the treble-winning side just three years earlier. Him and Andy Cole had been devastating up front.

I was walking around the training ground with him when Alex came out of his office and wished us both a good morning. I went and had breakfast with Yorkie before heading out for training. Alex spotted me and called me over to him. He said to me, "Do you want to be here for a long time?" I replied, "Yeah, I want to win everything and do as well as I can." He replied, "Well the first thing you should think about doing is not hanging around with him because he isn't going to be here."

I could hardly believe what I was hearing. "He was unbelievable. He won everything, but he's complacent now," added Alex. It really hit home that nobody was safe at the club.

Yorkie had been the king of Manchester after winning the treble. But the moment you start letting your standards slip, or if the intensity is not there in training sessions, then you've got to go. That conversation stayed with me for the rest of my time at Manchester United, not least because Yorkie left for Blackburn Rovers less than a week later.

I also learned it's best not to take Alex on, following a game against Benfica in the Champions League. We hadn't played well and he started shouting at me in the changing room after the game. I thought I had played okay and began shouting back at him. But I discovered the more I shouted at him, the more he shouted back and the more aggressive he became. He also got closer and closer. I was under the hairdryer and I can tell you that wasn't the best place to be!

Wayne Rooney

WAYNE ROONEY was the precocious Everton youngster signed by Alex in 2004 for £26 million who went on to become Manchester United's all-time record goalscorer. His 208 goals make him the Premier League's second top scorer and he also became England's record goalscorer with 53 goals from 120 caps before moving into management with Derby County.

One of Alex Ferguson's most important qualities was his man-management skills. As a manager he was, in my opinion, the best, but his man-management was what a lot of other bosses would struggle to match.

He knew the ins and outs of every player. How to speak to a player, how to get a reaction. He knew how to leave a player out of the team and end up with that player still thinking he's a great manager. I think he's the only one who could do that, leave someone out and the player still feels on top of the world. That's an incredible attribute to have.

I wasn't easy to handle at times, but he knew how to get a reaction from me. I may have played well when some others hadn't, but at half-time he would often direct his anger at me. It would sometimes end up as a shouting match with me having a go back at him, but he knew he was certain of a good reaction from me on the pitch.

That wouldn't have been the case if he had hollered at someone like Nani. If Sir Alex had spoken the same way to Nani as he did to me he would have been in tears and not gone out for the second half. But by yelling at me the message got through to the others. If he warned me to stop dribbling the penny would drop for Nani because in reality he had been guilty of over-doing that. It was very clever because then he would get a response from myself and the other players.

He did it with Giggsy as well, but if it had gone off between us at an away game then on the way home he would walk down the coach and give me or Giggsy a slap on the back of the head. That was his way of saying what had gone on was now finished.

I believe there is no harm in having a lively dressing room exchange or debate. At the end of the day, he was the manager and you had to respect his decisions. He never ever over-complicated things. Some of his team-talks were simple, 'You're Manchester United, now go out there and win the game'. Or, 'You 11 players are better than them so win the game'.

He would give us responsibility. If we got a player sent off we would work the new formation out on the pitch. If it didn't work out then he would change it. He would nearly always get his tactics right in the big games too. We would usually tire teams out. They would be dead on their feet after 70 minutes so there was never any panicking if we hadn't scored. It was no coincidence that we won many games late on. He knew what was effective and how to get the best out of you. The best advice I received from him was about me working too hard. At first I wondered what he meant, but I used to run as hard as I could for 90 minutes but tire in the last 10 minutes. The manager wanted his strikers to keep a bit in the tank, because that match-winning chance might not come until the 90th minute.

After listening to his advice I also used to practise finishing when I was tired. At the end of a training session I'd get a keeper and Eric Steele, the goalkeeping coach, and I'd do a continuous sprinting and shooting routine. By the fifth or sixth one I'd be shattered and out of breath, but if you learn how to finish when you're tired then it's much easier to put away a chance when you feel normal.

The only real time my relationship with the manager took a bit of a hit was when I asked to leave the club in 2010. I was frustrated with the way things were going. We'd sold Carlos Tevez and Cristiano Ronaldo and it came at the time when the club was offering me a new five-year contract. I was almost 25 and coming to the peak of my career and I wanted assurances about who we were bringing in to replace our big players who had left. I wanted to know if we were going to go for proven players who could fit straight into the team.

The manager told me that was none of my business. I said, "Fine, I respect your decision on that. You're the manager, but if you can't give me these assurances it's best that I leave the club." It was all quick and something I regret now.

A few days after speaking to Sir Alex I went to see David Gill, the Manchester United chief executive. He was obviously a lot calmer than Sir Alex was! Two or three days down the line I signed the new contract, but that hadn't stopped a few hoodie-wearing fans turning up at my house in the early hours of the morning protesting about my possible transfer. For a time afterwards there was still a bit of tension hanging over from my conversation with the manager. I just tried to keep my head down and score goals. At the time I knew what I wanted when I went in to see him, but in retrospect it probably wasn't my place as a young lad to go into his office and say what I did.

A couple of years earlier I'd been unhappy with him during an FA Cup quarter-final against Portsmouth at Old Trafford. It was the year Harry Redknapp's team went on to win it.

Our substitute keeper Tomasz Kuszczak had been sent off for up-ending Milan Baros in the penalty area. The manager put Rio Ferdinand in goal. It should have been me. I always used to go in goal once we had finished the normal training sessions. I'd practise all the goalkeeping techniques with our keepers. I suppose I still had energy to burn. So I would always say to the manager that any time our keeper gets sent off, put me in goal.

I think at the time of Portsmouth's penalty he couldn't risk me going in goal because if they scored we'd have been 1-0 down with not long to go and he would rather have me playing up front trying to save the game. Instead he put Rio in goal, but Sulley Muntari scored from the spot and we ended up being knocked out. The manager was upset with the surprise 1-0 defeat and I don't think he spoke to us all for about two weeks.

More than a decade later and Sir Alex was amongst the people I spoke to after becoming Derby County manager. It wasn't about how the team were playing or tactics, it was just a general chat. He said straight away that I could call him at any time if I needed a chat. I would be naïve not to seek the advice of someone like him because there's nothing better than learning from the very best.

Postscript

'Football has always been in his DNA. Retirement has not diluted that one ounce'

Visitors to Old Trafford never fail to pause for a few moments and gaze at the wonderful statue of arguably Manchester United's greatest ever manager.

And there has never ever been a single objection to the towering North Stand being renamed the Sir Alex Ferguson Stand. It's there for everyone to see – dignitaries, managers and officials – as they make their way onto the pitch which has echoed to the sound of outstanding success during the Laird of Old Trafford's stunning reign.

Safe to say the man himself takes it all in his stride as he continues to watch the club he rebuilt on most match days.

More often than not the cameras will pick him out, always smartly dressed – usually booted and suited – having travelled to an away game as well.

For Sir Alex football will always be in his DNA, retirement has not diluted it one ounce and there's still a fair few bottles of red wine devoured in the room he has kept at Old Trafford for special guests.

As another birthday milestone approaches (he's 80 on New Year's Eve) there's no sign that football's loss will be the local garden centre's gain on a Saturday or Sunday afternoon. His comeback from a near-death experience with a brain haemorrhage has been as breathtaking as some of his football exploits.

The tidal wave of emotion and well wishers was not only proof of his standing in the game but also of how he is perceived within football. He has always been one of the first on the phone to offer support and advice for a young manager who has just been sacked. Flowers will often arrive coupled with a short note after discovering a former staff member, football person or friend has been ill.

On the night it was announced that he was fighting for his life it was like the world had stopped. Shock was the first feeling on hearing the news and then a tremendous desire for him to recover – even from supporters of clubs who were traditional rivals. Like the fighter he has been throughout his life, the recovery was on.

He was desperate to not lose his memory and with the help of his close family set himself tasks like reciting some of his teams, also carefully writing them down – anything to stir the brain which had helped set him apart. His former players queued up to send him good wishes – seeing vulnerability for the first time after years of setting the agenda in his authoritative style.

There were nerves and a feeling of apprehension when he ventured out to Old Trafford for the first time after being given the all-clear to watch his beloved Manchester United. It had been rather eerie at times not seeing him at games, rather like the Colosseum without Julius Caesar. But in typical style he was back just four months after his collapse.

It was a hero's reception on that September 2018 day against Wolves. Once the stadium announcer informed an Old Trafford full house that the main man was back it prompted a standing ovation and a two-handed salute from Fergie, who was sitting next to his loyal former chief executive David Gill. "Who in the whole world of football, even in the world, is not happy with Sir Alex Ferguson back and healthy? Great news for everybody," declared United's manager at the time, Jose Mourinho.

Following Mourinho's departure, Sir Alex has been a sounding board for current manager Ole Gunnar Solskjaer and was instrumental in the second coming of Stretford End idol Cristiano Ronaldo. Once it was clear that Juventus were going to allow him to leave Turin and rivals Manchester City explored the possibility of luring him to the Etihad, the competitive juices once again coursed through Sir Alex's veins.

A quick phone call knocked that idea on the head and the player who has always seen Fergie as a second father was on his way to join up with Solskjaer's side. Like a fan there was no way he wanted to miss out on Ronaldo's unique skills. He will still remember Rio Ferdinand and company badgering him to sign a young Sporting Lisbon upstart who had run them ragged in a pre-season friendly in Portugal.

Ronaldo has never forgotten the painstaking time Fergie afforded him as he matured into one of the most outstanding players in Europe. There was a special bond between them, one that persuaded Ronaldo to delay a dream move to Real Madrid by a season. There was nothing in writing – it was just Sir Alex's word that he would be free to leave 12 months down the line.

Sir Alex has always delighted in his former players excelling elsewhere once they have delivered at United and he lapped up the forward's performances for Real Madrid, just hoping that one day he might become a United player once again. Now he has a ringside seat to watch the latest version of the exceptional showman. He is also proud that many of his players have become managers in their own right and has never tired of receiving calls asking for advice. If some want doors opening for jobs then have no fear, Sir Alex has the key. A word from the great man in a chairman's ear is worth its weight in gold. There are countless tales of some of his loyal troops stepping into management or coaching thanks to a quick call from the Scot.

After that it's up to them to survive in a cut-throat football world which demands instant success. The fact that he clocked up almost 27 years at Manchester United, allied to the deluge of silverware, tells its own unique story.

Few will argue he has been the most successful Old Trafford manager in their history – Sir Matt Busby will have some support as the club's founding father, transforming their fortunes with the Busby Babes and then having to rebuild after the horrors of Munich, but surely the garland belongs to the man from Govan. Sir Alex also had to rebuild in his own way – and one which survived the test of time.

As you have read, there have been a few hairdryers along the way but all in a good cause – ones which inevitably bring a smile to the 'victims' when they are retold. Safe to say there is only one Sir Alex Ferguson – one who thankfully is still with us to help celebrate that delightful fact.

John Richardson, September 2021

Honours

As a player:

St Johnstone
Scottish Division Two 1962/63
Falkirk
Scottish Division Two 1969/70

As a manager:

St Mirren
Scottish First Division 1976/77

Aberdeen
Scottish Premier Division 1979/80, 1983/84, 1984/85
Scottish Cup 1981/82, 1982/83, 1983/84, 1985/86
Scottish League Cup 1985/86
European Cup Winners' Cup 1982/83
European Super Cup 1983

Manchester United
Premier League 1992/93, 1993/94, 1995/96, 1996/97, 1998/99,
1999/00, 2000/01, 2002/03, 2006/07, 2007/08, 2008/09,
2010/11, 2012/13
FA Cup 1989/90, 1993/94, 1995/96, 1998/99, 2003/04
League Cup 1991/92, 2005/06, 2008/09, 2009/10
Community Shield 1990 (shared), 1993, 1994, 1996, 1997, 2003,
2007, 2008, 2010, 2011
Champions League 1998/99, 2007/08
European Cup Winners' Cup 1990/91
European Super Cup 1991
Intercontinental Cup 1999
FIFA Club World Cup 2008

Acknowledgements

Frank McGarvey: 'Totally Frank'. The Frank McGarvey Story
(Mainstream Publishing)
Kenny Dalglish: 'Dalglish My Autobiography'
(Hodder and Stoughton)
Rio Ferdinand: 'Rio My Story' (Headline Publishing)
The Manchester United Official Podcast. www.manutd.com
The United Way. Documentary directed by Mat Hodgson